FREE Test Taking Tips DVD Offer

To help us better serve you, we have developed a Test Taking Tips DVD that we would like to give you for FREE. **This DVD covers world-class test taking tips that you can use to be even more successful when you are taking your test.**

All that we ask is that you email us your feedback about your study guide. Please let us know what you thought about it – whether that is good, bad or indifferent.

To get your **FREE Test Taking Tips DVD**, email freedvd@studyguideteam.com with "FREE DVD" in the subject line and the following information in the body of the email:

     a. The title of your study guide.

     b. Your product rating on a scale of 1-5, with 5 being the highest rating.

     c. Your feedback about the study guide. What did you think of it?

     d. Your full name and shipping address to send your free DVD.

If you have any questions or concerns, please don't hesitate to contact us at freedvd@studyguideteam.com.

Thanks again!

ACT Prep Book 2017-2018

ACT Study Guide Review Team

Table of Contents

Quick Overview 1

Test-Taking Strategies 2

Introduction to the ACT 6

ACT English Test 8

    Production of Writing 8

    Knowledge of Language 12

    Conventions of Standard English 18

    Practice Questions 30

    Answers and Explanations 52

ACT Mathematics Test 63

    Number and Quantity 63

    Algebra 80

    Functions 87

    Geometry 95

    Statistics and Probability 101

    Practice Questions 106

    Answer Explanations 118

ACT Reading Test 126

    Key Ideas and Details 126

    Craft and Structure 128

    Integration of Knowledge and Ideas 135

    Practice Test 143

    Answer Explanations 157

ACT Science Test 163

    Practice Questions 173

    Answer Explanations 204

ACT Writing Test 208

    What to Expect 208

    Keys to Good Writing 208

    On Test Day 209

Final Thoughts 212

Quick Overview

As you draw closer to taking your exam, effective preparation becomes more and more important. Thankfully, you have this study guide to help you get ready. Use this guide to help keep your studying on track and refer to it often.

This study guide contains several key sections that will help you be successful on your exam. The guide contains tips for what you should do the night before and the day of the test. Also included are test-taking tips. Knowing the right information is not always enough. Many well-prepared test takers struggle with exams. These tips will help equip you to accurately read, assess, and answer test questions.

A large part of the guide is devoted to showing you what content to expect on the exam and to helping you better understand that content. Near the end of this guide is a practice test so that you can see how well you have grasped the content. Then, answer explanations are provided so that you can understand why you missed certain questions.

Don't try to cram the night before you take your exam. This is not a wise strategy for a few reasons. First, your retention of the information will be low. Your time would be better used by reviewing information you already know rather than trying to learn a lot of new information. Second, you will likely become stressed as you try to gain a large amount of knowledge in a short amount of time. Third, you will be depriving yourself of sleep. So be sure to go to bed at a reasonable time the night before. Being well-rested helps you focus and remain calm.

Be sure to eat a substantial breakfast the morning of the exam. If you are taking the exam in the afternoon, be sure to have a good lunch as well. Being hungry is distracting and can make it difficult to focus. You have hopefully spent lots of time preparing for the exam. Don't let an empty stomach get in the way of success!

When travelling to the testing center, leave earlier than needed. That way, you have a buffer in case you experience any delays. This will help you remain calm and will keep you from missing your appointment time at the testing center.

Be sure to pace yourself during the exam. Don't try to rush through the exam. There is no need to risk performing poorly on the exam just so you can leave the testing center early. Allow yourself to use all of the allotted time if needed.

Remain positive while taking the exam even if you feel like you are performing poorly. Thinking about the content you should have mastered will not help you perform better on the exam.

Once the exam is complete, take some time to relax. Even if you feel that you need to take the exam again, you will be well served by some down time before you begin studying again. It's often easier to convince yourself to study if you know that it will come with a reward!

Test-Taking Strategies

1. Predicting the Answer

When you feel confident in your preparation for a multiple-choice test, try predicting the answer before reading the answer choices. This is especially useful on questions that test objective factual knowledge or that ask you to fill in a blank. By predicting the answer before reading the available choices, you eliminate the possibility that you will be distracted or led astray by an incorrect answer choice. You will feel more confident in your selection if you read the question, predict the answer, and then find your prediction among the answer choices. After using this strategy, be sure to still read all of the answer choices carefully and completely. If you feel unprepared, you should not attempt to predict the answers. This would be a waste of time and an opportunity for your mind to wander in the wrong direction.

2. Reading the Whole Question

Too often, test takers scan a multiple-choice question, recognize a few familiar words, and immediately jump to the answer choices. Test authors are aware of this common impatience, and they will sometimes prey upon it. For instance, a test author might subtly turn the question into a negative, or he or she might redirect the focus of the question right at the end. The only way to avoid falling into these traps is to read the entirety of the question carefully before reading the answer choices.

3. Looking for Wrong Answers

Long and complicated multiple-choice questions can be intimidating. One way to simplify a difficult multiple-choice question is to eliminate all of the answer choices that are clearly wrong. In most sets of answers, there will be at least one selection that can be dismissed right away. If the test is administered on paper, the test taker could draw a line through it to indicate that it may be ignored; otherwise, the test taker will have to perform this operation mentally or on scratch paper. In either case, once the obviously incorrect answers have been eliminated, the remaining choices may be considered. Sometimes identifying the clearly wrong answers will give the test taker some information about the correct answer. For instance, if one of the remaining answer choices is a direct opposite of one of the eliminated answer choices, it may well be the correct answer. The opposite of obviously wrong is obviously right! Of course, this is not always the case. Some answers are obviously incorrect simply because they are irrelevant to the question being asked. Still, identifying and eliminating some incorrect answer choices is a good way to simplify a multiple-choice question.

4. Don't Overanalyze

Anxious test takers often overanalyze questions. When you are nervous, your brain will often run wild, causing you to make associations and discover clues that don't actually exist. If you feel that this may be a problem for you, do whatever you can to slow down during the test. Try taking a deep breath or counting to ten. As you read and consider the question, restrict yourself to the particular words used by the author. Avoid thought tangents about what the author *really* meant, or what he or she was *trying* to say. The only things that matter on a multiple-choice test are the words that are actually in the question. You must avoid reading too much into a multiple-choice question, or supposing that the writer meant something other than what he or she wrote.

5. No Need for Panic

It is wise to learn as many strategies as possible before taking a multiple-choice test, but it is likely that you will come across a few questions for which you simply don't know the answer. In this situation, avoid panicking. Because most multiple-choice tests include dozens of questions, the relative value of a single wrong answer is small. Moreover, your failure on one question has no effect on your success elsewhere on the test. As much as possible, you should compartmentalize each question on a multiple-choice test. In other words, you should not allow your feelings about one question to affect your success on the others. When you find a question that you either don't understand or don't know how to answer, just take a deep breath and do your best. Read the entire question slowly and carefully. Try rephrasing the question a couple of different ways. Then, read all of the answer choices carefully. After eliminating obviously wrong answers, make a selection and move on to the next question.

6. Confusing Answer Choices

When working on a difficult multiple-choice question, there may be a tendency to focus on the answer choices that are the easiest to understand. Many people, whether consciously or not, gravitate to the answer choices that require the least concentration, knowledge, and memory. This is a mistake. When you come across an answer choice that is confusing, you should give it extra attention. A question might be confusing because you do not know the subject matter to which it refers. If this is the case, don't eliminate the answer before you have affirmatively settled on another. When you come across an answer choice of this type, set it aside as you look at the remaining choices. If you can confidently assert that one of the other choices is correct, you can leave the confusing answer aside. Otherwise, you will need to take a moment to try to better understand the confusing answer choice. Rephrasing is one way to tease out the sense of a confusing answer choice.

7. Your First Instinct

Many people struggle with multiple-choice tests because they overthink the questions. If you have studied sufficiently for the test, you should be prepared to trust your first instinct once you have carefully and completely read the question and all of the answer choices. There is a great deal of research suggesting that the mind can come to the correct conclusion very quickly once it has obtained all of the relevant information. At times, it may seem to you as if your intuition is working faster even than your reasoning mind. This may in fact be true. The knowledge you obtain while studying may be retrieved from your subconscious before you have a chance to work out the associations that support it. Verify your instinct by working out the reasons that it should be trusted.

8. Key Words

Many test takers struggle with multiple-choice questions because they have poor reading comprehension skills. Quickly reading and understanding a multiple-choice question requires a mixture of skill and experience. To help with this, try jotting down a few key words and phrases on a piece of scrap paper. Doing this concentrates the process of reading and forces the mind to weigh the relative importance of the question's parts. In selecting words and phrases to write down, the test taker thinks about the question more deeply and carefully. This is especially true for multiple-choice questions that are preceded by a long prompt.

9. Subtle Negatives

One of the oldest tricks in the multiple-choice test writer's book is to subtly reverse the meaning of a question with a word like *not* or *except*. If you are not paying attention to each word in the question, you can easily be led astray by this trick. For instance, a common question format is, "Which of the following is…?" Obviously, if the question instead is, "Which of the following is not…?," then the answer will be quite different. Even worse, the test makers are aware of the potential for this mistake and will include one answer choice that would be correct if the question were not negated or reversed. A test taker who misses the reversal will find what he or she believes to be a correct answer and will be so confident that he or she will fail to reread the question and discover the original error. The only way to avoid this is to practice a wide variety of multiple-choice questions and to pay close attention to each and every word.

10. Reading Every Answer Choice

It may seem obvious, but you should always read every one of the answer choices! Too many test takers fall into the habit of scanning the question and assuming that they understand the question because they recognize a few key words. From there, they pick the first answer choice that answers the question they believe they have read. Test takers who read all of the answer choices might discover that one of the latter answer choices is actually *more* correct. Moreover, reading all of the answer choices can remind you of facts related to the question that can help you arrive at the correct answer. Sometimes, a misstatement or incorrect detail in one of the latter answer choices will trigger your memory of the subject and will enable you to find the right answer. Failing to read all of the answer choices is like not reading all of the items on a restaurant menu: you might miss out on the perfect choice.

11. Spot the Hedges

One of the keys to success on multiple-choice tests is paying close attention to every word. This is never more true than with words like *almost*, *most*, *some*, and *sometimes*. These words are called "hedges" because they indicate that a statement is not totally true or not true in every place and time. An absolute statement will contain no hedges, but in many subjects, like literature and history, the answers are not always straightforward or absolute. There are always exceptions to the rules in these subjects. For this reason, you should favor those multiple-choice questions that contain hedging language. The presence of qualifying words indicates that the author is taking special care with his or her words, which is certainly important when composing the right answer. After all, there are many ways to be wrong, but there is only one way to be right! For this reason, it is wise to avoid answers that are absolute when taking a multiple-choice test. An absolute answer is one that says things are either all one way or all another. They often include words like *every*, *always*, *best*, and *never*. If you are taking a multiple-choice test in a subject that doesn't lend itself to absolute answers, be on your guard if you see any of these words.

12. Long Answers

In many subject areas, the answers are not simple. As already mentioned, the right answer often requires hedges. Another common feature of the answers to a complex or subjective question are qualifying clauses, which are groups of words that subtly modify the meaning of the sentence. If the question or answer choice describes a rule to which there are exceptions or the subject matter is complicated, ambiguous, or confusing, the correct answer will require many words in order to be expressed clearly and accurately. In essence, you should not be deterred by answer choices that seem excessively long. Oftentimes, the author of the text will not be able to write the correct answer without offering some qualifications and modifications. Your job is to read the answer choices thoroughly and completely and to select the one that most accurately and precisely answers the question.

13. Restating to Understand

Sometimes, a question on a multiple-choice test is difficult not because of what it asks but because of how it is written. If this is the case, restate the question or answer choice in different words. This process serves a couple of important purposes. First, it forces you to concentrate on the core of the question. In order to rephrase the question accurately, you have to understand it well. Rephrasing the question will concentrate your mind on the key words and ideas. Second, it will present the information to your mind in a fresh way. This process may trigger your memory and render some useful scrap of information picked up while studying.

14. True Statements

Sometimes an answer choice will be true in itself, but it does not answer the question. This is one of the main reasons why it is essential to read the question carefully and completely before proceeding to the answer choices. Too often, test takers skip ahead to the answer choices and look for true statements. Having found one of these, they are content to select it without reference to the question above. Obviously, this provides an easy way for test makers to play tricks. The savvy test taker will always read the entire question before turning to the answer choices. Then, having settled on a correct answer choice, he or she will refer to the original question and ensure that the selected answer is relevant. The mistake of choosing a correct-but-irrelevant answer choice is especially common on questions related to specific pieces of objective knowledge, like historical or scientific facts. A prepared test taker will have a wealth of factual knowledge at his or her disposal, and should not be careless in its application.

15. No Patterns

One of the more dangerous ideas that circulates about multiple-choice tests is that the correct answers tend to fall into patterns. These erroneous ideas range from a belief that B and C are the most common right answers, to the idea that an unprepared test-taker should answer "A-B-A-C-A-D-A-B-A." It cannot be emphasized enough that pattern-seeking of this type is exactly the WRONG way to approach a multiple-choice test. To begin with, it is highly unlikely that the test maker will plot the correct answers according to some predetermined pattern. The questions are scrambled and delivered in a random order. Furthermore, even if the test maker was following a pattern in the assignation of correct answers, there is no reason why the test taker would know which pattern he or she was using. Any attempt to discern a pattern in the answer choices is a waste of time and a distraction from the real work of taking the test. A test taker would be much better served by extra preparation before the test than by reliance on a pattern in the answers.

Introduction to the ACT

Function of the Test

The ACT is one of two national standardized college entrance examinations (the SAT being the other). Most prospective college students take the ACT or the SAT, and it is increasingly common for students to take both. All four-year colleges and universities in the United States accept the ACT for admissions purposes, and some require it. Some of those schools also use ACT subject scores for placement purposes. Sixteen states also require all high school juniors to take the ACT as part of the states' school evaluation efforts.

The vast majority of people taking the ACT are high school juniors and seniors who intend to apply to college. Traditionally, the SAT was more commonly taken than the ACT, particularly among students on the East and West coasts. However, the popularity of the ACT has grown dramatically in recent years and is now commonly taken by students in all fifty states. In fact, starting in 2013, more test takers took the ACT than the SAT. In 2015, 1.92 million students took the ACT. About 28 percent of 2015 high school graduates taking the ACT met the test's college-readiness benchmarks in all four subjects, while 31 percent met none of the benchmarks.

Test Administration

The ACT is offered on six dates throughout the year in the U.S. and Canada, and on five of those same dates in other countries. The registration fee includes score reports for four colleges, with additional reports available for purchase. There is a separate registration fee for the optional writing section.

On test dates, the ACT is administered at test centers throughout the world. The test centers are usually high schools or colleges, with several locations usually available in significant population centers.

Test takers can retake the ACT as frequently as the test is offered, up to a maximum of twelve times; although, individual colleges may have limits on how many retakes they will consider. Scores from the various sections cannot be combined from different sessions. The ACT does provide reasonable accommodations to test takers with professionally-documented disabilities.

Test Format

The ACT consists of 215 multiple-choice questions in four subject areas (English, mathematics, reading, and science) and takes about three hours and thirty minutes to complete. It also has an optional writing test, which takes an additional forty minutes.

The English section is 45 minutes long and contains 75 questions on usage, language mechanics, and rhetorical skills. The Mathematics section is 60 minutes long and contains 60 questions on algebra, geometry, and elementary trigonometry. Calculators that meet the ACT's calculator policy are permitted on the Mathematics section. The Reading section is 35 minutes long and contains four written passages with ten questions per passage. The Science section is 35 minutes long and contains 40 questions.

The Writing section is forty minutes long and is always given at the end so that test takers not wishing to take it may leave after completing the other four sections. This section consists of one essay in which students must analyze three different perspectives on a broad social issue. Although the Writing section is optional, some colleges do require it.

Section	Length	Questions
English	45 minutes	75
Mathematics	60 minutes	60
Reading	35 minutes	40
Science	35 minutes	40
Writing (optional)	40 minutes	1 essay

Scoring

Test takers receive a score between 1 and 36 for each of the four subject areas. Those scores are averaged together to give a Composite Score, which is the primary score reported as an "ACT score." The most prestigious schools typically admit students with Composite ACT Scores in the low 30's. Other selective schools typically admit students with scores in the high 20's. Traditional colleges more likely admit students with scores in the low 20's, while community colleges and other more open schools typically accept students with scores in the high teens. In 2015, the average composite score among all test takers (including those not applying to college) was 21.

Recent/Future Developments

In 2015, the Writing section underwent several changes. The allotted time extended 10 minutes (from 30 to 40 minutes) and the scoring changed to a scale from 1 to 36 (as with the other subject and Composite scores), rather than the previous scale from 2 to 12. The test also began asking test takers to give an opinion on a subject in light of three different perspectives provided by the test prompt, Lastly, the ACT began reporting four new "subscores," providing different ways to combine and evaluate the results of the various sections.

Beginning in September 2016, the scoring of the writing section changed back to a 2 to 12 scale.

ACT English Test

Production of Writing

Topic Development

<u>Identifying the Position and Purpose</u>
When it comes to an author's writing, readers should always identify a position or stance. No matter how objective a text may seem, readers should assume the author has preconceived beliefs. One can reduce the likelihood of accepting an invalid argument by looking for multiple articles on the topic, including those with varying opinions. If several opinions point in the same direction and are backed by reputable peer-reviewed sources, it's more likely that the author has a valid argument. Positions that run contrary to widely held beliefs and existing data should invite scrutiny. There are exceptions to the rule, so readers should be careful consumers of information.

While themes, symbols, and motifs are buried deep within the text and can sometimes be difficult to infer, an author's purpose is usually obvious from the beginning. There are four purposes of writing: to inform, to persuade, to describe, and to entertain. Informative writing presents facts in an accessible way. Persuasive writing appeals to emotions and logic to inspire the reader to adopt a specific stance. Readers should be wary of this type of writing, as it can mask a lack of objectivity with powerful emotion. Descriptive writing is designed to paint a picture in the reader's mind, while texts that entertain are often narratives designed to engage and delight the reader.

The various writing styles are usually blended, with one purpose dominating the rest. A persuasive text, for example, might begin with a humorous tale to make readers more receptive to the persuasive message, or a recipe in a cookbook designed to inform might be preceded by an entertaining anecdote that makes the recipes more appealing.

Identify the Purposes of Parts of Texts

Writing can be classified under four passage types: narrative, expository, technical, and persuasive. Although these types are not mutually exclusive, one form tends to dominate the rest. By recognizing the *type* of passage being read, readers gain insight into *how* they should read. A narrative passage intended to entertain can sometimes be read more quickly if the details are discernible. A technical document, on the other hand, might require a close read, because skimming the passage might cause the reader to miss salient details.

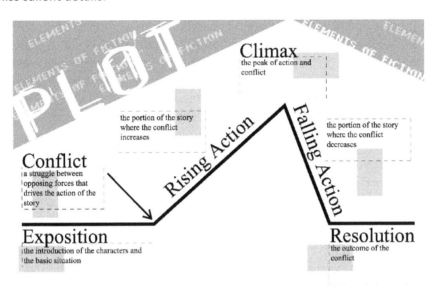

Narrative, at its core, is the art of storytelling. For a narrative to exist, certain elements must be present. It must have characters. While many characters are human, characters can be defined as anything that thinks, acts, and talks like a human. For example, many recent movies, such as *Lord of the Rings* and *The Chronicles of Narnia*, include animals, fantastical creatures, and even trees that behave like humans. Narratives also must have a plot or sequence of events. Typically, those events follow a standard plot diagram, but recent trends start *in medias res* or in the middle (nearer the climax). In this instance, foreshadowing and flashbacks often fill in plot details. Along with characters and a plot, there must also be conflict. Conflict is usually divided into two types: internal and external. Internal conflict indicates the character is in turmoil. One can imagine an angel on one shoulder and the devil on the other, arguing it out. Internal conflicts are presented through the character's thoughts. External conflicts are visible. Types of external conflict include person versus person, person versus nature, person versus technology, person versus the supernatural, or a person versus fate.

Expository texts are detached and to the point, while other types of writing — persuasive, narrative, and descriptive — are livelier. Since expository writing is designed to instruct or inform, it usually involves directions and steps written in second person (the "you" voice) and lacks any persuasive or narrative elements. Sequence words such as *first, second,* and *third,* or *in the first place, secondly,* and *lastly* are often given to add fluency and cohesion. Common examples of expository writing include instructor's lessons, cookbook recipes, and repair manuals.

Due to its empirical nature, technical writing is filled with steps, charts, graphs, data, and statistics. The goal of technical writing is to advance understanding in a field through the scientific method. Experts such as teachers, doctors, or mechanics use words unique to the profession in which they operate. These words, which often incorporate acronyms, are called *jargon*. Technical writing is a type of expository writing, but is not meant to be understood by the general public. Instead, technical writers assume readers have received a formal education in a particular field of study and need no explanation as to what the jargon means. One can imagine a doctor trying to understand a diagnostic reading for a car or a mechanic trying to interpret lab results. Only professionals with proper training will fully comprehend the text.

Persuasive texts are designed to change opinions and attitudes. The topic, stance, and arguments are found in the thesis, which is positioned near the end of the introduction. Later supporting paragraphs offer relevant quotations, paraphrases, and summaries from primary or secondary sources, which are then interpreted, analyzed, and evaluated. The goal of persuasive writers is not to stack quotes, but to develop original ideas by using sources as a starting point. Good persuasive writing makes powerful arguments with valid sources and thoughtful analyses. Poor persuasive writing is riddled with bias and logical fallacies. Sometimes, logical and illogical arguments are sandwiched together in the same text. Therefore, readers should employ skepticism when reading persuasive arguments.

Determine Whether a Text Has Met Its Intended Goal
Authors typically make it very easy for readers to identify the purpose of a passage: to entertain, inform, or persuade. The author's purpose might be determined through the formatting or organization of the text (such as through headings or a thesis statement), or through the presentation of ideas.

For example, if the author's purpose is to entertain, he or she might use humorous language or share a personal story. The use of personal anecdotes or experiences indicates that the intent is probably to entertain. Description is also often used in writing that seeks to entertain, although some authors choose this as a distinctive purpose. Descriptive writing paints a picture with words, and an author will use various adjectives and adverbs that entail the five senses (sight, sound, touch, smell, and taste) to do this.

If the author's purpose is to inform, the passage will likely contain facts, figures, and studies. The goal in such a passage is to educate readers; therefore, authors typically do this in a very straightforward way. The informative passage uses a clear thesis statement, which usually appears at the end of the introduction. The information will be presented in a fair, balanced manner, without the use of the author's opinion. There may be some elements of entertaining language or even a bias in the way the information is presented, but overall, the informative passage will be a clear presentation of facts.

When the author's intent is to persuade, he or she may employ other types of writing to engage the reader. There may be personal details or humorous language used to draw on the emotions of the reader. The persuasive writer might also include facts and figures to drive a point home. A persuasive passage might also present the point at the beginning, but it will most likely be in the form of a claim.

It's important for readers to be able to identify an author's purpose and determine whether the author has achieved that purpose effectively and consistently.

Organization, Unity, and Cohesion

Main Ideas and Supporting Details
Topics and main ideas are critical parts of writing. The *topic* is the subject matter of the piece. An example of a topic would be is *global warming*.

The *main idea* is what the writer wants to say about that topic. A writer may make the point that global warming is a growing problem that must be addressed in order to save the planet. Therefore, the topic is global warming, and the main idea is that it's *a serious problem needing to be addressed*. The topic can be expressed in a word or two, but the main idea should be a complete thought.

An author will likely identify the topic immediately within the title or the first sentence of the passage. The main idea is usually presented in the introduction. In a single passage, the main idea may be identified in the first or last sentence, but it will most likely be directly stated and easily recognized by the reader. Because it is not always stated immediately in a passage, it's important that readers carefully read the entire passage to identify the main idea.

The main idea should not be confused with the thesis statement. A *thesis statement* is a clear statement of the writer's specific stance and can often be found in the introduction of a nonfiction piece. The thesis is a specific sentence (or two) that offers the direction and focus of the discussion.

In order to illustrate the main idea, a writer will use *supporting details*, which provide evidence or examples to help make a point. Supporting details are typically found in nonfiction pieces that seek to inform or persuade the reader.

For example, in the example of global warming, where the author's main idea is to show the seriousness of this growing problem and the need for change, supporting details would be critical for effectively making that point. Supporting details used here might include *statistics* on an increase in global temperatures and *studies* showing the impact of global warming on the planet. The author could also include *projections* for future climate change in order to illustrate potential lasting effects of global warming.

It's important that readers evaluate the author's supporting details to be sure that they are credible, provide evidence of the author's point, and directly support the main idea. Although shocking statistics grab readers' attention, their use may provide ineffective information in the piece. Details like this are crucial to understanding the passage and evaluating how well the author presents his or her argument and evidence.

Parts of the Essay
The *introduction* of an essay has to do a few important things:

- Establish the topic of the essay in original wording
- Clarify the significance/importance of the topic or the purpose for writing
- Offer a thesis statement that identifies the writer's own viewpoint on the topic (typically one or two brief sentences as a clear, concise explanation of the main point on the topic)

Body paragraphs reflect the ideas developed in the middle of an essay. Body paragraphs should include the following:

- A topic sentence that identifies the sub-point (e.g., a reason why, a way how, a cause or effect)
- A detailed explanation of the point, explaining why the writer thinks the point is valid
- Illustrative examples, such as personal examples or real-world examples, that support and validate the point (i.e., "prove" the point)
- A concluding sentence that connects the examples, reasoning, and analysis of the point being made

The *conclusion*, or final paragraph, should be brief and should reiterate the focus, clarifying why the discussion is significant or important. It is important that writers avoid adding specific details or new ideas to this paragraph. The purpose of the conclusion is to sum up what has been said to bring the discussion to a close.

Knowledge of Language

Precision

People often think of precision in terms of math, but precise word choice is another key to successful writing. Since language itself is imprecise, it's important for the writer to find the exact word or words to convey the full, intended meaning of a given situation. For example:

> The number of deaths has gone down since seat belt laws started.

There are several problems with this sentence. First, the word *deaths* is too general. From the context, it's assumed that the writer is referring only to deaths caused by car accidents. However, without clarification, the sentence lacks impact and is probably untrue. The phrase *gone down* might be accurate, but a more precise word would provide more information and greater accuracy. Did the numbers show a slow and steady decrease in highway fatalities or a sudden drop? If the latter is true, the writer is missing a chance to make his or her point more dramatically. Instead of *gone down* the author could substitute *plummeted*, *fallen drastically*, or *rapidly diminished* to bring the information to life. Also, the phrase *seat belt laws* is unclear. Does it refer to laws requiring cars to include seat belts or to laws requiring drivers and passengers to use them? Finally, *started* is not a strong verb. Words like *enacted* or *adopted* are more direct and make the content more real. When put together, these changes create a far more powerful sentence:

> The number of highway fatalities has plummeted since laws requiring seat belt usage were enacted.

However, it's important to note that precise word choice can sometimes be taken too far. If the writer of the sentence above takes precision to an extreme, it might result in the following:

> The incidence of high-speed, automobile accident-related fatalities has decreased 75% and continued to remain at historical lows since the initial set of federal legislations requiring seat belt use were enacted in 1992.

This sentence is extremely precise, but it takes so long to achieve that precision that it suffers from a lack of clarity. Precise writing is about finding the right balance between information and flow. This is also an issue of conciseness (discussed in the next section).

The last thing for writers to consider with precision is a word choice that's not only unclear or uninteresting, but also confusing or misleading. For example:

> The number of highway fatalities has become hugely lower since laws requiring seat belt use were enacted.

In this case, the reader might be confused by the word *hugely*. Huge means large, but here the writer uses *hugely* in an incorrect and awkward manner. Although most readers can decipher this, doing so disconnects them from the flow of the writing and makes the writer's point less effective.

Concision

"Less is more" is a good rule for writers to follow when composing a sentence. Unfortunately, writers often include extra words and phrases that seem necessary at the time, but add nothing to the main idea. This confuses the reader and creates unnecessary repetition. Writing that lacks conciseness is usually guilty of excessive wordiness and redundant phrases. Here's an example containing both of these issues:

> When legislators decided to begin creating legislation making it mandatory for automobile drivers and passengers to make use of seat belts while in cars, a large number of them made those laws for reasons that were political reasons.

There are several empty or "fluff" words here that take up too much space. These can be eliminated while still maintaining the writer's meaning. For example:

- *decided to begin* could be shortened to *began*
- *making it mandatory for* could be shortened to *requiring*
- *make use of* could be shortened to *use*
- *a large number* could be shortened to *many*

In addition, there are several examples of redundancy that can be eliminated:

- legislators decided to begin creating legislation and made those laws
- automobile drivers and passengers and while in cars
- reasons that were political reasons

These changes are incorporated as follows:

> When legislators began requiring drivers and passengers to use seat belts, many of them did so for political reasons.

There are many general examples of redundant phrases, such as *add an additional, complete and total, time schedule,* and *transportation vehicle.* If asked to identify a redundant phrase on the exam, test takers should look for words that are close together with the same (or similar) meanings.

Consistency in Style and Tone

Style and tone are often thought to be the same thing. Though they're closely related, there are important differences to keep in mind. The easiest way to do this is to remember that style creates and affects tone. More specifically, style is *how the writer uses words* to create the desired tone for his or her writing.

Style

Style can include any number of technical writing choices, and some may have to be analyzed on the test. A few examples of style choices include:

- Sentence Construction: When presenting facts, does the writer use shorter sentences to create a quicker sense of the supporting evidence, or does he or she use longer sentences to elaborate and explain the information?

- Technical Language: Does the writer use jargon to demonstrate his or her expertise in the subject, or do the writer use ordinary language to help the reader understand things in simple terms?

- Formal Language: Does the writer refrain from using contractions such as *won't* or *can't* to create a more formal tone, or does he or she use a colloquial, conversational style to connect to the reader?

- Formatting: Does the writer use a series of shorter paragraphs to help the reader follow a line of argument, or does he or she use longer paragraphs to examine an issue in great detail and demonstrate his or her knowledge of the topic?

On the exam, test takers should examine the writer's style and how his or her writing choices affect the way the text comes across.

Tone

Tone refers to the writer's attitude toward the subject matter. Tone is usually explained in terms of a work of fiction. For example, the tone conveys how the writer feels about the characters and the situations in which they're involved. Nonfiction writing is sometimes thought to have no tone at all; however, this is incorrect.

A lot of nonfiction writing has a neutral tone, which is an important one for the writer to use. A neutral tone demonstrates that the writer is presenting a topic impartially and letting the information speak for itself. On the other hand, nonfiction writing can be just as effective and appropriate if the tone isn't neutral. The following short passage provides an example of tone in nonfiction writing:

> Seat belts save more lives than any other automobile safety feature. Many studies show that airbags save lives as well; however, not all cars have airbags. For instance, some older cars don't. Furthermore, air bags aren't entirely reliable. For example, studies show that in 15% of accidents airbags don't deploy as designed, but, on the other hand, seat belt malfunctions are extremely rare. The number of highway fatalities has plummeted since laws requiring seat belt usage were enacted.

In this passage, the writer mostly chooses to retain a neutral tone when presenting information. If instead, the author chose to include his or her own personal experience of losing a friend or family member in a car accident, the tone would change dramatically. The tone would no longer be neutral and would show that the writer has a personal stake in the content, allowing him or her to interpret the information in a different way. When analyzing tone, the reader should consider what the writer is trying to achieve in the text and how they *create* the tone using style.

Word Parts

By analyzing and understanding Latin, Greek, and Anglo-Saxon word roots, prefixes, and suffixes, one can better understand word meanings. Of course, people can always look words up if a dictionary or thesaurus if available, but meaning can often be gleaned on the spot if the reader learns to dissect and examine words.

A word can consist of the following combinations:

- root
- root + suffix
- prefix + root
- prefix + root + suffix

For example, if someone was unfamiliar with the word *submarine* they could break the word into its parts.

prefix + root

sub + marine

It can be determined that *sub* means *below* as in *subway* and *subpar*. Additionally, one can determine that *marine* refers to *the sea* as in *marine life*. Thus, it can be figured that *submarine* refers to something below the water.

Roots

Roots are the basic components of words. Many roots can stand alone as individual words, but others must be combined with a prefix or suffix to be a word. For example, *calc* is a root but it needs a suffix to be an actual word (*calcium*).

Prefixes

A *prefix* is a word, letter, or number that is placed before another. It adjusts or qualifies the root word's meaning. When written alone, prefixes are followed by a dash to indicate that the root word follows. Some of the most common prefixes are the following:

Prefix	Meaning	Example
dis-	not or opposite of	disabled
in-, im-, il-, ir-	not	illiterate
re-	again	return
un-	not	unpredictable
anti-	against	antibacterial
fore-	before	forefront
mis-	wrongly	misunderstand
non-	not	nonsense
over-	more than normal	overabundance
pre-	before	preheat
super-	above	superman

Suffixes

A suffix is a letter or group of letters added at the end of a word to form another word. The word created from the root and suffix is either a different tense of the same root (*help + ed = helped*) or a new word (*help + ful = helpful*). When written alone, suffixes are preceded by a dash to indicate that the root word comes before.

Some of the most common suffixes are the following:

Suffix	Meaning	Example
-ed	makes a verb past tense	washed
-ing	makes a verb a present participle verb	washing
-ly	to make characteristic of	lovely
-s, -es	to make more than one	chairs, boxes
-able	can be done	deplorable
-al	having characteristics of	comical
-est	comparative	greatest
-ful	full of	wonderful
-ism	belief in	communism
-less	without	faithless
-ment	action or process	accomplishment
-ness	state of	happiness
-ize, -ise	to render, to make	sterilize, advertise
-cede, -ceed, -sede	go	concede, proceed, supersede

Here are some helpful tips:

- When adding a suffix that starts with a vowel (for example, -ed) to a one-syllable root whose vowel has a short sound and ends in a consonant (for example, *stun*), the final consonant of the root (*n*) gets doubled.

  stun + ed = stun*n*ed

- Exception: If the past tense verb ends in *x* such as *box*, the *x* does not get doubled.

  box + ed = boxed

- If adding a suffix that starts with a vowel (*-er*) to a multi-syllable word ending in a consonant (*begin*), the consonant (*n*) is doubled.

  begin + er = begin*n*er

- If a short vowel is followed by two or more consonants in a word such as *i+t+c+h = itch*, the last consonant should not be doubled.

  itch + ed = itched

- If adding a suffix that starts with a vowel (*-ing*) to a word ending in *e* (for example, *name*), that word's final *e* is generally (but not always) dropped.

  name + ing = naming
  exception: manage + able = manageable

- If adding a suffix that starts with a consonant (*-ness*) to a word ending in *e* (*complete*), the *e* generally (but not always) remains.

  complete + ness = completeness
  exception: judge + ment = judgment

- There is great diversity on handling words that end in *y*. For words ending in a vowel + *y*, nothing changes in the original word.

  play + ed = played

- For words ending in a consonant + *y*, the *y* id changed to i when adding any suffix except for – *ing*.

  marry + ed = married
  marry + ing = marrying

Conventions of Standard English

Sentence Structure and Formation

Sentence Structure

Simple sentence: composed of one independent clause

Many people watch hummingbirds.

Note that it has one subject and one verb; however, a simple sentence can have a compound subject and/or a compound verb.

Adults and children often enjoy watching and photographing hummingbirds.

Compound sentence: composed of two independent clauses

The wind knocked down lots of trees, but no trees in my yard were affected.

Complex sentence: composed of one independent clause and one dependent clause

Although the wind knocked down lots of trees, no trees in my yard were affected.

Sentence Fluency

Learning and utilizing the mechanics of structure will encourage effective, professional results, and adding some creativity will elevate one's writing to a higher level.

First, the basic elements of sentences will be reviewed.

A *sentence* is a set of words that make up a grammatical unit. The words must have certain elements and be spoken or written in a specific order to constitute a complete sentence that makes sense.

1. A sentence must have a *subject* (a noun or noun phrase). The subject tells whom or what the sentence is addressing (i.e. what it is about).

2. A sentence must have an *action* or *state of being* (*a verb*). To reiterate: A verb forms the main part of the predicate of a sentence. This means that it explains what the noun is doing.

3. A sentence must convey a complete thought.

When examining writing, readers should be mindful of grammar, structure, spelling, and patterns. Sentences can come in varying sizes and shapes, so the point of grammatical correctness is not to stamp out creativity or diversity in writing. Rather, grammatical correctness ensures that writing will be enjoyable and clear. One of the most common methods successful test takers employ to catch errors is to mouth the words as they read them. Many typos are fixed automatically by the brain, but mouthing the words often circumvents this instinct and helps one read what's actually on the page. Often, grammar errors are caught not by memorization of grammar rules but by the training of one's mind to know whether something *sounds* right or not.

<u>Types of Sentences</u>
There isn't an overabundance of absolutes in grammar, but here is one: every sentence in the English language falls into one of four categories.

Declarative: a simple statement that ends with a period

The price of milk per gallon is the same as the price of gasoline.

Imperative: a command, instruction, or request that ends with a period

Buy milk when you stop to fill up your car with gas.

Interrogative: a question that ends with a question mark

Will you buy the milk?

Exclamatory: a statement or command that expresses emotions like anger, urgency, or surprise and ends with an exclamation mark

Buy the milk now!

Declarative sentences are the most common type, probably because they are comprised of the most general content, without any of the bells and whistles that the other three types contain. They are, simply, declarations or statements of any degree of seriousness, importance, or information.

Imperative sentences often seem to be missing a subject. The subject is there, though; it is just not visible or audible because it is *implied*. For example:

Buy the milk when you fill up your car with gas.

In this sentence, *you* is the implied subject, the one to whom the command is issued. This is sometimes called *the understood you* because it is understood that *you* is the subject of the sentence.

Interrogative sentences—those that ask questions—are defined as such from the idea of the word *interrogation*, the action of questions being asked of suspects by investigators. Although that is serious business, interrogative sentences apply to all kinds of questions.

To exclaim is at the root of *exclamatory* sentences. These are made with strong emotions behind them. The only technical difference between a declarative or imperative sentence and an exclamatory one is the exclamation mark at the end. The example declarative and imperative sentences can both become an exclamatory one simply by putting an exclamation mark at the end of the sentences.

The price of milk per gallon is the same as the price of gasoline!

Buy milk when you stop to fill up your car with gas!

After all, someone might be really excited by the price of gas or milk, or they could be mad at the person that will be buying the milk! However, as stated before, exclamation marks in abundance defeat their own purpose! After a while, they begin to cause fatigue! When used only for their intended purpose, they can have their expected and desired effect.

Transitions

Transitions are the glue use to make organized thoughts adhere to one another. Transitions are the glue that helps put ideas together seamlessly, within sentences and paragraphs, between them, and (in longer documents) even between sections. Transitions may be single words, sentences, or whole paragraphs (as in the prior example). Transitions help readers to digest and understand what to feel about what has gone on and clue readers in on what is going on, what will be, and how they might react to all these factors. Transitions are like good clues left at a crime scene.

Parallel Structure in a Sentence

Parallel structure, also known as parallelism, refers to using the same grammatical form within a sentence. This is important in lists and for other components of sentences.

> Incorrect: At the recital, the boys and girls were dancing, singing, and played musical instruments.

> Correct: At the recital, the boys and girls were dancing, singing, and playing musical instruments.

Notice that in the first example, *played* is not in the same verb tense as the other verbs nor is it compatible with the helping verb *were*. To test for parallel structure in lists, try reading each item as if it were the only item in the list.

> The boys and girls were dancing.

> The boys and girls were singing.

> The boys and girls were played musical instruments.

Suddenly, the error in the sentence becomes very clear. Here's another example:

Incorrect: After the accident, I informed the police *that Mrs. Holmes backed* into my car, *that Mrs. Holmes got out* of her car to look at the damage, and *she was driving* off without leaving a note.

Correct: After the accident, I informed the police *that Mrs. Holmes backed* into my car, *that Mrs. Holmes got out* of her car to look at the damage, and *that Mrs. Holmes drove off* without leaving a note.

Correct: After the accident, I informed the police that Mrs. Holmes *backed* into my car, *got out* of her car to look at the damage, and *drove off* without leaving a note.

Note that there are two ways to fix the nonparallel structure of the first sentence. The key to parallelism is consistent structure.

Punctuation

Ellipses

An *ellipsis* (. . .) consists of three handy little dots that can speak volumes on behalf of irrelevant material. Writers use them in place of a word(s), line, phrase, list contents, or paragraph that might just as easily have been omitted from a passage of writing. This can be done to save space or to focus only on the specifically relevant material.

> Exercise is good for some unexpected reasons. Watkins writes, "Exercise has many benefits such as . . . reducing cancer risk."

In the example above, the ellipsis takes the place of the other benefits of exercise that are more expected.

The ellipsis may also be used to show a pause in sentence flow.

> "I'm wondering . . . how this could happen," Dylan said in a soft voice.

Commas

A *comma* (,) is the punctuation mark that signifies a pause or a breath between parts of a sentence. It denotes a break in the flow. As with so many aspects of writing structure, authors will benefit by reading their writing aloud or mouthing the words. This can be particularly helpful if one is uncertain about whether the comma is needed.

In a complex sentence—one that contains a subordinate (dependent) clause or clauses—the clauses should be separated with commas.

> I will not pay for the steak, because I don't have that much money.

Here, the purpose of each comma usage is to designate an interruption in flow. Readers should also notice how the last clause is dependent because it requires the earlier independent clauses to make sense.

A comma should be used on both sides of an interrupting phrase.

> I will pay for the ice cream, *chocolate and vanilla,* and I will eat it all myself.

The words forming the phrase in italics are nonessential (extra) information. To determine if a phrase is nonessential, one can try reading the sentence without the phrase and see if it's still coherent.

A comma is not necessary in this next sentence because no interruption—nonessential or extra information—has occurred. Again, when uncertain, sentences can be read aloud.

> I will pay for his chocolate and vanilla ice cream and I will eat it all myself.

If the nonessential phrase comes at the beginning of a sentence, a comma should only go at the end of the phrase. If the phrase comes at the end of a sentence, a comma should only go at the beginning of the phrase.

Other types of interruptions include the following:

- Interjections: Oh no, I am not going.
- Abbreviations: Barry Potter, M.D., specializes in heart disorders.
- Direct addresses: Yes, Claudia, I am tired and going to bed.
- Parenthetical phrases: His wife, lovely as she was, was not helpful.
- Transitional phrases: Also, it is not possible.

The second comma in the following sentence is called an Oxford comma.

> I will pay for ice cream, syrup, and pop.

It is a comma used after the second-to-last item in a series of three or more items. It comes before the word *or* or *and*. Not everyone uses the Oxford comma; it is optional, but many believe it is needed. The comma functions as a tool to reduce confusion in writing. So, if omitting the Oxford comma would cause confusion, then it's best to include it.

Commas are used in math to mark the place of thousands in numerals, breaking them up so they are easier to read. Other uses for commas are in dates (*March 19, 2016*), letter greetings (*Dear Sally,*), and in between cities and states (*Louisville, KY*).

Semicolons
The *semicolon* (*;*) might be described as a heavy-handed comma. Consider these two examples:

> I will pay for the ice cream and I will pay for the syrup, but I will not pay for the steak.

> I will pay for the ice cream and I will pay for the syrup; I will not pay for the steak.

What's the difference? The first example has a comma and a conjunction separating the two independent clauses. The second example does not have a conjunction, but there are two independent clauses in the sentence, so something more than a comma is required. In this case, a semicolon is used.

Two independent clauses can only be joined in a sentence by either a comma and conjunction or a semicolon. If one of those tools is not used, the sentence will be a run-on. It is worth reiterating that while the clauses are independent, they need to be closely related in order to be contained in one sentence.

Another use for the semicolon is to separate items in a list when the items themselves require commas.

> The family lived in Phoenix, Arizona; Oklahoma City, Oklahoma; and Raleigh, North Carolina.

Colons
Colons (*:*) have many miscellaneous functions. Colons can be used to proceed further information or a list. In these cases, a colon should only follow an independent clause.

> Humans take in sensory information through five basic senses: sight, hearing, smell, touch, and taste.

> The meal includes the following components:

> - Caesar salad
> - spaghetti
> - garlic bread
> - cake

> The family got what they needed: a reliable vehicle.

While a comma is more common, a colon can also precede a formal quotation.

> He said to the crowd: "Let's begin!"

A colon is used after the greeting in a formal letter.

> Dear Sir:

> To Whom It May Concern:

In the writing of time, a colon separates the minutes from the hour (*4:45 p.m.*). The colon can also be used to indicate a ratio between two numbers (*50:1*).

Hyphens
The *hyphen* (-) is a little hash mark that can be used to join words to show that they are linked.

honey-covered biscuits

Some words always require hyphens, even if not serving as an adjective.

merry-go-round

Hyphens always go after certain prefixes like *anti-* & *all-*.

Hyphens should also be used when the absence of the hyphen would cause a strange vowel combination (*semi-engineer*) or confusion. For example, *re-collect* should be used to describe something being gathered twice, rather than being written as *recollect*, which means to remember.

Parentheses and Dashes
Parentheses are half-round brackets that look like this: ( ). They set off a word, phrase, or sentence that is an afterthought, explanation, or side note relevant to the surrounding text, but not essential to it. A pair of commas is often used to set off this sort of information, but parentheses are generally used for information that would not fit well within a sentence or that the writer deems not important enough to be structurally part of the sentence.

The picture of the heart (see above) shows the major parts you should memorize.

Mount Everest is one of three mountains in the world that are over 28,000 feet high (K2 and Kanchenjunga are the other two).

The sentences above are complete without the parenthetical statements. In the first example, *see above* would not have fit well within the flow of the sentence. The second parenthetical statement could have been a separate sentence, but the writer deemed the information not pertinent to the topic.

The dash (—) is a mark longer than a hyphen used as a punctuation mark in sentences and to set apart a relevant thought. Even after plucking out the line separated by the dash marks, the sentence will be intact and make sense.

Looking out the airplane window at the landmarks—Lake Clarke, Thompson Community College, and the bridge—she couldn't help but feel excited to be home.

The dash's use is similar to that of parentheses or a pair of commas. So, what's the difference? Many believe that using dashes makes the clause within them stand out while using parentheses is subtler. It's advised to not use dashes when commas could be used instead.

Quotation Marks

Here are some instances where *quotation marks* should be used:

- Dialogue for characters in narratives. When characters speak, the first word should always be capitalized and the punctuation goes inside the quotes. For example:

  Janie said, "The tree fell on my car during the hurricane."

- Around titles of songs, short stories, essays, and chapter in books
- To emphasize a certain word
- To refer to a word as the word itself

Apostrophes

This punctuation mark, the *apostrophe* (') is a versatile little mark. It has a few different functions:

- Quotes: Apostrophes are used when a second quote is needed within a quote.

  In my letter to my friend, I wrote, "The girl had to get a new purse, and guess what Mary did? She said, 'I'd like to go with you to the store.' I knew Mary would buy it for her."

- Contractions: Another use for an apostrophe in the quote above is a contraction. *I'd* is used for *I would*.

- Possession: An apostrophe followed by the letter *s* shows possession (*Mary's* purse). If the possessive word is plural, the apostrophe generally just follows the word.

  The trees' leaves are all over the ground.

Usage

Spelling might or might not be important to some, or maybe it just doesn't come naturally, but those who are willing to discover some new ideas and consider their benefits can learn to spell better and improve their writing. Misspellings reduce a writer's credibility and can create misunderstandings. Spell checkers built into word processors are not a substitute for accuracy. They are neither foolproof nor without error. In addition, a writer's misspelling of one word may also be a valid (but incorrect) word. For example, a writer intending to spell *herd* might accidentally type *s* instead of *d* and unintentionally spell *hers*. Since *hers* is a word, it would not be marked as a misspelling by a spell checker. In short, writers should use spell check, but not rely on them.

Guidelines for Spelling

Saying and listening to a word serves as the beginning of knowing how to spell it. Writers should keep these subsequent guidelines in mind, remembering there are often exceptions because the English language is replete with them.

Guideline #1: Syllables must have at least one vowel. In fact, every syllable in every English word has a vowel.

- dog
- haystack
- answering

- *abstentious*
- *simple*

Guideline #2: The long and short of it. When the vowel has a short vowel sound as in *mad* or *bed,* only the single vowel is needed. If the word has a long vowel sound, add another vowel, either alongside it or separated by a consonant: bed/*bead*; mad/*made.* When the second vowel is separated by two spaces—*madder*—it does not affect the first vowel's sound.

Guideline #3: Suffixes. Refer to the examples listed above.

Guideline #4: Which comes first; the *i* or the *e*? Remember the saying, "*I* before *e* except after *c* or when sounding as *a* as in *neighbor* or *weigh*." Keep in mind that these are only guidelines and that there are always exceptions to every rule.

Guideline #5: Vowels in the right order. Another helpful rhyme is, "When two vowels go walking, the first one does the talking." When two vowels are in a row, the first one often has a long vowel sound and the other is silent. An example is *team.*

If one has difficulty spelling words, he or she can determine a strategy to help. Some people work on spelling by playing word games like Scrabble or Words with Friends. Others use phonics, which is sounding words out by slowly and surely stating each syllable. People try repeating and memorizing spellings as well as picturing words in their head, or they may try making up silly memory aids. Each person should experiment and see what works best.

Homophones

Homophones are two or more words that have no particular relationship to one another except their identical pronunciations. Homophones make spelling English words fun and challenging. Examples include:

Common Homophones
affect, effect
allot, a lot
barbecue, barbeque
bite, byte
brake, break
capital, capitol
cash, cache
cell, sell
colonel, kernel
do, due, dew
dual, duel
eminent, imminent
flew, flu, flue
gauge, gage
holy, wholly
it's, its
knew, new
libel, liable
principal, principle
their, there, they're
to, too, two
yoke, yolk

Irregular Plurals

Irregular plurals are words that aren't made plural the usual way.

- Most nouns are made plural by adding –*s* (book*s*, television*s*, skyscraper*s*).

- Most nouns ending in *ch, sh, s, x,* or *z* are made plural by adding –*es* (church*es,* marsh*es*).

- Most nouns ending in a vowel + *y* are made plural by adding –*s* (day*s,* toy*s*).

- Most nouns ending in a consonant + *y,* are made plural by the -*y* becoming -*ies* (baby becomes *babies*).

- Most nouns ending in an *o* are made plural by adding –*s* (piano*s,* photo*s*).

- Some nouns ending in an *o,* though, may be made plural by adding –*es* (example: potato*es,* volcano*es*), and, of note, there is no known rhyme or reason for this!

- Most nouns ending in an *f* or *fe* are made plural by the *-f* or *-fe* becoming *-ves*! (example: wolf becomes *wolves*).

- Some words function as both the singular and plural form of the word (fish, deer).

- Other exceptions include *man* becomes *men, mouse* becomes *mice, goose* becomes *geese,* and *foot* becomes *feet.*

Contractions

The basic rule for making *contractions* is one area of spelling that is pretty straightforward: combine the two words by inserting an apostrophe (') in the space where a letter is omitted. For example, to combine *you* and *are*, drop the *a* and put the apostrophe in its place: *you're*.

he + is = he's

you + all = y'all (informal, but often misspelled)

Note that *it's*, when spelled with an apostrophe, is always the contraction for *it is*. The possessive form of the word is written without an apostrophe as *its*.

Correcting Misspelled Words

A good place to start looking at commonly misspelled words here is with the word *misspelled*. While it looks peculiar, look at it this way: *mis* (the prefix meaning *wrongly*) + *spelled* = *misspelled*.

The following table includes examples of words that writers often misspell:

Commonly Misspelled Words			
accept	committee	intelligence	possess
acceptable	conceive	intercede	precede
accidentally	congratulations	interest	prevalent
accommodate	courtesy	irresistible	privilege
accompany	deceive	jewelry	pronunciation
acknowledgement	desperate	judgment	protein
acquaintance	discipline	library	publicly
acquire	disappoint	license	questionnaire
address	dissatisfied	maintenance	recede
aesthetic	eligible	maneuver	receive
aisle	embarrass	mathematics	recommend
altogether	especially	mattress	referral
amateur	exaggerate	millennium	relevant
apparent	exceed	miniature	restaurant
appropriate	existence	mischievous	rhetoric
arctic	experience	misspell	rhythm
asphalt	extraordinary	mortgage	schedule
associate	familiar	necessary	sentence
attendance	February	neither	separate
auxiliary	fiery	nickel	sergeant
available	finally	niece	similar
balloon	forehead	ninety	supersede
believe	foreign	noticeable	surprise
beneficial	foremost	obedience	symmetry
benign	forfeit	occasion	temperature
bicycle	glamorous	occurrence	tragedy
brief	government	omitted	transferred
business	grateful	operate	truly
calendar	handkerchief	parallel	usage
campaign	harass	pastime	valuable
candidate	hygiene	permissible	vengeance
category	hypocrisy	perseverance	villain
cemetery	ignorance	personnel	Wednesday
changeable	incredible	persuade	weird

Capitalization

Here's a non-exhaustive list of things that should be capitalized:

- The first word of every sentence
- The first letter of proper nouns (World War II)
- Holidays (Valentine's Day)
- Days of the week and months of the year (Tuesday, March)
- The first word, last word, and all major words in the titles of books, movies, songs, and other creative works (*To Kill a Mockingbird,* note that *a* is lowercase since it's not a major word, but *to* is capitalized since it's the first word of the title.
- Titles when preceding a proper noun (President Roberto Gonzales, Aunt Judy)

When simply using a word such as *president* or *secretary*, though, the word is not capitalized.

Officers of the new business must include a *president* and *treasurer*.

Seasons—*spring*, *fall*, etc.—are not capitalized.

North, *south*, *east*, and *west* are capitalized when referring to regions but are not when being used for directions. In general, if it's preceded by *the* it should be capitalized.

I'm from the South.

I drove south.

Practice Questions

Focus: Students must make revising and editing decisions on the context of a passage on a career-related topic.

Aircraft Engineers

The knowledge of an aircraft engineer is acquired through years of education, and special (3) licenses are required. Ideally, an individual will begin his or her preparation for the profession in high school by taking chemistry, physics, trigonometry, and calculus. Such curricula will aid in one's pursuit of a bachelor's degree in aircraft engineering, which requires several physical and life sciences, mathematics, and design courses.

(4) Some of universities provide internship or apprentice opportunities for the students enrolled in aircraft engineer programs. A bachelor's in aircraft engineering is commonly accompanied by a master's degree in advanced engineering or business administration. Such advanced degrees enable an individual to position himself or herself for executive, faculty, and/or research opportunities. (5)These advanced offices oftentimes require a Professional Engineering (PE) license which can be obtained through additional college courses, professional experience, and acceptable scores on the Fundamentals of Engineering (FE) and Professional Engineering (PE) standardized assessments.

Once the job begins, this line of work requires critical thinking, business skills, problem solving, and creativity. This level of (7) expertise (8) allows aircraft engineers to apply mathematical equations and scientific processes to aeronautical and aerospace issues or inventions. (10) For example, aircraft engineers may test, design, and construct flying vessels such as airplanes, space shuttles, and missile weapons. As a result, aircraft engineers are compensated with generous salaries. In fact, in May 2014, the lowest 10 percent of all American aircraft engineers earned less than $60,110 while the highest paid ten-percent of all American aircraft engineers earned $155,240. (11) In May 2015, the United States Bureau of Labor Statistics (BLS) reported that the median annual salary of aircraft engineers was $107, 830. (13)Conversely, (15) employment opportunities for aircraft engineers are projected to decrease by 2 percent by 2024. This decrease may be the result of a decline in the manufacturing industry. Nevertheless, aircraft engineers who know how to utilize modeling and simulation programs, fluid dynamic software, and robotic engineering tools are projected to remain the most employable.

2015 Annual Salary of Aerospace Engineers

Source: Bureau of Labor Statistics

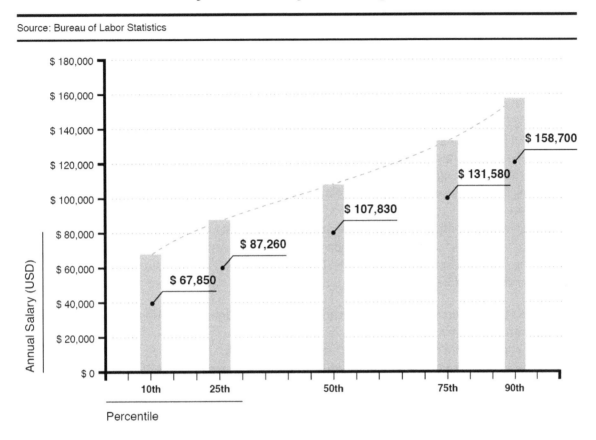

1. What is the purpose of this passage?
    a. To define the terms that will be discussed in the following paragraphs
    b. To demonstrate the correlation between aircraft engineer's extensive education and their pay
    c. To identify the skills that are required in order to become an aircraft engineer
    d. To define the roles of an aircraft engineer

2. What type of text is utilized in the passage?
    a. Argumentative
    b. Narrative
    c. Biographical
    d. Informative

3.
    a. NO CHANGE
    b. Will be
    c. May be
    d. Should be

4.
    a. NO CHANGE
    b. Some of universities provided internship or apprentice opportunities
    c. Some of universities provide internship or apprenticeship opportunities
    d. Some universities provide internship or apprenticeship opportunities

5.
    a. NO CHANGE
    b. These advanced positions oftentimes require acceptable scores on the Fundamentals of Engineering (FE) and Professional Engineering (PE) standardized assessments in order to achieve a Professional Engineering (PE) license. Additional college courses and professional experience help.
    c. These advanced offices oftentimes require acceptable scores on the Fundamentals of Engineering (FE) and Professional Engineering (PE) standardized assessments to gain the Professional Engineering (PE) license which can be obtained through additional college courses, professional experience.
    d. These advanced positions oftentimes require a Professional Engineering (PE) license which is obtained by acceptable scores on the Fundamentals of Engineering (FE) and Professional Engineering (PE) standardized assessments. Further education and professional experience can help prepare for the assessments.

6. "The knowledge of an aircraft engineer is acquired through years of education." Which statement serves to support this claim?
    a. Aircraft engineers are compensated with generous salaries.
    b. Such advanced degrees enable an individual to position himself or herself for executive, faculty, or research opportunities.
    c. Ideally, an individual will begin his or her preparation for the profession in high school by taking chemistry, physics, trigonometry, and calculus.
    d. Aircraft engineers who know how to utilize modeling and simulation programs, fluid dynamic software, and robotic engineering tools will be the most employable.

7. What is the meaning of "expertise" in the marked sentence?
    a. Care
    b. Skill
    c. Work
    d. Composition

8.
    a. NO CHANGE
    b. Inhibits
    c. Requires
    d. Should

9. In the third paragraph, which of the following claims is supported?
    a. This line of work requires critical thinking, business skills, problem solving, and creativity.
    b. Aircraft engineers are compensated with generous salaries.
    c. The knowledge of an aircraft engineer is acquired through years of education.
    d. Those who work hard are rewarded accordingly.

10.
    a. NO CHANGE
    b. Therefore,
    c. However,
    d. Furthermore,

11.
    a. NO CHANGE
    b. May of 2015, the United States Bureau of Labor Statistics (BLS) reported that the median annual salary of aircraft engineers was $107, 830.
    c. In May of 2015 the United States Bureau of Labor Statistics (BLS) reported that the median annual salary of aircraft engineers was $107, 830.
    d. In May, 2015, the United States Bureau of Labor Statistics (BLS) reported that the median annual salary of aircraft engineers was $107, 830.

12. Which accurately describes the use of introductions and conclusions in this passage?
    a. No introduction and no conclusion
    b. An introduction and a conclusion
    c. No introduction but a conclusion
    d. An introduction but no conclusion

13.
    a. NO CHANGE
    b. Similarly,
    c. In other words,
    d. Accordingly,

14. The author's attitude on the future of aircraft engineers can best be described as
    a. Pessimistic
    b. Optimistic
    c. Proud
    d. Unconvinced

15.
    a. NO CHANGE
    b. Employment opportunities for aircraft engineers will be projected to decrease by 2 percent in 2024.
    c. Employment opportunities for aircraft engineers is projected to decrease by 2 percent in 2024.
    d. Employment opportunities for aircraft engineers were projected to decrease by 2 percent in 2024.

History/ Social Studies

Focus: Students must make revising and editing decisions on the context of a passage on a history/social studies topic.

Attacks of September 11th

On September 11th 2001, a group of terrorists hijacked four American airplanes. The terrorists crashed the planes into the World Trade Center in New York City, the

Pentagon in Washington D.C., and a field in Pennsylvania. Nearly 3,000 people died during the attacks, which propelled the United States into a "War on Terror".

About the Terrorists

Terrorists commonly use fear and violence to achieve political goals. The nineteen terrorists who orchestrated and implemented the attacks of September 11th were militants associated with al-Qaeda, an Islamic extremist group founded by Osama bin Landen, Abdullah Azzam, and others in the late 1980s. (18) Bin Laden orchestrated the attacks as a response to what he felt was American injustice against Islam and hatred towards Muslims. In his words, "Terrorism against America deserves to be praised."

Islam is the religion of Muslims, who live mainly in South and Southwest Asia and Sub-Saharan Africa. The majority of Muslims practice Islam peacefully. However, fractures in Islam have led to the growth of Islamic extremists who strictly oppose Western influences. They seek to institute stringent Islamic law and destroy those who (20) violate Islamic code.

In November 2002, bin Laden provided the explicit motives for the 9/11 terror attacks. According to this list, America's support of Israel, military presence in Saudi Arabia, and other anti-Muslim actions were the causes.

The Timeline of the Attacks

The morning of September 11 began like any other for most Americans. Then, at 8:45 a.m., a Boeing 767 plane crashed into the north tower of the World Trade Center in New York City. Hundreds were instantly killed. Others were trapped on higher floors. The (22) crash was initially thought to be a freak accident. When a second plane flew directly into the south tower eighteen minutes later, it was determined that America was under attack.

At 9:45 a.m., a third plane slammed into the Pentagon, America's military headquarters in Washington D.C. The jet fuel of this plane caused a major fire and partial building collapse that resulted in nearly 200 deaths. By 10:00 a.m., the south tower of the World Trade Center collapsed. Thirty minutes later, the north tower followed suit.

While this was happening, a fourth plane that departed from New Jersey, United Flight 93, was hijacked. The passengers learned of the attacks that occurred in New York and Washington D.C. and realized that they faced the same fate as the other planes that crashed. The passengers were determined to overpower the terrorists in an effort to prevent the deaths of additional innocent American citizens. Although the passengers were successful in (23) diverging the plane, it crashed in a western Pennsylvania field and killed everyone on board. The plane's final target remains uncertain, but many believe that United Flight 93 was heading for the White House.

Heroes and Rescuers

Close to 3,000 people died in the World Trade Center attacks. This figure includes 343 New York City firefighters and paramedics, 23 New York City police officers, and 37 Port Authority officers. Nevertheless, thousands of men and women in service worked (26) valiantly to evacuate the buildings, save trapped workers, extinguish infernos, uncover victims trapped in fallen rubble, and tend to nearly 10,000 injured individuals.

About 300 rescue dogs played a major role in the after-attack salvages. Working twelve-hour shifts, the dogs scoured the rubble and alerted paramedics when they found signs of life. While doing so, the dogs served as a source of comfort and therapy for the rescue teams.

Initial Impacts on America

The attacks of September 11, 2001 resulted in the immediate suspension of all air travel. No flights could take off from or land on American soil. (27) American airports and airspace closed to all national and international flights. Therefore, over five hundred flights had to turn back or be redirected to other countries. Canada alone received 226 flights and thousands of stranded passengers. (28) Needless to say, as canceled flights are rescheduled, air travel became backed up and chaotic for quite some time.

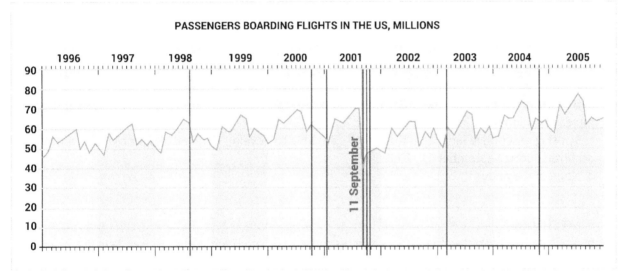

PASSENGERS BOARDING FLIGHTS IN THE US, MILLIONS

At the time of the attacks, George W. Bush was the president of the United States. President Bush announced that "We will make no distinction between the terrorists who committed these acts and those who harbor them." The rate of hate crimes against American Muslims spiked, despite President Bush's call for the country to treat them with respect.

Additionally, relief funds were quickly arranged. The funds were used to support families of the victims, orphaned children, and those with major injuries. In this way, the tragic event brought the citizens together through acts of service towards those directly impacted by the attack.

Long-term Effects of the Attacks

Over the past fifteen years, the attacks of September 11th have transformed the United States' government, travel safety protocols, and international relations. Anti-terrorism legislation became a priority for many countries as law enforcement and intelligence agencies teamed up to find and defeat alleged terrorists.

Present George W. Bush announced a War on Terror. He (29) desired to bring bin Laden and al-Qaeda to justice and prevent future terrorist networks from gaining strength. The War in Afghanistan began in October of 2001 when the United States and British forces bombed al-Qaeda camps. (30) The Taliban, a group of fundamental Muslims who protected Osama bin Laden, was overthrown on December 9, 2001. However, the war continued in order to defeat insurgency campaigns in neighboring countries. Ten years later, the United State Navy SEALS killed Osama bin Laden in Pakistan. During 2014, the United States declared the end of its involvement in the War on Terror in Afghanistan.

Museums and memorials have since been erected to honor and remember the thousands of people who died during the September 11th attacks, including the brave rescue workers who gave their lives in the effort to help others.

16. How does the author structure the text?
    a. Cause and effect
    b. Compare and contrast
    c. Chronological sequence
    d. Problem and solution

17. How does the structure of the text help readers better understand the topic?
    a. By stating that anti-terrorism legislation was a priority for many countries, the reader can determine which laws were made and how they changed the life in the country.
    b. By placing the events in the order that they occurred, readers are better able to understand how the day unfolded.
    c. By using descriptive language, the readers are able to develop detailed images of the events that occurred during September 11, 2001.
    d. None of the above

18.
    a. NO CHANGE
    b. Bin Laden orchestrated the attacks as a response to what he felt was American injustice against Islam, and hatred towards Muslims.
    c. Bin Laden orchestrated the attacks, as a response to what he felt was American injustice against Islam and hatred towards Muslims.
    d. Bin Laden orchestrated the attacks as responding to what he felt was American injustice against Islam and hatred towards Muslims.

19. How could the author best express that most Muslims are peaceful people?
    a. By describing the life of a Muslim after the attacks.
    b. By including an anecdote about a Muslim friend.
    c. By reciting details from religious texts.
    d. By explicitly stating that fact.

20. What word could be used in exchange for "violate"?
    a. Respect
    b. Defile
    c. Deny
    d. Obey

21. What technique does the author use to highlight the impact of United Flight 93?
   a. An image of the crash
   b. An allusion to illustrate what may have occurred had the passengers not taken action
   c. An anecdote about a specific passenger
   d. A point of view consideration, where the author forces the reader to think about how he or she would have responded to such a situation

22. Which of the following would not be an appropriate replacement for the underlined portion of the sentence?
   a. First crash was thought to be
   b. Initial crash was thought to be
   c. Thought was that the initial crash
   d. Initial thought was that the crash was

23.
   a. NO CHANGE
   b. Diverting
   c. Converging
   d. Distracting

24. What statement is best supported by the graph included in this passage?
   a. As canceled flights were rescheduled, air travel became backed up and chaotic for quite some time.
   b. Over five hundred flights had to turn back or be redirected to other countries.
   c. Canada alone received 226 flights and thousands of stranded passengers.
   d. The attacks of September 11, 2001 resulted in the immediate suspension of all air travel.

25. What is the purpose of the last paragraph?
   a. It shows that beautiful art can be used to remember a past event.
   b. It demonstrates that Americans will always remember the 9/11 attacks and the lives that were lost.
   c. It explains how America fought back after the attacks.
   d. It provides the author with an opportunity to explain how the location of the towers is used today.

26. Which choice would adequately replace "valiantly"?
   a. Courage
   b. Fortitude
   c. Bravely
   d. Stealthily

27.
   a. NO CHANGE
   b. American airports and airspace close to all national and international flights.
   c. American airports and airspaces closed to all national and international flights.
   d. American airspace and airports were closed to all national and international flights.

28.
a. NO CHANGE
b. As canceled flights are rescheduled, air travel became backed up and chaotic for quite some time.
c. Needless to say, as canceled flights were rescheduled, air travel became backed up and chaotic for quite some time.
d. Needless to say, as canceled flights are rescheduled, air travel became backed up and chaotic over a period of time.

29.
a. NO CHANGE
b. Perceived
c. Intended
d. Assimilated

30.
a. NO CHANGE
b. The Taliban was overthrown on December 9, 2001. They were a group of fundamental Muslims who protected Osama bin Laden. However, the war continued in order to defeat insurgency campaigns in neighboring countries.
c. The Taliban, a group of fundamental Muslims who protected Osama bin Laden, on December 9, 2001 was overthrown. However, the war continued in order to defeat insurgency campaigns in neighboring countries.
d. Osama bin Laden's fundamental Muslims who protected him were called the Taliban and overthrown on December 9, 2001. Yet the war continued in order to defeat the insurgency campaigns in neighboring countries.

Humanities

Focus: Students must make revising and editing decisions on the context of a passage on a humanities-related topic.

Fred Hampton

Fred Hampton desired to see lasting social change for African American people through nonviolent means and community recognition. (32) As a result, he became an African American activist during the American Civil Rights Movement and led the Chicago chapter of the Black Panther Party.

Hampton's Education

Hampton was born and raised in Maywood of Chicago, Illinois in 1948. (33) Gifted academically and a natural athlete, he became a (34) stellar baseball player in high school. (35) After graduating from Proviso East High School in 1966, he later went on to study law at Triton Junior College.

While studying at Triton, Hampton joined and became a leader of the National Association for the Advancement of Colored People (NAACP). (36) As a result of his leadership, the NAACP gained more than 500 members. Hampton worked relentlessly to acquire recreational facilities in the neighborhood and improve the educational resources provided to the impoverished black community of Maywood.

The Black Panthers

The Black Panther Party (BPP) was another activist group that formed around the same time as the NAACP. Hampton was quickly attracted to the Black Panther's approach to the fight for equal rights for African Americans. (37) Hampton eventually joined the chapter and relocated to downtown Chicago to be closer to its headquarters.

His (38) charismatic personality, organizational abilities, sheer determination, and rhetorical skills enabled him to quickly rise through the chapter's ranks. (39) Hampton soon became the leader of the Chicago chapter of the BPP where he organized rallies, taught political education classes, and established a free medical clinic. He also took part in the community police supervision project and played an (40) instrumental role in the BPP breakfast program for impoverished African American children.

Hampton's greatest achievement as the leader of the BPP may be his fight against street gang violence in Chicago. In 1969, Hampton held a press conference where he made the gangs agree to a nonaggression pact known as the Rainbow Coalition. As a result of the pact, a multiracial alliance between blacks, Puerto Ricans, and poor youth was developed.

Assassination

As the Black Panther Party's popularity and influence grew, the Federal Bureau of Investigation (FBI) placed the group under constant surveillance. In an attempt to (42) neutralize the party, the FBI launched several harassment campaigns against the BPP, raided its headquarters in Chicago three times, and arrested over one hundred of the group's members. Hampton was shot during such a raid that occurred on the morning of December 4[th,] 1969.

In 1976, seven years after the event, it was revealed that William O'Neal, Hampton's trusted bodyguard, was an undercover FBI agent. (43) O'Neal provided the FBI with detailed floor plans of the BPP's headquarters, identifying the exact location of Hampton's bed. It was because of these floor plans that the police were able to target and kill Hampton.

The assassination of Hampton fueled outrage amongst the African American community. It was not until years after the assassination that the police admitted wrongdoing. The Chicago City Council now (44) commemorates December 4th as Fred Hampton Day.

31. How does the author structure the text?
    a. Problem and solution
    b. Compare and contrast
    c. Cause and effect
    d. Chronology/sequence

32.
  a. NO CHANGE
  b. As a result he became an African American activist
  c. As a result: he became an African American activist
  d. As a result of, he became an African American activist

33. What word could be used in place of the underlined description?
  a. Vacuous
  b. Energetic
  c. Intelligent
  d. Athletic

34. What term could be used in place of the underlined word?
  a. Outrageous
  b. Adequate
  c. Passionate
  d. Outstanding

35. How could this sentence be rewritten without changing its meaning?
  a. Graduating from Proviso East High School, Hampton studied law at Triton Junior College in 1966.
  b. Hampton graduated from Proviso East High School and studied law at Triton Junior College in 1966.
  c. Hampton went on to study law at Triton Junior College after graduating from Proviso East High School in 1966.
  d. None of the above

36. Which of the following statements, if true, would further validate the selected sentence?
  a. Several of these new members went on to earn scholarships.
  b. With this increase in numbers, Hampton was awarded a medal for his contribution to the NAACP.
  c. Many of these new members would go on to hold high positions in the organization, often accrediting Hampton for his encouragement and guidance.
  d. The NAACP has been growing steadily every year.

37. How else could this sentence be re-structured while maintaining the context of the fourth paragraph?
  a. NO CHANGE
  b. Eventually, Hampton joined the chapter and relocated to downtown Chicago to be closer to its headquarters.
  c. Nevertheless, Hampton joined the chapter and relocated to downtown Chicago to be closer to its headquarters.
  d. Hampton then joined the chapter and relocated to downtown Chicago to be closer to its headquarters

38. What word is synonymous with the underlined description?
  a. Egotistical
  b. Obnoxious
  c. Chauvinistic
  d. Charming

39.
   a. NO CHANGE
   b. As the leader of the BPP, Hampton: organized rallies, taught political education classes, and established a free medical clinic.
   c. As the leader of the BPP, Hampton; organized rallies, taught political education classes, and established a free medical clinic.
   d. As the leader of the BPP, Hampton—organized rallies, taught political education classes, and established a medical free clinic.

40. What term could best replace the underlined word?
   a. Loud
   b. Musical
   c. Influential
   d. Insignificant

41. The author develops the idea that Frank Hampton should not have been killed at the hands of the police. Which could best be used to support that claim?
   a. The manner in which the police raided the BPP headquarters.
   b. The eventual admission from the police that they were wrong in killing Hampton.
   c. The description of previous police raids that resulted in the arrest of hundreds BPP members.
   d. All of the above.

42.
   a. NO CHANGE
   b. Accommodate
   c. Assuage
   d. Praise

43. How could this sentence be rewritten without losing its original meaning?
   a. NO CHANGE
   b. O'Neal provided the FBI with detailed floor plans of the BPP's headquarters, which identified the exact location of Hampton's bed.
   c. O'Neal provided the FBI with detailed floor plans and Hampton's bed.
   d. O'Neal identified the exact location of Hampton's bed that provided the FBI with detailed floor plans of the BPP's headquarters.

44. What word could be used in place of the underlined word?
   a. Disregards
   b. Memorializes
   c. Communicates
   d. Denies

45. How would the author likely describe the FBI during the events of the passage?
   a. Corrupt
   b. Confused
   c. Well-intended
   d. Prejudiced

Science

Focus: Students must make revising and editing decisions on the context of a passage on a scientific topic.

<u>Here Comes the Flood!</u>

A flood occurs when an area of land that is normally dry becomes submerged with water. Floods have affected Earth since the beginning of time and are caused by many different factors. <u>(52) Flooding can occur slowly or within seconds and can submerge small regions or extend over vast areas of land.</u> Their impact on society and the environment can be harmful or helpful.

What Causes Flooding?

Floods may be caused by natural phenomenon, induced by the activities of humans and other animals, or the failure of an infrastructure. Areas located near bodies of water are prone to flooding as are low-lying regions.

Global warming is the result of air pollution that prevents the sun's radiation from being emitted back into space. Instead, the radiation is trapped in Earth and results in global warming. The warming of the Earth has resulted in climate changes. As a result, floods have been occurring with increasing regularity. Some claim that the increased temperatures on Earth may cause the icebergs to melt. They fear that the melting of icebergs will cause the <u>(53) oceans levels</u> to rise and flood coastal regions.

Local Sea Level Rise and Tidal Flooding, 1970-2012

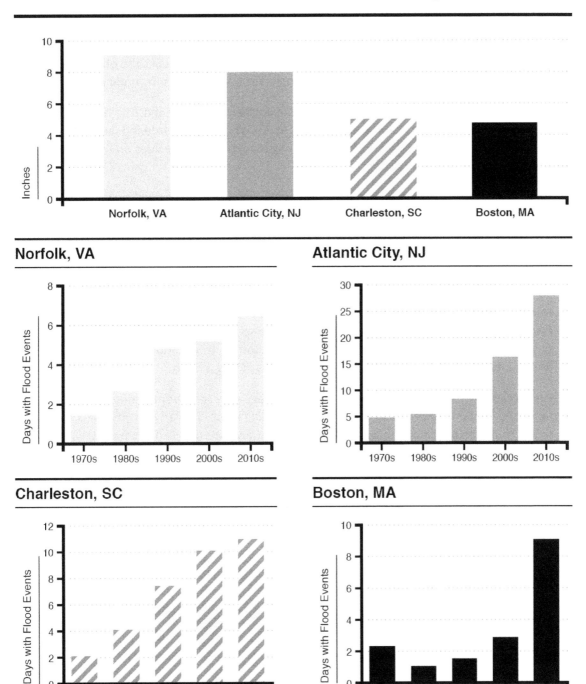

Most commonly, flooding is caused by excessive rain. The ground is not able to absorb all the water produced by a sudden heavy rainfall or rainfall that occurs over a prolonged period of time. Such rainfall may cause the water in rivers and other bodies

43

of water to overflow. The excess water can cause dams to break. Such events can cause flooding of the surrounding riverbanks or coastal regions.

Flash flooding can occur without warning and without rainfall. Flash floods may be caused by a river being blocked by a glacier, avalanche, landslide, logjam, a beaver's obstruction, construction, or dam. Water builds behind such a blockage. Eventually, the mass and force of the built-up water become so extreme that it causes the obstruction to break. Thus, enormous amounts of water rush out towards the surrounding areas.

Areal or urban flooding occurs because the land has become hardened. The hardening of land may result from urbanization or drought. Either way, the hardened land prevents water from seeping into the ground. Instead, the water resides on top of the land.

Finally, flooding may result after severe hurricanes, tsunamis, or tropical cyclones. Local defenses and infrastructures are no matches for the tidal surges and waves caused by these natural phenomena. Such events are bound to result in the flooding of nearby coastal regions or estuaries.

A Flood's After-Effects

Flooding can result in severe devastation of nearby areas. Flash floods and tsunamis can result in sweeping waters that travel at destructive speeds. Fast-moving water has the power to demolish all obstacles in its path such as homes, trees, bridges, and buildings. Animals, plants, and humans may all lose their lives during a flood.

Floods can also cause pollution and infection. Sewage may seep from drains or septic tanks and contaminate drinking water or surrounding lands. Similarly, toxins, fuels, debris from annihilated buildings, and other hazardous materials can leave water unusable for consumption. (54) As the water begins to drain, mold may begin to grow. As a result, residents of flooded areas may be left without power, drinkable water, or be exposed to toxins and other diseases.

(55) Although often associated with devastation, not all flooding results in adverse circumstances. For millions of years, peoples have inhabited floodplains of rivers. (57) Examples include the Mississippi Valley of the United States, the Nile River in Egypt, and the Tigris River of the Middle East. The flooding of such rivers (58) caused nutrient-rich silts to be deposited on the floodplains. Thus, after the floods recede, an extremely fertile soil is left behind. This soil is conducive to the agriculture of bountiful crops and has sustained the diets of humans for millennium.

Proactive Measures Against Flooding

Technologies now allow scientists to predict where and when flooding is likely to occur. Such technologies can also be used (59) to project the severity of an anticipated flood. In this way, local inhabitants can be warned and take preventative measures such a boarding up their homes, gathering necessary provisions, and moving themselves and possessions to higher grounds.

The (60) picturesque views of coastal regions and rivers have long enticed people to build near such locations. Due to the costs associated with the repairs needed after the flooding of such residencies, many governments now require inhabitants of flood-prone areas to purchase flood insurance and build flood-resistant structures. Pictures of all items within a building or home should be taken so that proper reimbursement for losses can be made in the event that a flood does occur.

Staying Safe During a Flood

If a forecasted flood does occur, then people should retreat to higher ground such as a mountain, attic, or roof. Flooded waters may be contaminated, contain hidden debris, or travel at high speeds. Therefore, people should not attempt to walk or drive through a flooded area. To prevent electrocution, electrical outlets and downed power lines need to be avoided.

The Flood Dries Up

Regardless of the type or cause of a flood, floods can result in detrimental alterations to nearby lands and serious injuries to nearby inhabitants. By understanding flood cycles, civilizations can learn to take advantage of flood seasons. By taking the proper precautionary measures, people can stay safe when floods occur. Thus, proper knowledge can lead to safety and prosperity during such an adverse natural phenomenon.

46. What type of text is utilized in the passage?
    a. Informative
    b. Argumentative
    c. Biographical
    d. Narrative

47. What is the main idea of this passage?
    a. All floods are harmful, so precautionary measures ought to be taken.
    b. When people take the proper precautionary measures, all floods can be helpful to civilizations that are located near the floods.
    c. Floods can be caused by several different factors and can be helpful or harmful to civilizations.
    d. None of the above

48. How does the author help the reader focus on the key points of the passage?
    a. The author divides the text into sections.
    b. The author gives explicit definitions for unknown or uncommon terms.
    c. The author uses pictures that illustrate the text.
    d. None of the above

49. Which accurately describes the use of introductions and conclusions in this passage?
    a. An introduction but no conclusion
    b. No introduction but a conclusion
    c. An introduction and a conclusion
    d. No introduction and no conclusion

50. What information from the graphs could be used to support the claims found in the third paragraph?
    a. Between 1970-1980, Boston experienced a decrease in the number of days with flood events.
    b. Between 1970-1980, Atlantic City, New Jersey did not experience an increase in the number of days with flood events.
    c. Since 1970, the number of days with floods has decreased in major coastal cities across America.
    d. Since 1970, sea levels have risen along the East Coast.

51. One of the headings is entitled "A Floods After-Effects." How should this heading be rewritten?
    a. A Flood's After-Effect
    b. A Flood's After-Effects
    c. A Floods After-Affect
    d. A Flood's After-Affects

52. Which of the following revisions can be made to the sentence that will still maintain the original meaning while making the sentence more concise?
    a. NO CHANGE
    b. Flooding can either be slow or occur within seconds. It doesn't take long to submerge small regions or extend vast areas of land.
    c. Flooding occurs slowly or rapidly submerging vast areas of land.
    d. Vast areas of land can be flooded slowly or within seconds.

53.
    a. NO CHANGE
    b. Ocean levels
    c. Ocean's levels
    d. Levels of the oceans

54. Which choice best maintains the pattern of the first sentence of the paragraph?
    a. NO CHANGE
    b. As the rain subsides and the water begins to drain, mold may begin to grow.
    c. Mold may begin to grow as the water begins to drain.
    d. The water will begin to drain and mold will begin to grow.

55.
    a. NO CHANGE
    b. Although often associated with devastation not all flooding results
    c. Although often associated with devastation. Not all flooding results
    d. While often associated with devastation, not all flooding results

56. What is the author's intent of the final paragraph?
    a. To explain that all bad occurrences eventually come to an end.
    b. To summarize the key points within the passage.
    c. To explain that, with time, all flooded lands will eventually dry.
    d. To relay a final key point about floods.

57. The author is considering deleting this sentence from the tenth paragraph. Should the sentence be kept or deleted?
    a. Kept, because it provides examples of floodplains that have been successfully inhabited by civilizations.
    b. Kept, because it provides an example of how floods can be beneficial.
    c. Deleted, because it blurs the paragraph's focus on the benefits of floods.
    d. Deleted, because it distracts from the overall meaning of the paragraph.

58.
    a. NO CHANGE
    b. Cause
    c. Causing
    d. Causes

59.
    a. NO CHANGE
    b. Projecting
    c. Project
    d. Projected

60. Which term could best replace the underlined word?
    a. Colorful
    b. Drab
    c. Scenic
    d. Candid

Literature

Focus: Students must make revising and editing decisions on the context of a reflective essay on literature.

Distrust in the Odyssey

In *The Odyssey*, Odysseus develops out of his experiences and the people he meets along his journey home. Many of his encounters involve female characters, some of whom offer Odysseus aid in his journey. (62) However, several of these characters deceive and even pose great danger to the hero. (63)This makes his journey home harder, it forces Odysseus himself to change and adapt in order to deal with the challenges. By the time Odysseus reaches home, he has become notably distrustful of women and even those who have true intentions. It is this sense of caution that ultimately serves Odysseus in successfully defeating the suitors of Penelope upon his return home.

Odysseus would not have been able to defeat the suitors without stealth and deception. He had (65) to conceal himself in order to achieve revenge. This is something we see earlier in Odysseus' encounter with Polyphemus the Cyclops. While not female, Polyphemus displayed feminine qualities characterized by his 'womb-like cave'. (66) Entering into the dwelling Odysseus directly demanded hospitality- Polyphemus instead butchered his men in spite of custom. In order to survive the encounter, Odysseus (67) relinquishes his true identity by telling Polyphemus his name is 'Nobody'. After the carnage of his men, he does not entrust the Cyclops with his true name. Rather, Odysseus uses disguise and cunning to trick Polyphemus into reopening the cave. When he emerges he is then reborn again as Odysseus.

This pattern is echoed again when Odysseus reaches Ithaca: "I look for endless ground to be spattered by the blood and brains of the suitors, these men who are eating all your substance away. But come now, let me make you so that no mortal can recognize you." (13: 394-397) Here Athena reveals her plan to disguise Odysseus as he makes his move against the suitors. Why do this? Why would Odysseus embrace the idea? With Polyphemus, Odysseus entered the cave trusting he would be received as a welcomed guest, but he wasn't. (68) Clearly, Odysseus isn't making the same mistake twice in trusting people to automatically abide by custom. Using a disguise allowed Odysseus to apply strategy in a similar manner he had with Polyphemus. This passage specifically describes the suitors as eating away at Odysseus' substance, seeming to further the parallel with Polyphemus who devoured Odysseus' men. (70) Also like with Polyphemus, Odysseus only reveals his true identity when he knows his plan has succeeded. The disguise concept presents a strategic role, but it also sheds further light on the impact of Odysseus' travels. To conceal (71) ones identity is to withhold trust.

The Circe episode matches Odysseus against someone he already knows to be untrustworthy. It is known that Circe welcomes all men who (72) enter upon her island with food and drink, but this is a deception meant to ensnare them. This xenia, or hospitality, that Odysseus would have been accustomed to, turns out to be farce. She violates the trust of her guests by turning them into swine, thus making her a deceitful host- and specifically- a woman Odysseus cannot trust. In order to (73) assure his and the crew's safety, Odysseus must look past her empty courtesy and deceive her in a way that will remedy the situation. With the knowledge of Circe's dark intentions (and Hermes' instructions), Odysseus attempts to out-maneuver Circe by making her think he will kill her (10: 321-323). By doing this he is taking on deceitful qualities so as to ensure he can bend her to proper behavior, which works. Still untrusting of Circe's submission though, Odysseus makes her swear a formal oath: "I would not be willing to go to bed with you unless you can bring yourself, O goddess, to swear me a great oath that there is no other evil hurt you devise against me." (10:342-344) Even though Odysseus tamed Circe, he is still distrustful. The 'great' oath becomes a final assurance that she is sincere. Until he knows for certain that no more treachery can befall him (the oath), he does not partake in showing any form of trust.

In the Land of the Dead, Odysseus encounters Agamemnon, who describes his own murder at the hand of his wife, Klytaimestra. Not only is this an example of a wife's betrayal, but a betrayal that appears close to Odysseus' own situation. (74) Like Agamemnon, Odysseus is returning home to his wife. However, Agamemnon didn't realize his wife had foul intentions, he trusted her to receive him with open arms:

"See, I had been thinking that I would be welcome to my children and thralls of my household when I came home, but she with thoughts surpassing grisly splashed the shame on herself and on the rest of her sex, on women still to come, even on the one whose acts are virtuous." (11: 430-434)

Clearly this is a cautionary story for Odysseus. After telling Odysseus of Klytaimestra's betrayal, Agamemnon warns Odysseus that all women are inherently distrustful. Now by this time Odysseus has already been deceived and nearly killed by female/female-like characters. Agamemnon's logic seems to back up what he already experienced. (75) As the text progresses, Odysseus encounters the Sirens and Calypso, who seem to corroborate the idea that women are bad news. However, what is most impressionable on Odysseus is Agamemnon's distrust of even virtuous women, "even on the one whose acts are virtuous". Who is to say that they cannot turn against him like Klytaimestra did against Agamemnon. This seems to cement in Odysseus a fear of betrayal, being welcomed in, just to be hurt.

61. What is the primary purpose of the passage?
    a. Inform the audience about the perils of Odysseus
    b. Argue that the Odyssey is a sexist text
    c. Prove that Odysseus' distrust of women was developed by past experiences which ultimately aided him in returning home
    d. Argue that femme-fatales were a key archetype in Ancient Greek literature

62.
    a. NO CHANGE
    b. However these
    c. However several of these
    d. Several of these

63.
    a. NO CHANGE
    b. This makes his journey home harder it forces Odysseus himself to change and adapt
    c. This makes his journey home harder which forces Odysseus to change and adapt
    d. This makes his journey home harder, forcing Odysseus to change and adapt

64. What function do the quotations provide in the passage?
    a. The quotes from The Odyssey help illustrate what the author is talking about
    b. The author provides these quotes to show where he gained his views on the text
    c. The quotes provide textual evidence to back up the writer's views
    d. All of the above are correct

65.
    a. NO CHANGE
    b. To be concealed
    c. Concealed
    d. Concealing

66. The author is trying to revise this sentence. He also wants to make it clear that Polyphemus' lack of hospitality violated Ancient Greek custom. Which of the following would be the best revision of this sentence?

    a. Odysseus directly entering into the dwelling and demanded hospitality – Polyphemus instead butchered his men in spite of custom.

    b. Odysseus entered Polyphemus' dwelling expecting to be received with customary hospitality, but instead, his men were butchered.

    c. Odysseus expected Polyphemus to receive him with hospitality, but instead, his men were butchered in gross opposition of what the custom demands.

    d. Polyphemus butchered Odysseus' men without any regard to hospitality.

67.

    a. NO CHANGE

    b. Conceals

    c. Withholds

    d. Surrenders

68.

    a. NO CHANGE

    b. Clearly Odysseus isn't making the same mistake twice in trusting people to automatically abide by custom.

    c. Clearly, Odysseus isn't making the same mistake twice; trusting people to automatically abide by custom.

    d. Odysseus isn't making the same mistake twice in trusting people, clearly, to automatically abide by custom.

69. Which statement would the author most likely use to describe Odysseus?

    a. Odysseus' naturally cautious nature proved an important asset for him in the Odyssey

    b. Odysseus is the noblest king of Ithaca

    c. Odysseus' guile is his greatest asset

    d. Odysseus has been molded by his journey to be naturally suspect of women and conventional situations

70.

    a. NO CHANGE

    b. As he did with Polyphemus

    c. As he did before

    d. With the exact method as he had with Polyphemus

71.

    a. NO CHANGE

    b. One's

    c. Someone's

    d. Oneself

72.
  a. NO CHANGE
  b. Land upon
  c. Arrive on
  d. Crash on

73.
  a. NO CHANGE
  b. Ensure
  c. Prevent
  d. Vindicate

74. The author is contemplating eliminating this sentence from the passage. Should he or should he not keep it within the text?
  a. Remove the sentence; it merely repeats the one before it
  b. Keep the sentence because it clarifies Agamemnon's and Odysseus' connection
  c. Keep the sentence because it helps transition into the next sentence and the quote after that
  d. Remove the sentence because the information is irrelevant

75.
  a. NO CHANGE
  b. As the text progresses Odysseus
  c. The text progresses with Odysseus
  d. As Odysseus progresses in the text

Answers and Explanations

1. B: In general, the first paragraph introduces the idea(s) or makes a claim(s) that will be discussed, explained, and/or supported throughout an essay or passage. Although Choices *D* and *C* include details from the passage, the statements don't encompass the meaning of the entire text. Choice *A* is neither a part of nor the reason for the passage. Therefore, Choice *B* is the correct answer.

2. D: This passage is informative, choice *D*, because it is nonfiction and factual. The passage's intent is not to state an opinion, discuss an individual's life, or tell a story. Thus, the passage is not argumentative Choice *A*, biographical, choice *C*, or narrative, choice *B*.

3. C: The next paragraph states that "These advanced offices oftentimes require a Professional Engineering (PE) license which can be obtained through additional college courses, professional experience, and acceptable scores on the Fundamentals of Engineering (FE) and Professional Engineering (PE) standardized assessments. Since the word "oftentimes" is used instead of always, Choice *C* is the best response.

4. D: To begin, *of* is not required here. *Apprenticeship* is also more appropriate in this context than *apprentice opportunities*, *apprentice* describes an individual in an apprenticeship, not an apprenticeship itself. Both of these changes are needed, making choice *D* the correct answer.

5. D: To begin, the selected sentence is a run-on, and displays discombobulated information. Thus, the sentence does need revision, making choice *A* wrong. The main objective of the selected section of the passage is to communicate that many positions (*positions* is a more suitable term than *offices,* as well) require a PE license, which is gained by scoring well on the FE and PE assessments. This must be the primary focus of the revision. It is necessary to break the sentence into two, to avoid a run-on. Choice *B* fixes the run-on aspect, but the sentence is indirect and awkward in construction. It takes too long to establish the importance of the PE license. Choice *C* is wrong for the same reason and it is a run on. Choice *D* is correct because it breaks the section into coherent sentences and emphasizes the main point the author is trying to communicate: the PE license is required for some higher positions, it's obtained by scoring well on the two standardized assessments, and college and experience can be used to prepare for the assessments in order to gain the certification.

6. C: Any time a writer wants to validate a claim, he or she ought to provide factual information that proves or supports that claim: "beginning his or her preparation for the profession in high school" supports the claim that aircraft engineers undergo years of education. For this reason, Choice *C* is the correct response. However, completing such courses in high school does not guarantee that aircraft engineers will earn generous salaries, choice *A*, become employed in executive positions, choice *B*, or stay employed, choice *D*.

7. B: Choice *B* is correct because "skill" is defined as having certain aptitude for a given task. Choice *C* is incorrect because "work" does not directly denote "critical thinking, business skills, problem solving, and creativity.", choice *A*, is incorrect because the word "care" doesn't fit into the context of the passage, and choice *D*, "composition," is incorrect because nothing in this statement points to the way in which something is structured.

8. C: *Allows* is inappropriate because it does not stress what those in the position of aircraft engineers actually need to be able to do. *Requires* is the only alternative that fits because it actually describes necessary skills of the job.

9. B: The third paragraph discusses reports made by the United States Bureau of Labor Statistics (BLS) in regards to the median, upper 10 percent, and lower 10 percent annual salaries of aircraft engineers in 2015. Therefore, this paragraph is used to support the claim that aircraft engineers are compensated with generous salaries, choice B. The paragraph has nothing to do with an aircraft engineer's skill set ,choice A, education, choice C, or incentive program, choice D.

10. A: The correct response is choice A because this statement's intent is to give examples as to how aircraft engineers apply mathematical equations and scientific processes towards aeronautical and aerospace issues and/or inventions. The answer is not "therefore", choice B, or "furthermore", choice D, because no causality is being made between ideas. Two items are neither being compared nor contrasted, so "however" choice C is also not the correct answer.

11. A: No change is required. The comma is properly placed after the introductory phrase "In May of 2015." Choice B is missing the word "in." Choice C does not separate the introductory phrase from the rest of the sentence. Choice D places an extra, and unnecessary, comma prior to 2015.

12. D: The first paragraph outlines the concepts that are discussed throughout the passage. Thus, this paragraph serves as the passage's introduction. The second paragraph provides specific details of the concepts introduced in the first paragraph. However, there is no conclusion in this passage. A conclusion would summarize the key concepts addressed throughout the passage. Since there is an introduction but no conclusion, choice D is the correct response. Since there is an introduction, choice A and choice C are incorrect. Since there is no conclusion, choice B is incorrect.

13. A: The word "conversely" best demonstrates the opposite sentiments in this passage. Choice B is incorrect because it denotes agreement with the previous statement. Choice C is incorrect because the sentiment is not restated, but opposed. Choice D is incorrect because the previous statement is not a cause for the sentence in question.

14. B: While it is likely that the author admires or is even proud of the work aircraft engineers do, this is inconclusive. Clearly the author is not pessimistic; the author expresses a positive attitude on the subject. *Unconvinced* is totally irrelevant. This leaves choice B *optimistic*. In the final paragraph, the author indicates that aircraft engineers with marketable skills will continue to find areas that require their work.

15. A: Choice A is the correct answer because the projections are taking place in the present, even though they are making reference to a future date.

History/ Social Studies

16. C: The author explains the events of September 11, 2001 in the order that they occurred. Therefore, the author structures the text chronologically. For this reason, Choice C is the correct response. Similarities or differences are not being made between two or more objects or ideas. Therefore, the author does not use a compare and contrast text structure, choice B. The passage does not solely focus on the reasons for the attacks. Therefore, the passage does not utilize the cause and effect text structure choice A. Terrorism still occurs around the world. Thus, the issue still remains. Choice D is incorrect because no solution to the problem of terrorism was created.

17. B: The passage contains clearly labeled subheadings. These subheadings inform the reader what will be addressed in upcoming paragraphs. Choice *A* is incorrect because the anti-terrorism laws of other countries were never addressed in the passage. The text is written in an informative manner; overly descriptive language is not utilized. Therefore, Choice *C* is incorrect. Choice *D* is incorrect because as mentioned, the structure of the text does help in the manner described in Choice *B*.

18. A: No change is needed. Choices *B* and *C* utilize incorrect comma placements. Choice *D* utilizes an incorrect verb tense (responding).

19. D: The third paragraph states "The majority of Muslims practice Islam peacefully". Therefore, the author explicitly states that most Muslims are peaceful peoples, choice D. Choices *B, C,* and *A* are not included in the passage and are incorrect.

20. B: The term "violate" implies a lack of respect or compliance. "Defile" means to degrade or show no respect. Therefore, choice *B* is the correct answer. Choice *A* is incorrect because "respect" is the opposite of violate. To "deny" is to refuse, so choice *C* is not the answer because the weight of the word "deny" is not as heavy as the word "violate." To "obey" is to follow orders, so choice *D* is not the answer.

21. B: An allusion is a direct or indirect literary reference or figure of speech towards a person, place, or event. By referencing the diversion of the airplanes to alternate locations, the author uses an allusion (Choice *B*) to highlight the impact of United Flight 93. Although a graph depicting the decline in the number of aircraft passengers is provided, an image is not. Therefore, Choice *A* is not the answer. The passage does not tell the story from a single passenger's point of view. Thus, Choice *C* and Choice *D* are not the answers.

22. C: All of the choices except choice *C* go with the flow of the original underlined portion of the sentence and communicate the same idea. Choice *C*, however, does not take into account the rest of the sentence and therefore, becomes awkward and incorrect.

23. B: Although "diverging" means to separate from the main route and go in a different direction, it is used awkwardly and unconventionally in this sentence. Therefore, Choice *A* is not the answer. Choice *B* is the correct answer because it implies that the passengers distracted the terrorists, which caused a change in the plane's direction. "Converging", choice *C*, is incorrect because it implies that the plane met another in a central location. Although the passengers may have distracted the terrorists, they did not distract the plane. Therefore, Choice *D* is incorrect.

24. D: The graph shows the number of people (in millions) boarding United States' flights between 1996-2005. The graph includes a vertical red line that indicates the dip in the number people that boarded U.S. flights on September 11, 2001. Therefore, the graph illustrates the effects of suspending air travel immediately after the attacks, choice D. The graph does not show where the flights were redirected, choice *B*, the number of passengers that other countries received as a result of the redirected air travel, choice *C*, or the resulting flight schedule implications (Choice *A*).

25. B: The last paragraph explains that museums and monuments have been erected to honor those who died as a result of the attacks and those who risked their lives to save the injured. Thus, the paragraph serves to explain the lasting impact on America and honor those impacted by the event, choice B. The design of the museums and monuments are not described, so Choice *A* is incorrect. Choice *C* is incorrect because America's War on Terror was not discussed in the last paragraph. Choice *D* is incorrect, because although the previous location of the towers was converted into a park, this was not mentioned in the passage.

26. C: Choice *D* has nothing to do with the sentence and can be easily eliminated. Choices *A* and *B* are both synonymous with "valiantly" but are both used as nouns, not adjectives, which is required. However, Choice *C*, "bravely", is used as an adjective and is synonymous with *valiantly*. Thus choice *C* is correct.

27. D: Airspace and airports must be closed by people; they don't just close themselves, so it is proper to include an action to indicate that they were sealed off. Choice *B* is wrong because the verb *close* is in the incorrect tense. Choice *C* is also wrong because *airspace* does not need to become *airspaces* and the issue still remains: while there is action, it is not in the proper form to indicate human action. Choice *D* is correct because it correctly uses the helping verb "were", which indicates human action.

28. C: This sentence contains improper verb agreement in the fragment "as canceled flights are rescheduled." "Are" is a present-tense verb while "rescheduled" is a past-tense verb. Because the attacks occurred in the past, both verbs need to be written in the past tense, as done in Choice *C*.

29. C: *Desired* communicates wishing or direct motive, so the goal here is to pick a term that communicates a similar meaning, if not better. To begin, Choices *B* and *C* have irrelevant meanings and wouldn't serve the sentence at all. However, *intended* means planned or meant to. *Intended* is a far better choice than *desired,* because it would communicate goals and strategy more than simply saying that Bush desired to do something.

30. A: While choice *B* isn't necessarily wrong, it lacks the direct nature that the original sentence has. Also by breaking up the sentences like this, the reader becomes confused because the connection between the Taliban's defeat and ongoing war is now separated by a second sentence that is not necessary. Choice *C* corrects this problem but the fluidity of the sentence is marred because of the awkward construction of the first sentence. Choice *D* begins well, but lacks the use of *was* before overthrown, which discombobulates the sentence. While *yet* provides an adequate transition for the next sentence, the term *however* is more appropriate. Thus, the original structure of the two sentences is correct, making Choice *A,* NO CHANGE, the correct answer.

Humanities

31. D: The author explains the events of Fred Hampton's life in the order that they occurred. Therefore, the author structures the text chronologically, choice D. Similarities or differences are not being made between two or more objects or ideas. So, the author does not use a compare and contrast text structure, choice B. Although the author alludes to the impact of Fred Hampton's life, the text is not structured such that this is its main purpose. Therefore, the passage does not utilize the cause and effect text structure (Choice C). Choice A is incorrect because the passage ends with Fred Hampton's assassination.

32. A: The comma after *result* is necessary for the sentence structure, making it an imperative component. The original sentence is correct, making Choice *A* correct. For the reason just listed, Choice *B* is incorrect because it lacks the crucial comma that introduces a new idea. Choice *C* is incorrect because a colon is unnecessary, and Choice *D* is wrong because the addition of "of" is both unnecessary and incorrect when applied to the rest of the sentence.

33. C: To be "gifted" is to be talented. "Academically" refers to education. Therefore, Fred Hampton was intellectually talented, or intelligent, choice C. Choice *B* is incorrect because it refers to a level of energy or activity. Choice *A* is incorrect because "vacuous" means the opposite of being gifted academically. Choice *D* is incorrect because it refers to one's physical build and/or abilities.

34. D: In this sentence, "stellar" implies an exceptional performance. Thus, the word can be used interchangeably with the term "outstanding", choice D. Choice *B* is incorrect because "adequate" implies a mediocre or moderate performance. Choice *C* is incorrect because "passionate" is used to describe one's feelings towards another person, place, or event. Choice *A* is incorrect because an "outrageous performance" would be shockingly abnormal, inadequate, bold, or startling.

35. C: Choice *C* maintains that Hampton began college after graduating Proviso East High School in 1966. Choices *A* and *B* are incorrect because these sentences infer that Hampton graduated high school *and* started college in 1966, the same time, which might not necessarily be true. Choice *C* is the most consistent choice with the original sentence.

36. C: The goal for this question is to select a sentence that not only affirms, or backs up, the selected statement, but could also appear after it and flows with the rest of the piece. Choice *A* is irrelevant to the sentence; just because new members earned scholarships this doesn't necessarily mean that this was testament of Hampton's leadership or that this actually benefitted the NAACP. Choice *B* is very compelling. If Hampton got an award for the increase in numbers, this could bolster the idea that he was the direct cause of the rise in numbers and that he was of great value to the organization. However, it does not say directly that he was the cause of the increase and that this was extremely beneficial to the NAACP. Let's keep looking. Choice *C* is a much better choice than Choice *B*. Choice *C* has the new members directly accrediting Hampton for his leadership; the fact that such new members went on to hold high positions is also testament to Hampton's leadership. Thus, Choice *C* is correct. Choice *D* does nothing for the underlined section.

37. B: Choice *B* moves the word "eventually" to the beginning of the sentences. By using the term as an introductory word, continuity from one sentence to another is created. Meanwhile, the syntax is not lost. Choice *A* is incorrect because the sentence requires a proper transition. Choice *C* is incorrect because the sentence does not contain surprising or contrasting information, as is indicated by the introductory word "nevertheless." Choice *D* is incorrect -because the term "then" implies that Hampton's relocation to the BPP's headquarters in Chicago occurred shortly or immediately after leading the NAACP.

38. D: An individual with a charismatic personality is charming and appealing to others. Therefore, Choice *D* is the correct answer. Choice *A* is incorrect because someone with an egotistical personality is conceited or self-serving. Choice *B* is incorrect because "obnoxious" is the opposite of charismatic. Choice *C* is incorrect because someone with a chauvinistic personality is aggressive or prejudiced towards one's purpose, desire, or sex.

39. A: No change is needed: Choice *A*. The list of events accomplished by Hampton is short enough that each item in the list can be separated by a comma. Choice *B* is incorrect. Although a colon can be used to introduce a list of items, it is not a conventional choice for separating items within a series. Semicolons are used to separate at least three items in a series that have an internal comma. Semicolons can also be used to separate clauses in a sentence that contain internal commas intended for clarification purposes. Neither of the two latter uses of semicolons is required in the example sentence. Therefore, Choice *C* is incorrect. Choice *D* is incorrect because a dash is not a conventional choice for punctuating items in a series.

40. C: "Instrumental" is synonymous with being influential, involved, or helpful. Therefore, Choice *C* is correct. Although the term "instrumental" has the word "instrument" in it, the term has nothing to do with instruments or music. Therefore, Choices *A* and *B* are incorrect. Choice *D* is incorrect because the word "insignificant" is the opposite of "instrumental."

41. D: Claims can be supported with evidence or supporting details found within the text. Choice *D* is correct because Choices *A, B,* and *C* are all either directly stated or alluded to within the passage.

42. A: The term *neutralize* means to counteract, or render ineffective, which is exactly what the FBI is wanting to do. Accommodate means to be helpful or lend aid, which is the opposite of *neutralize*. Therefore choice *B* is wrong. *Assuage* means to ease, while *praise* means to express warm feeling, so they are in no way close to the needed context. Therefore, *neutralize* is the best option, making Choice *A,* NO CHANGE, the correct answer.

43. B: The order of the original sentence suggests that the floor plans that were provided to the FBI by O'Neal enabled the FBI to identify the exact location of Hampton's bed. This syntax is maintained in Choice *B.* Therefore, Choice *B* is correct, which makes Choice *A* incorrect. Choice *C* is incorrect because the sentence's word order conveys the meaning that O'Neal provided the FBI with Hampton's bed as well as the floor plans. Choice *D* is incorrect because it implies that it was the location of the bed that provided the FBI with the headquarters' floor plans.

44. B: "Commemorates" means to honor, celebrate, or memorialize a person or event. Therefore, Choice *B* is correct. Choice *A* is incorrect because "disregards" is the opposite of "commemorates." Choice *C* is incorrect because to communicate means to converse or to speak. Choice *D* is incorrect because to "deny" means to reject, negate, refuse, or rebuff.

45. D: From the context of the passage, it is clear that the author does not think well of the FBI and their investigation of Hampton and the Black Panthers. Choices *B* and *C* can be easily eliminated. "Well intended" is positive, which is not a characteristic that he would probably attribute to the FBI in the passage. Nor would he think they were "confused", but deliberate in their methods. Choice *A,* "corrupt", is very compelling; he'd likely agree with this, but Choice *D,* "prejudiced" is better. The FBI may not have been corrupt but there certainly seemed to have particular dislike/distrust for the Black Panthers. Thus Choice *D,* "prejudiced", is correct.

Science

46. A: This passage is informative (choice A) because it is nonfiction and factual. The passage's intent is not to state an opinion, discuss an individual's life, or tell a story. Thus, the passage is not argumentative , choice *B,* biographical, choice *C,* or narrative, choice *D.*

47. C: The main idea of a text is the central idea or main point. Choice *C* is correct because the text talks about the type of floods and the effects of floods. Choice *A* is incorrect because not all floods are harmful. For example, the passage described how some floods are helpful in creating fertile soils for crops grown in floodplains. Choice *B* is incorrect because not all floods are helpful. For example, the text describes the detrimental effects of tsunamis and flash floods. Choice *D* is incorrect.

48. A: This passage is divided into five subsections. Thus, Choice *A* is correct. Choice *B* is incorrect because explicit definitions to new words are not provided. Choice *C* is incorrect; although a graph is used to depict supporting information about floods, pictures are not provided. Choice *D* is incorrect.

49. C: The first paragraph outlines the concepts that are discussed throughout the passage. Thus, this paragraph serves as the passage's introduction. The paragraphs found in the body of the text provide specific details of the concepts introduced in the first paragraph. The final paragraph serves as a summary and conclusion of the topics addressed throughout the text. Since the text has both an introduction and conclusion, Choice *C* is correct. Since the text does include a conclusion, Choice *A* and Choice *D* are incorrect. Since the text does include an introduction, Choice *B* is incorrect.

50. D: All of the cities included in the graphs are along the East Coast of the United States. All of the bars on the graphs show an increase in sea level or the number of days with flood events since 1970. Therefore, the author chose to include the graphs to support the claim that sea levels have risen along the East Coast since 1970, choice D. Choice *A* and Choice *B* are incorrect because the bars above 1970 on Boston's graph and Atlantic City's graph are shorter than the graphs' bars above 1980. Therefore, between 1970-1980, both cities experienced an increase in the number of days with flood events. Choice *C* is incorrect because the bars increase in height on all of the cities' graphs, showing an increase in the number of days with floods along the entire East coast.

51. B: Although "affect" and "effect" sound the same, they have different meanings. "Affect" is used as a verb. It is defined as the influence of a person, place, or event on another. "Effect" is used as a noun. It is defined as the result of an event. Therefore, the latter ought to be used in the heading. For this reason, Choices *C* and *D* are incorrect. Because the effect is a result of the flood, a possessive apostrophe is needed for the singular noun "flood." For this reason, Choice *A* is incorrect and Choice *B* is correct.

52. D: Again, the objective for questions like this is to determine if a revision is possible within the choices and if it can adhere to the specific criteria of the question; in this case, we want the sentence to maintain the original meaning while being more concise, or shorter. Choice *B* can be eliminated. The meaning of the original sentence is split into two distinct sentences. The second of the two sentences is also incorrectly constructed. Choice *C* is very intriguing but there is a jumble of verbs present in: "Flooding occurs slowly or rapidly submerging" that it makes the sentence awkward and difficult to understand without the use of a comma after *rapidly*, making it a poor construction. Choice *C* is wrong. Choice *D* is certainly more concise and it is correctly phrased; it communicates the meaning message that flooding can overtake great lengths of land either slowly or very fast. The use of "Vast areas of land" infers that smaller regions or small areas can flood just as well. Thus, Choice *D* is a good revision that maintains the meaning of the original sentence while being concise and more direct. This rules out Choice *A* in the process.

53. B: In this sentence, the word *ocean* does not require an *s* after it to make it plural because "ocean levels" is plural. Therefore choices *A* and *C* are incorrect. Because the passage is referring to multiple – if not all ocean levels – *ocean* does not require an apostrophe (*'s*) because that would indicate that only one ocean is the focus, which is not the case. Choice *D* does not fit well into the sentence and, once again, we see that *ocean* has an *s* after it. This leaves Choice *B,* which correctly completes the sentence and maintains the intended meaning.

54. C: Choice *C* is the best answer because it most closely maintains the sentence pattern of the first sentence of the paragraph, which begins with a noun and passive verb phrase. Choice *A* and *C* are incorrect. Choice *B* is incorrect because it does not maintain the sentence pattern of the first sentence of the paragraph. Instead, Choice *B* shifts the placement of the modifying prepositional phrase to the beginning of the sentence. Choice *D* is incorrect because it does not maintain the sentence pattern established by the first sentence of the paragraph. Instead, Choice *D* is an attempt to combine two independent clauses.

55. A: Choice *C* can be eliminated because creating a new sentence with *not* is grammatically incorrect and it throws off the rest of the sentence. Choice *B* is wrong because a comma is definitely needed after *devastation* in the sentence. Choice *D* is also incorrect because "while" is a poor substitute for "although". *Although* in this context is meant to show contradiction with the idea that floods are associated with devastation. Therefore, none of these choices would be suitable revisions because the original was correct: NO CHANGE, Choice *A*, is the correct answer.

56. B: Choice *B* is the correct answer because the final paragraph summarizes key points from each subsection of the text. Therefore, the final paragraph serves as the conclusion. A concluding paragraph is often found at the end of a text. It serves to remind the reader of the main points of a text. Choice *A* is incorrect because the last paragraph does not just mention adverse effects of floods. For example, the paragraph states "By understanding flood cycles, civilizations can learn to take advantage of flood seasons." Choice *C* is incorrect; although the subheading mentions the drying of floods, the phenomena is not mentioned in the paragraph. Finally, Choice *D* is incorrect because no new information is presented in the last paragraph of the passage.

57. A: Idea and claims are best expressed and supported within a text through examples, evidence, and descriptions. Choice *A* is correct because it provides examples of rivers that support the tenth paragraph's claim that "not all flooding results in adverse circumstances." Choice *B* is incorrect because the sentence does not explain how floods are beneficial. Therefore, Choices *C* and *D* are incorrect.

58. D: In the sentence, *caused* is an incorrect tense, making choice *A* wrong. Choice *B* is incorrect because this used as a noun, we need *cause* in verb form. Choices *C* and *D* are very compelling. *Causing,* choice *C*, is a verb and it is in the present continuous tense, which appears to agree with the verb *flooding,* but it is incorrectly used. This leaves choice *D, causes,* which does fit because it is in the indefinite present tense. Fitting each choice into the sentence and reading it in your mind will also reveal that choice *D, causes,* correctly completes the sentence. Apply this method to all the questions when possible.

59. A: To *project* means to anticipate or forecast. This goes very well with the sentence because it describes how new technology is trying to estimate flood activity in order to prevent damage and save lives. "Project" in this case needs to be assisted by "to" in order to function in the sentence. Therefore, Choice *A* is correct. Choices *B* and *D* are the incorrect tenses. Choice *C* is also wrong because it lacks *to.*

60. C: *Picturesque* is an adjective used for an attractive, scenic, or otherwise striking image. Thus, Choice *C* is correct. Choice *A* is incorrect because although "colorful" can be included in a picturesque view, it does not encompass the full meaning of the word. Choice *B* is incorrect because "drab" is the opposite of "picturesque." Choice *D* is incorrect because "candid" is defined as being frank, open, truthful, or honest.

Literature

61. C: While the text is clearly informative, there is a definite goal in the writing. The author is presenting evidence and key information to illustrate a specific point. Choice *A* is incorrect. Choices *B* and *D* are also incorrect because the author does not mention or directly state any of these things, but instead focuses on Odysseus' experiences and how, and why, they have shaped his character. This makes *C* the correct answer, which can also be seen clearly laid out in the first paragraph.

62. A: "However" is an appropriate word to begin this sentence since it illustrates the idea of contrast: some of the female Odysseus encountered were helpful, *however* some were clearly not. Therefore, we can eliminate Choice *D*. Choice *B* is also wrong because it eliminates the word "several", which is also useful in distinguishing that, while some female characters were benevolent, several were deceptive and even harmful. Choice *C* is wrong because it lacks the comma after "However". Thus, this part of the sentence requires no edits, making the choice *A*, NO CHANGE.

63. D: This portion of the sentence could certainly use revision, but one aspect that should definitely remain is the use of a comma in the structure. Eliminating the comma in this portion of the sentence will make the sentence a run-on and confuse the reader. A comma is needed to link these two ideas together, which makes choice *B* easy to eliminate. For this reason Choice *C* can also be ruled out. Even with the word "which" added for clarity, a comma is still necessary for the overall construction. Choice *D* has several very good modifications that both maintain the original meaning of the sentence and make it easier to read. In Choice *D*, the comma is included. Another good modification is eliminating *himself*, which is confusing and unnecessary. Changing "it forces" to "forcing" also makes the sentence clearer and eliminates word cluster. All these factors make *D* the correct answer, which means that Choice *A* wrong.

64. D: All of the answer choices are correct. Quotes from the original text serve to enlighten the reader about specific moments and context within the work, illustrate where the author gets their ideas, and also cite examples as evidence. The author does all of these things with the quotes, making *D* the correct answer. Be sure to read such questions carefully and consider how an author uses additional materials in the passage, such as quotes or graphs.

65. A: Choice *D* is wrong, *concealing* is the improper tense and it throws off the sentence. Choice *B* is a very good possibility, but the "be" is ultimately unnecessary in the context of the sentence, so it can be eliminated. Choice *C* is also very tempting because "concealed" would fit into the sentence, but it isn't as strong as the original "to conceal". This is so because "to conceal" suggests the active of use the word towards an objective. "Odysseus had concealed himself" is more passive than "Odysseus had to conceal". The latter suggests a more direct action, which is what the author is trying to communicate. This makes choice *A*, NO CHANGE, the best option.

66. C: Choice *D* can be ruled out. While this shorter option makes for a quicker transition into the next sentence, it does not convey the full depth of what the writer is trying to communicate. Sometimes shorter sentences are not always the answer! What will be the correct answer is a sentence that flows and communicates the message of the original sentence more effectively and with correct punctuation. Choice *A* can quickly be dismissed because of its grammatical errors and lack of necessary punctuation. Choice *B* seems to retain most of the same diction of the original sentence, but Choice *C* is more direct and better phrased. Choice *C* also gives the reader a better impression of how important hospitality is in context of the story and culture. Another note: in the original sentence, there needed to be a comma after "dwelling", but Choice *C* fixes this with commas after "hospitality" and "instead".

67. B: *Relinquishes* means to give up or to voluntarily cease control of something. This is not something Odysseus does because he does not surrender his true name, he just hides it, metaphorically becoming someone else. Choice *A* is wrong. Therefore, Choice *B*, *conceals*, is the best option because Odysseus does in fact hide (or conceal) his true identity behind a false name. He does not *withhold* (Choice *C*) his true identity, but offers an alternative. Choice *D* is synonymous with *relinquishes* and therefore, it is also wrong.

68. A: Reading through the sentence, one can see that it flows and uses proper punctuation and grammar, which means that no change is necessary; Choice *A* is the correct answer. Choice *B* lacks the necessary comma after "Clearly", making it wrong. Choice *C* utilizes an unnecessary semicolon. Choice *D* makes the sentence awkward by placing *clearly* in the middle of the sentence.

69. D: The opening passage basically sums up that Odysseus's distrust of women and those seeming to have honorable intentions can be attributed to the experiences he faced when trying to return to home to Ithaca. This distrust is something the author argues was developed through multiple experiences, not that Odysseus was naturally distrustful. While Odysseus' cleverness is what gets him through the trials he faced, this isn't what the author focused on in the passage. This makes Choice *D* the strongest answer.

70. B: This is a difficult question. While this section could use revision (making choice *A* wrong), the three remaining options are all plausible. The task then is to choose the best fitting option to revise the selected part of the sentence, bearing in mind how it will tie into the rest of the sentence as a whole. Choice *D* is a decent option, but much of it is unnecessary and already addressed in the remainder of the sentence that isn't underlined. Eliminate Choice *D*. Choice *C* is compelling, but it lacks the necessary information that the original sentence has: we need to have Polyphemus still in the sentence. Thus choice *C* is wrong. Choice *B* is the answer because it avoids the confusion of the original "also like", making the sentence flow while still being clear in what the author is communicating.

71. B: The issue with this word is that it lacks proper punctuation. "One" is referring to an individual, and it needs to show possession of "identity". Therefore, *ones* must have an apostrophe to show ownership and to be correct. Thus, choice *B one's*, is the correct answer.

72. C: The current phrase seems to repeat itself, and really refers more to beginning something rather than an arrival, so we can eliminate Choice *A*. Choices *B* and *D* are compelling but are somewhat specific. What must be communicated is that all men who reach the island, in whatever fashion, risked being seduced by Circe. Choice *C* is the most practical revision and is more direct, while allowing for other circumstances in which men come to Circe's island. In the end, "arrive on" also sounds better when plugged into the sentence.

73. B: *Assure* means to speak to someone in a way that eliminates doubt, or to guarantee. This indirectly relates to what Odysseus wants to do, but to *assure* specifically refers to speaking to someone. Choice *A* is wrong. The best choice is choice *B, ensure*, which means to make certain. Odysseus is trying to make certain that the crew and he will be safe by beating Circe at her own game. Choices *C* and *D* are totally irrelevant. *Vindicate* means to free from blame, while *prevent* means to stop from happening. Both terms would not suit the sentence.

74. B: Without this sentence, the reader must infer the connection between the two characters. It is better to let the short sentence remain to ensure that the reader will understand parallels between the two characters: both sought to return home, but when one did, his wife betrayed him. This is the primary reason for keeping the sentence, making Choice *B* the answer.

75. A: Changing the main construction of this section of the sentence will throw off the entire sentence. There must be a comma in place in order to separate ideas in this particularly long, but correct,

61

sentence. The way the author has already laid out this section of the sentence already laid out is correct therefore Choice *A*, NO CHANGE, is right.

ACT Mathematics Test

Number and Quantity

Numbers usually serve as an adjective representing a quantity of objects. They function as placeholders for a value. Numbers can be better understood by their type and related characteristics.

Integers

An integer is any number that has a nonzero decimal part. This includes all positive and negative whole numbers and zero. Fractions and decimals—which aren't whole numbers—aren't integers.

Prime Numbers

A *prime* number cannot be divided except by 1 and itself. A prime number has no other factors, which means that no other combination of whole numbers can be multiplied to reach that number. For example, the set of prime numbers between 1 and 27 is {2, 3, 5, 7, 11, 13, 17, 19, 23}.

The number 7 is a prime number because its only factors are 1 and 7. In contrast, 12 isn't a prime number, as it can be divided by other numbers like 2, 3, 4, and 6. Because they are composed of multiple factors, numbers like 12 are called *composite* numbers. All numbers greater than 1 that aren't prime numbers are composite numbers.

Even and Odd Numbers

An integer is *even* if one of its factors is 2, while those integers without a factor of 2 are *odd*. No numbers except for integers can have either of these labels. For example, 2, 40, -16, and 108 are all even numbers, while -1, 13, 59, and 77 are all odd numbers since they are integers that cannot be divided by 2 without a remainder. Numbers like 0.4, $\frac{5}{9}$, π, and $\sqrt{7}$ are neither odd nor even because they are not integers.

Decimals

A decimal number is designated by a decimal point, which indicates that what follows the point is a value that is less than 1 and is added to the integer number preceding the decimal point. The digit immediately following the decimal point is in the tenths place, the digit following the tenths place is in the hundredths place, and so on.

For example, the decimal number 1.735 has a value greater than 1 but less than 2. The 7 represents seven tenths of the unit 1 (0.7 or $\frac{7}{10}$); the 3 represents three hundredths of 1 (0.03 or $\frac{3}{100}$); and the 5 represents five thousandths of 1 (0.005 or $\frac{5}{1000}$).

Rational and Irrational Numbers

Rational numbers include all numbers that can be expressed as a fraction; in other words, rational numbers encompass all integers and all numbers with terminating or repeating decimals. That is, any rational number either will have a countable number of nonzero digits or will end with an ellipses or a bar (3.6666... or $3.\bar{6}$) to depict repeating decimal digits.

Some examples of rational numbers include 12, -3.54, $110.\overline{256}$, $\frac{-35}{10}$, and $4.\overline{7}$.

Irrational numbers include all real numbers that aren't rational. It can be thought of as any number with endless non-repeating digits to the right of the decimal point. They can be expressed as an endless decimal but never as a fraction. The most common irrational number is π, which has an endless and non-repeating decimal, but there are other well-known irrational numbers like e and $\sqrt{2}$.

Real Numbers

Defined by Descartes in the seventeenth century, *real numbers* include all numbers found on an infinite number line. All irrational and rational numbers are real numbers. Nonterminating decimal numbers and π are also real numbers. As the range of real numbers extends to both negative and positive infinity, the set of real numbers is complete and uncountable. This set is known as the complete ordered field of numbers.

Rounding Numbers

It's often convenient to round a number, which means to give an approximate figure to make it easier to compare amounts or perform mental math. When the digit is 5 or more, it gets rounded up. The rounded digit, and all subsequent digits, becomes 0, and the preceding digit goes up by 1. Here are some examples:

75 rounded to the nearest ten is 80

380 rounded to the nearest hundred is 400

22.697 rounded to the nearest hundredth is 22.70

When rounding for any digit that is below 5, the digit gets rounded down. The rounded digit, and all subsequent digits, becomes 0, and the preceding digit goes down by 1.

Here are some examples:

92 rounded to the nearest ten is 90

839 rounded to the nearest hundred is 800

22.64 rounded to the nearest hundredth is 22.60

Addition

Addition is the combination of two numbers so their quantities are added together cumulatively. The sign for an addition operation is the + symbol. For example, 9 + 6 = 15. The 9 and 6 combine to achieve a cumulative value, called a *sum.*

Addition holds the *commutative property*, which means that numbers in an addition equation can be switched without altering the result. The formula for the commutative property is a + b = b + a. The following examples can demonstrate how the commutative property works:

$$7 = 3 + 4 = 4 + 3 = 7$$

$$20 = 12 + 8 = 8 + 12 = 20$$

Addition also holds the associative property, which means that the grouping of numbers does not matter in an addition problem. In other words, the presence or absence of parentheses is irrelevant. The formula for the associative property is (a + b) + c = a + (b + c). Here are some examples of the associative property at work:

$$30 = (6 + 14) + 10 = 6 + (14 + 10) = 30$$

$$35 = 8 + (2 + 25) = (8 + 2) + 25 = 35$$

Subtraction

Subtraction is taking away one number from another, so their quantities are reduced. The sign designating a subtraction operation is the – symbol, and the result is called the *difference*. For example, 9 - 6 = 3. The number *6* detracts from the number *9* to reach the difference *3*.

Unlike addition, subtraction follows neither the commutative nor associative properties. The order and grouping in subtraction impact the result.

$$15 = 22 - 7 \neq 7 - 22 = -15$$

$$3 = (10 - 5) - 2 \neq 10 - (5 - 2) = 7$$

When working through subtraction problems involving larger numbers, it's necessary to regroup the numbers. The following practice problem uses regrouping:

$$\begin{array}{r} 3\ 2\ 5 \\ -\ 7\ 7 \\ \hline \end{array}$$

Here, it is clear that the ones and tens columns for 77 are greater than the ones and tens columns for 325. To subtract this number, one needs to borrow from the tens and hundreds columns. When borrowing from a column, subtracting 1 from the lender column will add 10 to the borrower column:

$$\begin{array}{r} {}^{3\text{-}1}\ {}^{10+2\text{-}1}\ {}^{10+5} \\ -\ \ \ \ 7\ \ \ \ \ 7 \\ \hline \end{array} = \begin{array}{r} 2\ \ 11\ \ 15 \\ -\ \ \ \ 7\ \ \ 7 \\ \hline 2\ \ \ 4\ \ \ 8 \end{array}$$

After ensuring that each digit in the top row is greater than the digit in the corresponding bottom row, subtraction can proceed as normal, and the answer is found to be 248.

Multiplication

Multiplication involves adding together multiple copies of a number. It is indicated by an × symbol or a number immediately outside of a parenthesis, e.g. 5(8-2). The two numbers being multiplied together are called *factors*, and their result is called a *product.* For example, $9 \times 6 = 54$. This can be shown alternatively by expansion of either the 9 or the 6:

$$9 \times 6 = 9 + 9 + 9 + 9 + 9 + 9 = 54$$

$$9 \times 6 = 6 + 6 + 6 + 6 + 6 + 6 + 6 + 6 + 6 = 54$$

Like addition, multiplication holds the commutative and associative properties:

$$115 = 23 \times 5 = 5 \times 23 = 115$$

$$84 = 3 \times (7 \times 4) = (3 \times 7) \times 4 = 84$$

Multiplication also follows the distributive property, which allows the multiplication to be distributed through parentheses. The formula for distribution is $a \times (b + c) = ab + ac$. This is clear after the examples:

$$45 = 5 \times 9 = 5(3 + 6) = (5 \times 3) + (5 \times 6) = 15 + 30 = 45$$

$$20 = 4 \times 5 = 4(10 - 5) = (4 \times 10) - (4 \times 5) = 40 - 20 = 20$$

Multiplication becomes slightly more complicated when multiplying numbers with decimals. The easiest way to answer these problems is to ignore the decimals and multiply as if they were whole numbers. After multiplying the factors, a decimal gets placed in the product. The placement of the decimal is determined by taking the cumulative number of decimal places in the factors.

For example:

$$
\begin{array}{r}
0.7 \\
\times\ 3 \\
\hline
2.1
\end{array}
\qquad
\begin{array}{r}
2.6 \\
\times\ 4.2 \\
\hline
10.92
\end{array}
\qquad
\begin{array}{r}
1.5 \\
\times\ 6.4 \\
\hline
9.60
\end{array}
$$

Starting with the first example, the first step is to ignore the decimal and multiply the numbers as though they were whole numbers, which results in a product of 21. The next step is to count the number of digits that follow a decimal (one, in this case). Finally, the decimal place gets moved that many positions to the left, because the factors have only one decimal place. The second example works the same way, except that there are two total decimal places in the factors, so the product's decimal is moved two places over. In the third example, the decimal should be moved over two digits, but the digit zero is no longer needed, so it is erased and the final answer is 9.6.

Division

Division and multiplication are inverses of each other in the same way that addition and subtraction are opposites. The signs designating the division operation are the ÷ and / symbols. In division, the second number divides into the first.

The number before the division sign is called the *dividend* or, if expressed as a fraction, the *numerator*. For example, in $a \div b$, a is the dividend, while in $\frac{a}{b}$, a is the numerator.

The number after the division sign is called the *divisor* or, if expressed as a fraction, the *denominator*. For example, in $a \div b$, b is the divisor, while in $\frac{a}{b}$, b is the denominator.

Like subtraction, division doesn't follow the commutative property, as it matters which number comes before the division sign, and division doesn't follow the associative or distributive properties for the same reason. For example:

$$\frac{3}{2} = 9 \div 6 \neq 6 \div 9 = \frac{2}{3}$$

$$2 = 10 \div 5 = (30 \div 3) \div 5 \neq 30 \div (3 \div 5) = 30 \div \frac{3}{5} = 50$$

$$25 = 20 + 5 = (40 \div 2) + (40 \div 8) \neq 40 \div (2 + 8) = 40 \div 10 = 4$$

If a divisor doesn't divide into a dividend an integer number of times, whatever is left over is termed the *remainder*. The remainder can be further divided out into decimal form by using long division; however, this doesn't always give a quotient with a finite number of decimal places, so the remainder can also be expressed as a fraction over the original divisor.

Division with decimals is similar to multiplication with decimals in that when dividing a decimal by a whole number, one should ignore the decimal and divide as if it was a whole number.

Upon finding the answer, or quotient, the decimal point is inserted at the decimal place equal to that in the dividend.

$$15.75 \div 3 = 5.25$$

When the divisor is a decimal number, both the divisor and dividend get multiplied by 10. This process is repeated until the divisor is a whole number, then one needs to complete the division operation as described above.

$$17.5 \div 2.5 = 175 \div 25 = 7$$

Exponents

An *exponent* is an operation used as shorthand for a number multiplied or divided by itself for a defined number of times.

$$3^7 = 3 \times 3 \times 3 \times 3 \times 3 \times 3 \times 3$$

In this example, the 3 is called the *base* and the 7 is called the *exponent*. The exponent is typically expressed as a superscript number near the upper right side of the base, but can also be identified as the number following a caret symbol (^). This operation is verbally expressed as "3 to the 7th power" or "3 raised to the power of 7." Common exponents are 2 and 3. A base raised to the power of 2 is referred to as having been "squared," while a base raised to the power of 3 is referred to as having been "cubed."

Several special rules apply to exponents. First, the Zero Power Rule finds that any number raised to the zero power equals 1. For example, 100^0, 2^0, $(-3)^0$ and 0^0 all equal 1 because the bases are raised to the zero power.

Second, exponents can be negative. With negative exponents, the equation is expressed as a fraction, as in the following example:

$$3^{-7} = \frac{1}{3^7} = \frac{1}{3 \times 3 \times 3 \times 3 \times 3 \times 3 \times 3}$$

Third, the Power Rule concerns exponents being raised by another exponent. When this occurs, the exponents are multiplied by each other:

$$(x^2)^3 = x^6 = (x^3)^2$$

Fourth, when multiplying two exponents with the same base, the Product Rule requires that the base remains the same and the exponents are added. For example, $a^x \times a^y = a^{x+y}$. Since addition and multiplication are commutative, the two terms being multiplied can be in any order.

$$x^3 x^5 = x^{3+5} = x^8 = x^{5+3} = x^5 x^3$$

Fifth, when dividing two exponents with the same base, the Quotient Rule requires that the base remains the same, but the exponents are subtracted. So, $a^x \div a^y = a^{x-y}$. Since subtraction and division are not commutative, the two terms must remain in order.

$$x^5 x^{-3} = x^{5-3} = x^2 = x^5 \div x^3 = \frac{x^5}{x^3}$$

Additionally, 1 raised to any power is still equal to 1, and any number raised to the power of 1 is equal to itself. In other words, $a^1 = a$ and $14^1 = 14$.

Exponents play an important role in scientific notation to present extremely large or small numbers as follows: $a \times 10^b$. To write the number in scientific notation, the decimal is moved until there is only one digit on the left side of the decimal point, indicating that the number a has a value between 1 and 10. The number of times the decimal moves indicates the exponent to which 10 is raised, here represented by b. If the decimal moves to the left, then b is positive, but if the decimal moves to the right, then b is negative. The following examples demonstrate these concepts:

$$3{,}050 = 3.05 \times 10^3$$

$$-777 = -7.77 \times 10^2$$

$$0.000123 = 1.23 \times 10^{-4}$$

$$-0.0525 = -5.25 \times 10^{-2}$$

Roots

The *square root symbol* is expressed as $\sqrt{}$ and is commonly known as the radical. Taking the root of a number is the inverse operation of multiplying that number by itself some number of times. For example, squaring the number 7 is equal to 7×7, or 49. Finding the square root is the opposite of finding an exponent, as the operation seeks a number that when multiplied by itself, equals the number in the square root symbol.

For example, $\sqrt{36} = 6$ because 6 multiplied by 6 equals 36. Note, the square root of 36 is also -6 since -6 × -6 = 36. This can be indicated using a plus/minus symbol like this: ±6. However, square roots are often just expressed as a positive number for simplicity, with it being understood that the true value can be either positive or negative.

Perfect squares are numbers with whole number square roots. The list of perfect squares begins with 0, 1, 4, 9, 16, 25, 36, 49, 64, 81, and 100.

Determining the square root of imperfect squares requires a calculator to reach an exact figure. It's possible, however, to approximate the answer by finding the two perfect squares that the number fits between. For example, the square root of 40 is between 6 and 7 since the squares of those numbers are 36 and 49, respectively.

Square roots are the most common root operation. If the radical doesn't have a number to the upper left of the symbol $\sqrt{}$, then it's a square root. Sometimes a radical includes a number in the upper left, like $\sqrt[3]{27}$, as in the other common root type—the cube root. Complicated roots, like the cube root, often require a calculator.

Parentheses

Parentheses separate different parts of an equation, and operations within them should be thought of as taking place before the outside operations take place. Practically, this means that the distinction between what is inside and outside of the parentheses decides the order of operations that the equation follows. Failing to solve operations inside the parentheses before addressing the part of the equation outside of the parentheses will lead to incorrect results.

For example, in $5 - (3 + 25)$, addition within the parentheses must be solved first. So $3 + 25 = 28$, leaving $5 - (28) = -23$. If this was solved using the incorrect order of operations, the solution might be found to be $5 - 3 + 25 = 2 + 25 = 27$, which would be wrong.

Equations often feature multiple layers of parentheses. To differentiate them, square brackets [ ] and braces { } are used in addition to parentheses. The innermost parentheses must be solved before working outward to larger brackets. For example, in $\{2 \div [5 - (3 + 1)]\}$, solving the innermost parentheses $(3 + 1)$ leaves $\{2 \div [5 - (4)]\}$. $[5 - (4)]$ is now the next smallest, which leaves $\{2 \div [1]\}$ in the final step, and 2 as the answer.

Order of Operations

When solving equations with multiple operations, special rules apply. These rules are known as the Order of Operations. The order is as follows: Parentheses, Exponents, Multiplication and Division from left to right, and Addition and Subtraction from left to right. A popular mnemonic device to help remember the order is Please Excuse My Dear Aunt Sally (PEMDAS). Evaluating the following two problems can help with understanding the Order of Operations:

$$4 + (3 \times 2)^2 \div 4$$

First, the operation within the parentheses must be completed, yielding: $4 + 6^2 \div 4$.

Second, the exponent is evaluated: $4 + 36 \div 4$.

Third, the division is conducted: $4 + 9$.

Fourth, addition is completed, giving the answer: 13.

$$2 \times (6 + 3) \div (2 + 1)^2$$

$$2 \times 9 \div (3)^2$$

$$2 \times 9 \div 9$$

$$18 \div 9$$

$$2$$

Positive and Negative Numbers

<u>Signs</u>
Aside from 0, numbers can be either positive or negative. The sign for a positive number is the plus sign or the + symbol, while the sign for a negative number is minus sign or the − symbol. If a number has no designation, then it's assumed to be positive.

<u>Absolute Values</u>
Both positive and negative numbers are valued according to their distance from 0. Both +3 and -3 can be considered using the following number line:

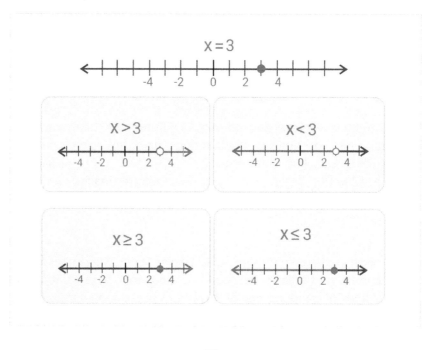

70

Both 3 and -3 are three spaces from 0. The distance from 0 is called its absolute value. Thus, both -3 and 3 have an absolute value of 3 since they're both three spaces away from 0.

An absolute number is written by placing | | around the number. So, $|3|$ and $|-3|$ both equal 3, as that's their common absolute value.

Implications for Addition and Subtraction

For addition, if all numbers are either positive or negative, they are simply added together. For example, 4 + 4 = 8 and -4 + -4 = -8. However, things get tricky when some of the numbers are negative and some are positive.

For example, with 6 + (-4), the first step is to take the absolute values of the numbers, which are 6 and 4. Second, the smaller value is subtracted from the larger. The equation becomes $6-4 = 2$. Third, the sign of the original larger number is placed on the sum. Here, 6 is the larger number, and it's positive, so the sum is 2.

Here's an example where the negative number has a larger absolute value: (-6) + 4. The first two steps are the same as the example above. However, on the third step, the negative sign must be placed on the sum, because the absolute value of (-6) is greater than 4. Thus, -6 + 4 = -2.

The absolute value of numbers implies that subtraction can be thought of as flipping the sign of the number following the subtraction sign and simply adding the two numbers. This means that subtracting a negative number will, in fact, be adding the positive absolute value of the negative number. Here are some examples:

$$-6 - 4 = -6 + -4 = -10$$

$$3 - -6 = 3 + 9 = 12$$

$$-3 - 2 = -3 + -2 = -5$$

Implications for Multiplication and Division

For multiplication and division, if both numbers are positive, then the product or quotient is always positive. If both numbers are negative, then the product or quotient is also positive. However, if the numbers have opposite signs, the product or quotient is always negative.

Simply put, the product in multiplication and quotient in division is always positive, unless the numbers have opposing signs, in which case it's negative. Here are some examples:

$$(-6) \times (-5) = 30$$

$$(-50) \div 10 = -5$$

$$8 \times |-7| = 56$$

$$(-48) \div (-6) = 8$$

If there are more than two numbers in a multiplication or division problem, then whether the product or quotient is positive or negative depends on the number of negative numbers in the problem. If there is an odd number of negatives, then the product or quotient is negative. If there is an even number of negative numbers, then the result is positive.

Here are some examples:

$$(-6) \times 5 \times (-2) \times (-4) = -240$$

$$(-6) \times 5 \times 2 \times (-4) = 240$$

Factorization

Factors are the numbers multiplied to achieve a product. Thus, every product in a multiplication equation has, at minimum, two factors. Of course, some products will have more than two factors. For the sake of most discussions, one can assume that factors are positive integers.

To find a number's factors, one should start with 1 and the number itself. The next step is to divide the number by 2, 3, 4, and so on, to see if any divisors can divide the number without a remainder. A list should be kept of those that do. This process can be stopped upon reaching either the number itself or another factor.

For example, to find the factors of 45, the first step is to start with 1 and 45. The next step is to try to divide 45 by 2, which fails. After this, 45 gets divided by 3. The answer is 15, so 3 and 15 are now factors. Dividing by 4 doesn't work, and dividing by 5 leaves 9. Lastly, dividing 45 by 6, 7, and 8 all don't work. The next integer to try is 9, but this is already known to be a factor, so the factorization is complete. The factors of 45 are 1, 3, 5, 9, 15 and 45.

Prime Factorization

Prime factorization involves an additional step after breaking a number down to its factors: breaking down the factors until they are all prime numbers. A prime number is any number that can only be divided by 1 and itself. The prime numbers between 1 and 20 are 2, 3, 5, 7, 11, 13, 17, and 19. As a simple test, numbers that are even or end in 5 are not prime.

When attempting to break 129 down into its prime factors, the factors are found first: 3 and 43. Both 3 and 43 are prime numbers, so that means the prime factorization is complete. If 43 was not a prime number, then it would also need to be factorized until all of the factors were expressed as prime numbers.

Common Factor

A common factor is a factor shared by two numbers. The following examples demonstrate how to find the common factors of 45 and 30:

- The factors of 45 are: 1, 3, 5, 9, 15, and 45.
- The factors of 30 are: 1, 2, 3, 5, 6, 10, 15, and 30.
- The common factors are 1, 3, 5, and 15.

Greatest Common Factor

The greatest common factor is the largest number among the shared, common factors. From the factors of 45 and 30, the common factors are 3, 5, and 15. Thus, 15 is the greatest common factor, as it's the largest number.

Least Common Multiple

The least common multiple is the smallest number that's a multiple of two numbers. For example, to find the least common multiple of 4 and 9, the multiples of 4 and 9 are found first. The multiples of 4 are 4, 8, 12, 16, 20, 24, 28, 32, 36, and so on. For 9, the multiples are 9, 18, 27, 36, 45, 54, etc. Thus, the least common multiple of 4 and 9 is 36, the lowest number where 4 and 9 share multiples.

If two numbers share no factors besides 1 in common, then their least common multiple will be simply their product. If two numbers have common factors, then their least common multiple will be their product divided by their greatest common factor. This can be visualized by the formula $LCM = \frac{x \times y}{GCF}$, where x and y are some integers and LCM and GCF are their least common multiple and greatest common factor, respectively.

Fractions

A fraction is an equation that represents a part of a whole, but can also be used to present ratios or division problems. An example of a fraction is $\frac{x}{y}$. In this example, x is called the *numerator,* while y is the *denominator.* The numerator represents the number of parts, and the denominator is the total number of parts. They are separated by a line or slash. In simple fractions, the numerator and denominator can be nearly any integer. However, the denominator of a fraction can never be zero, because dividing by zero is a function, which is undefined.

To visualize the basic idea of fractions, one can imagine that an apple pie has been baked for a holiday party, and the full pie has eight slices. After the party, there are five slices left. How could the amount of the pie that remains be expressed as a fraction? The numerator is 5 since there are two parts left, and the denominator is 8, since there were eight total slices in the whole pie. Thus, expressed as a fraction, the leftover pie totals $\frac{5}{8}$ of the original amount.

Fractions come in three different varieties: proper fractions, improper fractions, and mixed numbers. Proper fractions have a numerator less than the denominator, such as $\frac{3}{8}$, but improper fractions have a numerator greater than the denominator, such as $\frac{15}{8}$. Mixed numbers combine a whole number with a proper fraction, such as $3\frac{1}{2}$. Any mixed number can be written as an improper fraction by multiplying the integer by the denominator, adding the product to the value of the numerator, and dividing the sum by the original denominator. For example, $3\frac{1}{2} = \frac{3 \times 2 + 1}{2} = \frac{7}{2}$. Whole numbers can also be converted into fractions by placing the whole number as the numerator and making the denominator 1. For example, $3 = \frac{3}{1}$.

One of the most fundamental concepts of fractions is their ability to be manipulated by multiplication or division. This is possible since $\frac{n}{n} = 1$ for any non-zero integer. As a result, multiplying or dividing by $\frac{n}{n}$ will not alter the original fraction since any number multiplied or divided by 1 doesn't change the value of that number. Fractions of the same value are known as equivalent fractions. For example, $\frac{2}{4}, \frac{4}{8}, \frac{50}{100}$, and $\frac{75}{150}$ are equivalent, as they all equal $\frac{1}{2}$.

Although many equivalent fractions exist, they are easier to compare and interpret when reduced or simplified. The numerator and denominator of a simple fraction will have no factors in common other than 1. When reducing or simplifying fractions, the numerator and denominator are divided by the greatest common factor. A simple strategy is to divide the numerator and denominator by low numbers, like 2, 3, or 5 until arriving at a simple fraction, but the same thing could be achieved by determining the greatest common factor for both the numerator and denominator and dividing each by it. Using the first method is preferable when both the numerator and denominator are even, end in 5, or are obviously a multiple of another number. However, if no numbers seem to work, it will be necessary to factor the numerator and denominator to find the GCF. The following problems provide examples:

Simplify the fraction $\frac{6}{8}$:

Dividing the numerator and denominator by 2 results in $\frac{3}{4}$, which is a simple fraction.

Simplify the fraction $\frac{12}{36}$:

Dividing the numerator and denominator by 2 leaves $\frac{6}{18}$. This isn't a simplified fraction, as both the numerator and denominator have factors in common. Diving each by 3 results in $\frac{2}{6}$, but this can be further simplified by dividing by 2, to get $\frac{1}{3}$. This is the simplest fraction, as the numerator is 1. In cases like this, multiple division operations can be avoided by determining the greatest common factor between the numerator and denominator.

Simplify the fraction $\frac{18}{54}$ by dividing by the greatest common factor:

The first step is to determine the factors of the numerator and denominator. The factors of 18 are 1, 2, 3, 6, 9, and 18. The factors of 54 are 1, 2, 3, 6, 9, 18, 27, and 54. Thus, the greatest common factor is 18. Dividing $\frac{18}{54}$ by 18 leaves $\frac{1}{3}$, which is the simplest fraction. This method takes slightly more work, but it definitely arrives at the simplest fraction.

A *ratio* is a comparison between the relative sizes of two parts of a whole, separated by a colon. It's different from a fraction because, in a ratio, the second number represents the number of parts which aren't currently being referenced, while in a fraction, the second or bottom number represents the total number of parts in the whole. For example, if 3 pieces of an 8-piece pie were eaten, the number of uneaten parts expressed as a ratio to the number of eaten parts would be 5:3.

Equivalent ratios work just like equivalent fractions. For example, both 3:9 and 20:60 are equivalent ratios to 1:3 because both can be simplified to 1:3.

Operations with Fractions

Of the four basic operations that can be performed on fractions, the one that involves the least amount of work is multiplication. To multiply two fractions, the numerators are multiplied, the denominators are multiplied, and the products are placed together as a fraction. Whole numbers and mixed numbers can also be expressed as a fraction, as described above, which more easily facilitates multiplication with another fraction. The following problems provide examples:

$$1. \frac{2}{5} \times \frac{3}{4} = \frac{6}{20} = \frac{3}{10}$$

$$2. \frac{4}{9} \times \frac{7}{11} = \frac{28}{99}$$

Dividing fractions is similar to multiplication with one key difference. To divide fractions, the numerator and denominator of the second fraction are flipped, and then one proceeds as if it were a multiplication problem:

1. $\dfrac{7}{8} \div \dfrac{4}{5} = \dfrac{7}{8} \times \dfrac{5}{4} = \dfrac{35}{32}$

2. $\dfrac{5}{9} \div \dfrac{1}{3} = \dfrac{5}{9} \times \dfrac{3}{1} = \dfrac{15}{9} = \dfrac{5}{3}$

Addition and subtraction require more steps than multiplication and division, as these operations require the fractions to have the same denominator, also called a *common denominator*. It is always possible to find a common denominator by multiplying the denominators. However, when the denominators are large numbers, this method is unwieldy, especially if the answer must be provided in its simplest form. Thus, it's beneficial to find the least common denominator of the fractions—the least common denominator is incidentally also the least common multiple.

Once equivalent fractions have been found with common denominators, the numerators are simply added or subtracted to arrive at the answer:

1. $\dfrac{1}{2} + \dfrac{3}{4} = \dfrac{2}{4} + \dfrac{3}{4} = \dfrac{5}{4}$

2. $\dfrac{3}{12} + \dfrac{11}{20} = \dfrac{15}{60} + \dfrac{33}{60} = \dfrac{48}{60} = \dfrac{4}{5}$

3. $\dfrac{7}{9} - \dfrac{4}{15} = \dfrac{35}{45} - \dfrac{12}{45} = \dfrac{23}{45}$

4. $\dfrac{5}{6} - \dfrac{7}{18} = \dfrac{15}{18} - \dfrac{7}{18} = \dfrac{8}{18} = \dfrac{4}{9}$

Order of Rational Numbers

A common question type on the ACT asks test takers to order rational numbers from least to greatest or greatest to least. The numbers will come in a variety of formats, including decimals, percentages, roots, fractions, and whole numbers. These questions test for knowledge of different types of numbers and the ability to determine their respective values.

Whether the question asks to order the numbers from greatest to least or least to greatest, the crux of the question is the same—convert the numbers into a common format. Generally, it's easiest to write the numbers as whole numbers and decimals so they can be placed on a number line. The following examples illustrate this strategy:

1. Order the following rational numbers from greatest to least:

$$\sqrt{36}, 0.65, 78\%, \dfrac{3}{4}, 7, 90\%, \dfrac{5}{2}$$

Of the seven numbers, the whole number (7) and decimal (0.65) are already in an accessible form, so test takers should concentrate on the other five.

First, the square root of 36 equals 6. (If the test asks for the root of a non-perfect root, determine which two whole numbers the root lies between.) Next, the percentages should be converted to decimals. A percentage means "per hundred," so this conversion requires moving the decimal point two places to the left, leaving 0.78 and 0.9. Lastly, the fractions are evaluated: $\frac{3}{4} = \frac{75}{100} = 0.75; \frac{5}{2} = 2\frac{1}{2} = 2.5$

Now, the only step left is to list the numbers in the requested order:

$7, \sqrt{36}, \frac{5}{2}, 90\%, 78\%, \frac{3}{4}, 0.65$

2. Order the following rational numbers from least to greatest:

$2.5, \sqrt{9}, -10.5, 0.853, 175\%, \sqrt{4}, \frac{4}{5}$

$\sqrt{9} = 3$

$175\% = 1.75$

$\sqrt{4} = 2$

$\frac{4}{5} = 0.8$

From least to greatest, the answer is: $-10.5, \frac{4}{5}, 0.853, 175\%, \sqrt{4}, 2.5, \sqrt{9}$,

Percentages

Percentages can be thought of as fractions with a denominator of 100. In fact, percentage means "per hundred." Problems often require converting numbers from percentages, fractions, and decimals. The following explains how to work through those conversions.

Converting Fractions to Percentages: The fraction is converted by using an equivalent fraction with a denominator of 100. For example, $\frac{3}{4} = \frac{3}{4} \times \frac{25}{25} = \frac{75}{100} = 75\%$

Converting Percentages to Fractions: Percentages can be converted to fractions by turning the percentage into a fraction with a denominator of 100. Test takers should be wary of questions asking the converted fraction to be written in the simplest form. For example, $35\% = \frac{35}{100}$ which, although correctly written, has a numerator and denominator with a greatest common factor of 5, so it can be simplified to $\frac{7}{20}$.

Converting Percentages to Decimals: Because a percentage is based on "per hundred," decimals and percentages can be converted by multiplying or dividing by 100. Practically speaking, this always amounts to moving the decimal point two places to the right or left, depending on the conversion. To convert a percentage to a decimal, the decimal point is moved two places to the right and the % sign gets removed. To convert a decimal to a percentage, the decimal point is moved two places to the left and a "%" sign is added. Here are some examples:

65% = 0.65

0.33 = 33%

0.215 = 21.5%

99.99% = 0.9999

500% = 5.00

7.55 = 755%

Percentage Problems

Questions dealing with percentages can be difficult when they are phrased as word problems. These word problems almost always come in one of three varieties. The first type will ask to find what percentage of some number will equal another number. The second asks to determine what number is some percentage of another given number. The third will ask what number another number is a given percentage of.

One of the most important parts of correctly answering percentage word problems is to identify the numerator and the denominator. This fraction can then be converted into a percentage, as described in the previous section.

The following word problem shows how to make this conversion:

A department store carries several different types of footwear. The store is currently selling 8 athletic shoes, 7 dress shoes, and 5 sandals. What percentage of the store's footwear are sandals?

The first step is to calculate what serves as the 'whole', as this will be the denominator. How many total pieces of footwear does the store sell? The store sells 20 different types (8 athletic + 7 dress + 5 sandals).

In the next step, test takers need to determine which footwear type the question is specifically asking about. Sandals. Thus, 5 is the numerator.

Lastly, the resultant fraction must be expressed as a percentage. The first two steps indicate that $\frac{5}{20}$ of the footwear pieces are sandals. This fraction must now be converted into a percentage: $\frac{5}{20} \times \frac{5}{5} = \frac{25}{100} = 25\%$.

Vectors

A vector can be thought of as an abstract list of numbers or as giving a location in a space. For example, the coordinates (x, y) for points in the Cartesian plane are vectors. Each entry in a vector can be referred to by its location in the list: first, second, third, and so on. The total length of the list is the *dimension* of the vector. A vector is often denoted as such by putting an arrow on top of it, e.g. $\vec{v} = (v_1, v_2, v_3)$.

Adding Vectors Graphically and Algebraically

There are two basic operations for vectors. First, two vectors can be added together. Let $\vec{v} = (v_1, v_2, v_3), \vec{w} = (w_1, w_2, w_3)$. The the sum of the two vectors is defined to be $\vec{v} + \vec{w} = (v_1 + w_1, v_2 + w_2, v_3 + w_3)$. Subtraction of vectors can be defined similarly.

Vector addition can be visualized in the following manner. First, each vector can be visualized as an arrow. Then, the base of one arrow is placed at the tip of the other arrow. The tip of this first arrow now hits some point in space, and there will be an arrow from the origin to this point. This new arrow corresponds to the new vector. In subtraction, the direction of the arrow being subtracted is reversed.

For example, if adding together the vectors (-2, 3) and (4, 1), the new vector will be (-2 + 4, 3 + 1), or (2, 4). Graphically, this may be pictured in the following manner:

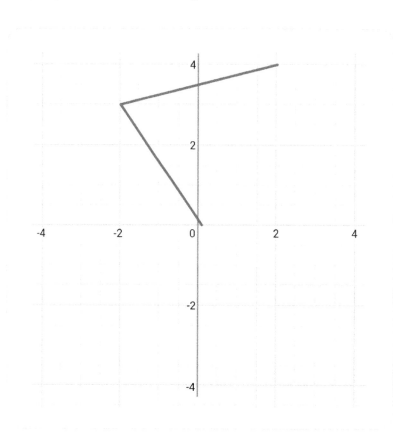

Performing Scalar Multiplications

The second basic operation for vectors is called *scalar multiplication*. Scalar multiplication is multiplying any vector by any real number, which is denoted here as a scalar. Let $\vec{v} = (v_1, v_2, v_3)$, and let a be an arbitrary real number. Then the scalar multiple $a\vec{v} = (av_1, av_2, av_3)$. Graphically, this corresponds to changing the length of the arrow corresponding to the vector by a factor, or scale, of a. That is why the real number is called a *scalar* in this instance.

As an example, let $\vec{v} = (2, -1, 1)$. Then $3\vec{v} = (3 \cdot 2, 3(-1), 3 \cdot 1) = (6, -3, 3)$.

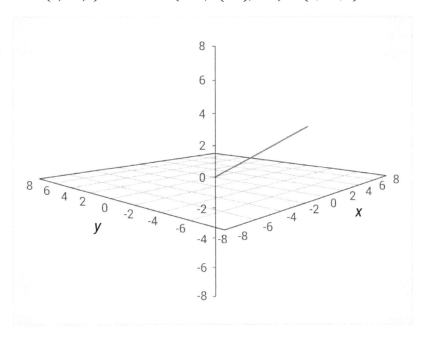

Note that scalar multiplication is *distributive* over vector addition, meaning that $a(\vec{v} + \vec{w}) = a\vec{v} + a\vec{w}$.

Determinants

A *matrix* is a rectangular arrangement of numbers in rows and columns. The *determinant* of a matrix is a special value that can be calculated for any square matrix.

Using the *square 2 x 2 matrix* $\begin{bmatrix} a & b \\ c & d \end{bmatrix}$, the determinant is $ad - bc$.

For example, the determinant of the matrix $\begin{bmatrix} -5 & 1 \\ 3 & 4 \end{bmatrix}$ is *-5(4) – 1(3) = -20 – 3 = -23*.

Using a *3 x 3 matrix* $\begin{bmatrix} a & b & c \\ d & e & f \\ g & h & i \end{bmatrix}$, the determinant is $a(ei - fh) - b(di - fg) + c(dh - eg)$.

For example, the determinant of the matrix $\begin{bmatrix} 2 & 0 & 1 \\ -1 & 3 & 2 \\ 2 & -2 & -1 \end{bmatrix}$ is

$$2(3(-1) - 2(-2)) - 0(-1(-1) - 2(2)) + 1(-1(-2) - 3(2))$$

$$= 2(-3 + 4) - 0(1 - 4) + 1(2 - 6)$$

$$= 2(1) - 0(-3) + 1(-4)$$

$$= 2 - 0 - 4 = -2$$

The pattern continues for larger square matrices.

Algebra

Solving for X in Proportions

Proportions are commonly used in word problems to find unknown values, such as x, that are some percent or fraction of a known number. Proportions are solved by cross-multiplying and then dividing to arrive at x. The following examples show how this is done:

1. $\frac{75\%}{90\%} = \frac{25\%}{x}$

To solve for x, the fractions must be cross-multiplied: ($75\% x = 90\% \times 25\%$). To make things easier, the percentages can be converted to decimals: ($0.9 \times 0.25 = 0.225 = 0.75x$). To get rid of the coefficient of x, each side must be divided by that same coefficient to get the answer $x = 0.3$. The question could ask for the answer as a percentage or fraction in lowest terms, which are 30% and $\frac{3}{10}$, respectively.

2. $\frac{x}{12} = \frac{30}{96}$

Cross-multiply: $96x = 30 \times 12$

Multiply: $96x = 360$

Divide: $x = 360 \div 96$

Answer: $x = 3.75$

3. $\frac{0.5}{3} = \frac{x}{6}$

Cross-multiply: $3x = 0.5 \times 6$

Multiply: $3x = 3$

Divide: $x = 3 \div 3$

Answer: $x = 1$

Observant test takers may have noticed there's a faster way to arrive at the answer. If there is an obvious operation being performed on the proportion, the same operation can be used on the other side of the proportion to solve for x. For example, in the first practice problem, 75% became 25% when divided by 3, and upon doing the same to 90%, the correct answer of 30% would have been found with much less legwork. However, these questions aren't always so intuitive, so it's a good idea for test takers to work through the steps, even if the answer seems apparent from the onset.

Translating Words into Math

When asked to rewrite a mathematical expression as a situation or translate a word problem into an expression, test takers should look for key words indicating addition, subtraction, multiplication, or division:

- *Addition*: add, altogether, together, plus, increased by, more than, in all, sum, and total
- *Subtraction*: minus, less than, difference, decreased by, fewer than, remain, and take away
- *Multiplication*: times, twice, of, double, and triple
- *Division*: divided by, cut up, half, quotient of, split, and shared equally

If a question asks to give words to a mathematical expression and says "equals," then an = sign must be included in the answer. Similarly, "less than or equal to" is expressed by the inequality symbol ≤, and "greater than or equal" to is expressed as ≥. Furthermore, "less than" is represented by <, and "greater than" is expressed by >.

Word Problems

Word problems can appear daunting, but prepared test takers shouldn't let the verbiage psyche them out. No matter the scenario or specifics, the key to answering them is to translate the words into a math problem. It is critical to keep in mind what the question is asking and what operations could lead to that answer. The following word problems highlight the most commonly tested question types.

Working with Money
Walter's Coffee Shop sells a variety of drinks and breakfast treats.

Price List	
Hot Coffee	$2.00
Slow Drip Iced Coffee	$3.00
Latte	$4.00
Muffins	$2.00
Crepe	$4.00
Egg Sandwich	$5.00

Costs	
Hot Coffee	$0.25
Slow Drip Iced Coffee	$0.75
Latte	$1.00
Muffins	$1.00
Crepe	$2.00
Egg Sandwich	$3.00

Walter's utilities, rent, and labor costs him $500 per day. Today, Walter sold 200 hot coffees, 100 slow drip iced coffees, 50 lattes, 75 muffins, 45 crepes, and 60 egg sandwiches. What was Walter's total profit today?

To accurately answer this type of question, the first step is to determine the total cost of making his drinks and treats, then determine how much revenue he earned from selling those products. After arriving at these two totals, the profit is measured by deducting the total cost from the total revenue.

Walter's costs for today:

200 hot coffees	× $0.25	= $50
100 slow drip iced coffees	× $0.75	= $75
50 lattes	× $1.00	= $50
75 muffins	× $1.00	= $75
45 crepes	× $2.00	= $90
60 egg sandwiches	× $3.00	= $180
Utilities, Rent, and Labor		= $500
Total costs		= $1,020

Walter's revenue for today:

200 hot coffees	× $2.00	= $400
100 slow drip iced coffees	× $3.00	= $300
50 lattes	× $4.00	= $200
75 muffins	× $2.00	= $150
45 crepes	× $4.00	= $180
60 egg sandwiches	× $5.00	= $300
Total revenue		= $1,530

Walter's $Profit = Revenue - Costs = \$1,530 - \$1,020 = \$510$

This strategy can be applied to other question types. For example, calculating salary after deductions, balancing a checkbook, and calculating a dinner bill are common word problems similar to business planning. In all cases, the most important step is remembering to use the correct operations. When a balance is increased, addition is used. When a balance is decreased, the problem requires subtraction. Common sense and organization are one's greatest assets when answering word problems.

Unit Rate

Unit rate word problems ask test takers to calculate the rate or quantity of something in a different value. For example, a problem might say that a car drove a certain number of miles in a certain number of minutes and then ask how many miles per hour the car was traveling. These questions involve solving proportions. Consider the following examples:

1. Alexandra made $96 during the first 3 hours of her shift as a temporary worker at a law office. She will continue to earn money at this rate until she finishes in 5 more hours. How much does Alexandra make per hour? How much money will Alexandra have made at the end of the day?

This problem can be solved in two ways. The first is to set up a proportion, as the rate of pay is constant. The second is to determine her hourly rate, multiply the 5 hours by that rate, and then adding the $96.

To set up a proportion, the money already earned (numerator) is placed over the hours already worked (denominator) on one side of an equation. The other side has x over 8 hours (the total hours worked in the day). It looks like this: $\frac{96}{3} = \frac{x}{8}$. Now, cross-multiply yields $768 = 3x$. To get x, the 768 is divided by 3, which leaves $x = 256$. Alternatively, as x is the numerator of one of the proportions, multiplying by its denominator will reduce the solution by one step. Thus, Alexandra will make $256 at the end of the day. To calculate her hourly rate, the total is divided by 8, giving $32 per hour.

Alternatively, it is possible to figure out the hourly rate by dividing $96 by 3 hours to get $32 per hour. Now her total pay can be figured by multiplying $32 per hour by 8 hours, which comes out to $256.

2. Jonathan is reading a novel. So far, he has read 215 of the 335 total pages. It takes Jonathan 25 minutes to read 10 pages, and the rate is constant. How long does it take Jonathan to read one page? How much longer will it take him to finish the novel? Express the answer in time.

To calculate how long it takes Jonathan to read one page, 25 minutes is divided by 10 pages to determine the page per minute rate. Thus, it takes 2.5 minutes to read one page.

Jonathan must read 120 more pages to complete the novel. (This is calculated by subtracting the pages already read from the total.) Now, his rate per page is multiplied by the number of pages. Thus, $120 \times 2.5 = 300$. Expressed in time, 300 minutes is equal to 5 hours.

3. At a hotel, $\frac{4}{5}$ of the 120 rooms are booked for Saturday. On Sunday, $\frac{3}{4}$ of the rooms are booked. On which day are more of the rooms booked, and by how many more?

The first step is to calculate the number of rooms booked for each day. This is done by multiplying the fraction of the rooms booked by the total number of rooms.

Saturday: $\frac{4}{5} \times 120 = \frac{4}{5} \times \frac{120}{1} = \frac{480}{5} = 96$ rooms

Sunday: $\frac{3}{4} \times 120 = \frac{3}{4} \times \frac{120}{1} = \frac{360}{4} = 90$ rooms

Thus, more rooms were booked on Saturday by 6 rooms.

4. In a veterinary hospital, the veterinarian-to-pet ratio is 1:9. The ratio is always constant. If there are 45 pets in the hospital, how many veterinarians are currently in the veterinary hospital?

A proportion is set up to solve for the number of veterinarians: $\frac{1}{9} = \frac{x}{45}$

Cross-multiplying results in $9x = 45$, which works out to 5 veterinarians.

Alternatively, as there are always 9 times as many pets as veterinarians, is it possible to divide the number of pets (45) by 9. This also arrives at the correct answer of 5 veterinarians.

5. At a general practice law firm, 30% of the lawyers work solely on tort cases. If 9 lawyers work solely on tort cases, how many lawyers work at the firm?

The first step is to solve for the total number of lawyers working at the firm, which will be represented here with x. The problem states that 9 lawyers work solely on torts cases, and they make up 30% of the total lawyers at the firm. Thus, 30% multiplied by the total, x, will equal 9. Written as equation, this is: $30\% \times x = 9$.

It's easier to deal with the equation after converting the percentage to a decimal, leaving $0.3x = 9$. Thus, $x = \frac{9}{0.3} = 30$ lawyers working at the firm.

6. Xavier was hospitalized with pneumonia. He was originally given 35mg of antibiotics. Later, after his condition continued to worsen, Xavier's dosage was increased to 60mg. What was the percent increase of the antibiotics? Round the percentage to the nearest tenth.

An increase or decrease in percentage can be calculated by dividing the difference in amounts by the original amount and multiplying by 100. Written as an equation, the formula is:

$$\frac{new\ quantity\ -\ old\ quantity}{old\ quantity} \times 100$$

Here, the question states that the dosage was increased from 35mg to 60mg, so these values are plugged into the formula to find the percentage increase.

$$\frac{60 - 35}{35} \times 100 = \frac{25}{35} \times 100 = .7142 \times 100 = 71.4\%$$

FOIL Method

FOIL is a technique for generating polynomials through the multiplication of binomials. A polynomial is an expression of multiple variables (for example, x, y, z) in at least three terms involving only the four basic operations and exponents. FOIL is an acronym for First, Outer, Inner, and Last. "First" represents the multiplication of the terms appearing first in the binomials. "Outer" means multiplying the outermost terms. "Inner" means multiplying the terms inside. "Last" means multiplying the last terms of each binomial.

After completing FOIL and solving the operations, *like terms* are combined. To identify like terms, test takers should look for terms with the same variable and the same exponent. For example, in $4x^2 - x^2 + 15x + 2x^2 - 8$, the $4x^2, -x^2$, and $2x^2$ are all like terms because they have the variable (x) and exponent (2). Thus, after combining the like terms, the polynomial has been simplified to $5x^2 + 15x - 8$.

The purpose of FOIL is to simplify an equation involving multiple variables and operations. Although it sounds complicated, working through some examples will provide some clarity:

1. Simplify $(x + 10)(x + 4) =$

$(x \times x)$ $+$ $(x \times 4)$ $+$ $(10 \times x)$ $+$ (10×4)
    First   Outer   Inner   Last

After multiplying these binomials, it's time to solve the operations and combine like terms. Thus, the expression becomes: $2x^2 + 4x + 10x + 40 = 2x^2 + 14x + 40$.

2. Simplify $2x (4x^3 - 7y^2 + 3x^2 + 4)$

Here, a monomial $(2x)$ is multiplied into a polynomial $(4x^3 - 7y^2 + 3x^2 + 4)$. Using the distributive property, the monomial get multiplied by each term in the polynomial. This becomes $2x(4x^3) - 2x(7y^2) + 2x(3x^2) + 2x(4)$.

Now, each monomial is simplified, starting with the coefficients:

$$(2 \times 4)(x \times x^3) - (2 \times 7)(x \times y^2) + (2 \times 3)(x \times x^2) + (2 \times 4)(x)$$

When multiplying powers with the same base, their exponents are added. Remember, a variable with no listed exponent has an exponent of 1, and exponents of distinct variables cannot be combined. This produces the answer:

$$8x^{1+3} - 14xy^2 + 6x^{1+2} + 8x = 8x^4 - 14xy^2 + 6x^3 + 8x$$

3. Simplify $(8x^{10}y^2z^4) \div (4x^2y^4z^7)$

The first step is to divide the coefficients of the first two polynomials: $8 \div 4 = 2$. The second step is to divide exponents with the same variable, which requires subtracting the exponents. This results in: $2(x^{10-2}y^{2-4}z^{4-7}) = 2x^8y^{-2}z^{-3}$.

However, the most simplified answer should include only positive exponents. Thus, $y^{-2}z^{-3}$ needs to be converted into fractions, respectively $\frac{1}{y^2}$ and $\frac{1}{z^3}$. Since the $2x^8$ has a positive exponent, it is placed in the numerator, and $\frac{1}{y^2}$ and $\frac{1}{z^3}$ are combined into the denominator, leaving $\frac{2x^8}{y^2z^3}$ as the final answer.

Rational Expressions

A *rational expression* is a fraction where the numerator and denominator are both polynomials. Some examples of rational expressions include the following: $\frac{4x^3y^5}{3z^4}$, $\frac{4x^3+3x}{x^2}$, and $\frac{x^2+7x+10}{x+2}$. Since these refer to expressions and not equations, they can be simplified but not solved. Using the rules in the previous *Exponents and Roots* section, some rational expressions with monomials can be simplified. Other rational expressions such as the last example, $\frac{x^2+7x+10}{x+2}$, require more steps to be simplified. First, the polynomial on top can be factored from $x^2 + 7x + 10$ into $(x + 5)(x + 2)$. Then the common factors can be canceled and the expression can be simplified to $(x + 5)$.

The following problem is an example of using rational expressions:

Reggie wants to lay sod in his rectangular backyard. The length of the yard is given by the expression $4x + 2$ and the width is unknown. The area of the yard is $20x + 10$. Reggie needs to find the width of the yard. Knowing that the area of a rectangle is length multiplied by width, an expression can be written to find the width: $\frac{20x+10}{4x+2}$, area divided by length. Simplifying this expression by factoring out 10 on the top and 2 on the bottom leads to this expression: $\frac{10(2x+1)}{2(2x+1)}$. Cancelling out the $2x + 1$ results in $\frac{10}{2} = 5$. The width of the yard is found to be 5 by simplifying the rational expression.

Rational Equations

A *rational equation* can be as simple as an equation with a ratio of polynomials, $\frac{p(x)}{q(x)}$, set equal to a value, where $p(x)$ and $q(x)$ are both polynomials. A rational equation has an equal sign, which is different from expressions. This leads to solutions, or numbers that make the equation true.

It is possible to solve rational equations by trying to get all of the x terms out of the denominator and then isolating them on one side of the equation. For example, to solve the equation $\frac{3x+2}{2x+3} = 4$, both sides get multiplied by $(2x + 3)$. This will cancel on the left side to yield $3x + 2 = 4(2x + 3)$, then $3x + 2 = 8x + 12$. Now, subtract $8x$ from both sides, which yields $-5x + 2 = 12$. Subtracting 2 from both sides results in $-5x = 10$. Finally, both sides get divided by -5 to obtain $x = -2$.

Sometimes, when solving rational equations, it can be easier to try to simplify the rational expression by factoring the numerator and denominator first, then cancelling out common factors. For example, to solve $\frac{2x^2-8x+6}{x^2-3x+2} = 1$, the first step is to factor $2x^2 - 8x + 6 = 2(x^2 - 4x + 3) = 2(x - 1)(x - 3)$. Then, factor $x^2 - 3x + 2$ into $(x - 1)(x - 2)$. This turns the original equation into $\frac{2(x-1)(x-3)}{(x-1)(x-2)} = 1$. The common factor of $(x - 1)$ can be canceled, leaving $\frac{2(x-3)}{x-1} = 1$. Now the same method used in the previous example can be followed. Multiplying both sides by $x - 1$ and performing the multiplication on the left yields $2x - 6 = x - 1$, which can be simplified to $x = 5$.

Rational Functions

A *rational function* is similar to an equation, but it includes two variables. In general, a rational function is in the form: $f(x) = \frac{p(x)}{q(x)}$, where $p(x)$ and $q(x)$ are polynomials. Refer to the *Functions* section for a more detailed definition of functions. Rational functions are defined everywhere except where the denominator is equal to zero. When the denominator is equal to zero, this indicates either a hole in the graph or an asymptote. An example of a function with an asymptote is shown below.

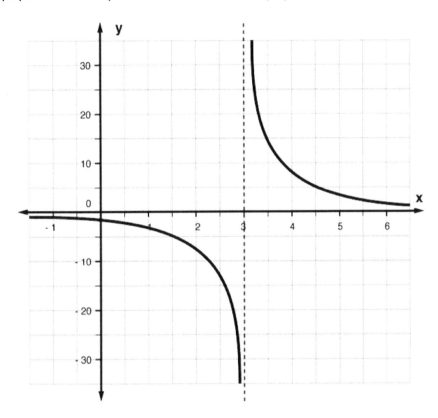

Functions

Algebraic Functions

A function is called *algebraic* if it is built up from polynomials by adding, subtracting, multplying, dividing, and taking radicals. This means that, for example, the variable can never appear in an exponent. Thus, polynomials and rational functions are algebraic, but exponential functions are not algebraic. It turns out that logarithms and trigonometric functions are not algebraic either.

A function of the form $f(x) = a_n x^n + a_{n-1} x^{n-1} + a_{n-2} x^{n-2} + \cdots + a_1 x + a_0$ is called a *polynomial function*. The value of n is called the *degree* of the polynomial. In the case where $n = 1$, it is called a *linear function*. In the case where $n = 2$, it is called a *quadratic function*. In the case where $n = 3$, it is called a *cubic function*.

When n is even, the polynomial is called *even*, and not all real numbers will be in its range. When n is odd, the polynomial is called *odd*, and the range includes all real numbers.

The graph of a quadratic function $f(x) = ax^2 + bx + c$ will be a parabola. To see whether or not the parabola opens up or down, it's necessary to check the coefficient of x^2, which is the value a. If the coefficient is positive, then the parabola opens upward. If the coefficient is negative, then the parabola opens downward.

The quantity $D = b^2 - 4ac$ is called the *discriminant* of the parabola. If the discriminant is positive, then the parabola has two real zeros. If the discriminant is negative, then it has no real zeros. If the discriminant is zero, then the parabola's highest or lowest point is on the x-axis, and it has a single real zero.

The highest or lowest point of the parabola is called the *vertex*. The coordinates of the vertex are given by the point $(-\frac{b}{2a}, -\frac{D}{4a})$. The roots of a quadratic function can be found with the quadratic formula, which is:

$$x = \frac{-b \pm \sqrt{b^2 - 4ac}}{2a}$$

A *rational function* is a function $f(x) = \frac{p(x)}{q(x)}$, where p and q are both polynomials. The domain of f will be all real numbers except the (real) roots of q. At these roots, the graph of f will have a *vertical asymptote*, unless they are also roots of p. Here is an example to consider:

$$p(x) = p_n x^n + p_{n-1} x^{n-1} + p_{n-2} x^{n-2} + \cdots + p_1 x + p_0$$

$$q(x) = q_m x^m + q_{m-1} x^{m-1} + q_{m-2} x^{m-2} + \cdots + q_1 x + q_0$$

When the degree of p is less than the degree of q, there will be a horizontal asymptote of $y = 0$. If p and q have the same degree, there will be a horizontal asymptote of $y = \frac{p_n}{q_n}$. If the degree of p is exactly one greater than the degree of q, then f will have an oblique asymptote along the line $y = \frac{p_n}{q_{n-1}} x + \frac{p_{n-1}}{q_{n-1}}$.

Exponential Functions

An *exponential function* is a function of the form $f(x) = b^x$, where b is a positive real number other than 1. In such a function, b is called the *base*.

The *domain* of an exponential function is all real numbers, and the *range* is all positive real numbers. There will always be a horizontal asymptote of $y = 0$ on one side. If b is greater than 1, then the graph will be increasing when moving to the right. If b is less than 1, then the graph will be decreasing when moving to the right. Exponential functions are one-to-one. The basic exponential function graph will go through the point (0, 1).

The following example demonstartes this more clearly:

Solve $5^{x+1} = 25$.

The first step is to get the x out of the exponent by rewriting the equation $5^{x+1} = 5^2$ so that both sides have a base of 5. Since the bases are the same, the exponents must be equal to each other. This leaves $x + 1 = 2$ or $x = 1$. To check the answer, the x-value of 1 can be substituted back into the original equation.

Logarithmic Functions

A *logarithmic function* is an inverse for an exponential function. The inverse of the base b exponential function is written as $\log_b(x)$, and is called the *base b logarithm*. The domain of a logarithm is all positive real numbers. It has the properties that $\log_b(b^x) = x$. For positive real values of x, $b^{\log_b(x)} = x$.

When there is no chance of confusion, the parentheses are sometimes skipped for logarithmic functions: $\log_b(x)$ may be written as $\log_b x$. For the special number e, the base e logarithm is called the *natural logarithm* and is written as $\ln x$. Logarithms are one-to-one.

When working with logarithmic functions, it is important to remember the following properties. Each one can be derived from the definition of the logarithm as the inverse to an exponential function:

- $\log_b 1 = 0$
- $\log_b b = 1$
- $\log_b b^p = p$
- $\log_b MN = \log_b M + \log_b N$
- $\log_b \dfrac{M}{N} = \log_b M - \log_b N$
- $\log_b M^p = p \log_b M$

When solving equations involving exponentials and logarithms, the following fact should be used:

If f is a one-to-one function, $a = b$ is equivalent to $f(a) = f(b)$.

Using this, together with the fact that logarithms and exponentials are inverses, allows for manipulations of the equations to isolate the variable as is demonstrated in the following example:

Solve $4 = \ln(x - 4)$.

Using the definition of a logarithm, the equation can be changed to $e^4 = e^{\ln(x-4)}$. The functions on the right side cancel with a result of $e^4 = x - 4$. This then gives $x = 4 + e^4$.

Trigonometric Functions

Trigonometric functions are built out of two basic functions, the *sine* and *cosine*, written as $\sin\theta$ and $\cos\theta$, respectively. Note that similar to logarithms, it is customary to drop the parentheses as long as the result is not confusing.

Sine and cosine are defined using the *unit circle*. If θ is the angle going counterclockwise around the origin from the x-axis, then the point on the unit circle in that direction will have the coordinates $(\cos\theta, \sin\theta)$.

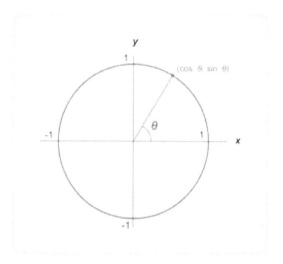

Since the angle returns to the start every 2π radians (or 360 degrees), the graph of these functions is *periodic*, with period 2π. This means that the graph repeats itself as one moves along the x-axis because $\sin\theta = \sin(\theta + 2\pi)$. Cosine works similarly.

From the unit circle definition, the sine function starts at 0 when $\theta = 0$. It grows to 1 as θ grows to $\pi/2$, and then back to 0 at $\theta = \pi$. Then it decreases to -1 as θ grows to $3\pi/2$, and goes back up to 0 at $\theta = 2\pi$.

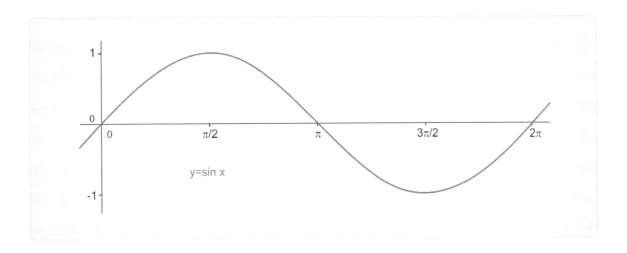

The graph of the cosine is similar. The cosine graph will start at 1, decreasing to 0 at $\pi/2$ and continuing to decrease to -1 at $\theta = \pi$. Then, it grows to 0 as θ grows to $3\pi/2$ and back up to 1 at $\theta = 2\pi$.

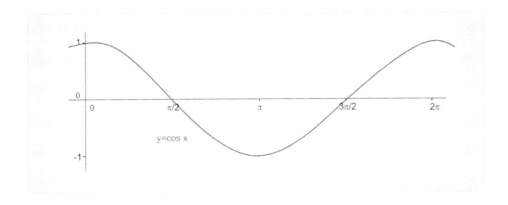

Another trigonometric function that is frequently used, is the *tangent* function. This is defined as the following equation: $\tan \theta = \frac{\sin \theta}{\cos \theta}$.

The tangent function is a period of π rather than 2π because the sine and cosine functions have the same absolute values after a change in the angle of π, but they flip their signs. Since the tangent is a ratio of the two functions, the changes in signs cancel.

The tangent function will be zero when sine is zero, and it will have a vertical asymptote whenever cosine is zero. The following graph shows the tangent function:

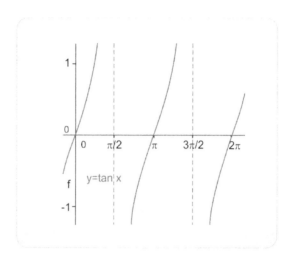

Three other trigonometric functions are sometimes useful. These are the *reciprocal* trigonometric functions, so named because they are just the reciprocals of sine, cosine, and tangent. They are the *cosecant*, defined as $\csc \theta = \frac{1}{\sin \theta}$, the *secant*, $\sec \theta = \frac{1}{\cos \theta}$, and the *cotangent*, $\cot \theta = \frac{1}{\tan \theta}$. Note that from the definition of tangent, $\cot \theta = \frac{\cos \theta}{\sin \theta}$.

In addition, there are three identities that relate the trigonometric functions to one another:

- $\cos \theta = \sin(\frac{\pi}{2} - \theta)$
- $\csc \theta = \sec\left(\frac{\pi}{2} - \theta\right)$
- $\cot \theta = \tan(\frac{\pi}{2} - \theta)$

Here is a list of commonly-needed values for trigonometric functions, given in radians, for the first quadrant:

Table for trigonometric functions

$\sin 0 = 0$	$\cos 0 = 1$	$\tan 0 = 0$
$\sin\dfrac{\pi}{6} = \dfrac{1}{2}$	$\cos\dfrac{\pi}{6} = \dfrac{\sqrt{3}}{2}$	$\tan\dfrac{\pi}{6} = \dfrac{\sqrt{3}}{3}$
$\sin\dfrac{\pi}{4} = \dfrac{\sqrt{2}}{2}$	$\cos\dfrac{\pi}{4} = \dfrac{\sqrt{2}}{2}$	$\tan\dfrac{\pi}{4} = 1$
$\sin\dfrac{\pi}{3} = \dfrac{\sqrt{3}}{2}$	$\cos\dfrac{\pi}{3} = \dfrac{1}{2}$	$\tan\dfrac{\pi}{3} = \sqrt{3}$
$\sin\dfrac{\pi}{2} = 1$	$\cos\dfrac{\pi}{2} = 0$	$\tan\dfrac{\pi}{2} = undefined$
$\csc 0 = undefined$	$\sec 0 = 1$	$\cot 0 = undefined$
$\csc\dfrac{\pi}{6} = 2$	$\sec\dfrac{\pi}{6} = \dfrac{2\sqrt{3}}{3}$	$\cot\dfrac{\pi}{6} = \sqrt{3}$
$\csc\dfrac{\pi}{4} = \sqrt{2}$	$\sec\dfrac{\pi}{4} = \sqrt{2}$	$\cot\dfrac{\pi}{4} = 1$
$\csc\dfrac{\pi}{3} = \dfrac{2\sqrt{3}}{3}$	$\sec\dfrac{\pi}{3} = 2$	$\cot\dfrac{\pi}{3} = \dfrac{\sqrt{3}}{3}$
$\csc\dfrac{\pi}{2} = 1$	$\sec\dfrac{\pi}{2} = undefined$	$\cot\dfrac{\pi}{2} = 0$

To find the trigonometric values in other quadrants, complementary angles can be used. The *complementary angle* is the smallest angle between the x-axis and the given angle.

Once the complementary angle is known, the following rule is used:

For an angle θ with complementary angle x, the absolute value of a trigonometric function evaluated at θ is the same as the absolute value when evaluated at x.

The correct sign for sine and cosine is determined by the x and y coordinates on the unit circle.

- Sine will be positive in quadrants I and II and negative in quadrants III and IV.
- Cosine will be positive in quadrants I and IV, and negative in II and III.
- Tangent will be positive in I and III, and negative in II and IV.

The signs of the reciprocal functions will be the same as the sign of the function of which they are the reciprocal. For example:

Find $\sin\frac{3\pi}{4}$.

The complementary angle must be found first. This angle is in the II quadrant, and the angle between it and the x-axis is $\frac{\pi}{4}$. Now, $\sin\frac{\pi}{4} = \frac{\sqrt{2}}{2}$. Since this is in the II quadrant, sine takes on positive values (the y coordinate is positive in the II quadrant). Therefore, $\sin\frac{3\pi}{4} = \frac{\sqrt{2}}{2}$.

In addition to the six trigonometric functions defined above, there are inverses for these functions. However, since the trigonometric functions are not one-to-one, one can only construct inverses for them on a restricted domain.

Usually, the domain chosen will be $[0, \pi)$ for cosine and $(-\frac{\pi}{2}, \frac{\pi}{2}]$ for sine. The inverse for tangent can use either of these domains. The inverse functions for the trigonometric functions are also called *arc functions*. In addition to being written with a -1 as the exponent to denote that the function is an inverse, they will sometimes be written with an "a" or "arc" in front of the function name, so $\cos^{-1}\theta = a\cos\theta = \arccos\theta$.

When solving equations that involve trigonometric functions, there are often multiple solutions. For example, $2\sin\theta = \sqrt{2}$ can be simplified to $\sin\theta = \frac{\sqrt{2}}{2}$. This has solutions $\theta = \frac{\pi}{4}, \frac{3\pi}{4}$, but in addition, because of the periodicity, any integer multiple of 2π can also be added to these solutions to find another solution.

The full set of solutions is $\theta = \frac{\pi}{4} + 2\pi k, \frac{3\pi}{4} + 2\pi k$ for all integer values of k. It is very important to remember to find all possible solutions when dealing with equations that involve trigonometric functions.

The name *trigonometric* comes from the fact that these functions play an important role in the geometry of triangles, particularly right triangles. Consider the right triangle shown in this figure:

The following hold true:

- $c\sin\theta = b$.
- $c\cos\theta = a$.
- $\tan\theta = \frac{b}{a}$.

- $b \csc \theta = c$.
- $a \sec \theta = c$.
- $\cot \theta = \frac{a}{b}$.

It is important to remember that the angles of a triangle must add up to π radians (180 degrees).

Geometry

Shapes and Solids

Perimeter is the distance measurement around something. It can be thought of as the length of the boundary, like a fence. In contrast, area is the space occupied by a defined enclosure, like a field enclosed by a fence.

The perimeter of a square is measured by adding together all of the sides. Since a square has four equal sides, its perimeter can be calculated by multiplying the length of one side by 4. Thus, the formula is $P = 4 \times s$, where s equals one side. The area of a square is calculated by squaring the length of one side, which is expressed as the formula $A = s^2$.

Like a square, a rectangle's perimeter is measured by adding together all of the sides. But as the sides are unequal, the formula is different. A rectangle has equal values for its lengths (long sides) and equal values for its widths (short sides), so the perimeter formula for a rectangle is $P = l + l + w + w = 2l + 2w$, where l equals length and w equals width. The area is found by multiplying the length by the width, so the formula is $A = l \times w$.

A triangle's perimeter is measured by adding together the three sides, so the formula is $P = a + b + c$, where $a, b,$ and c are the values of the three sides. The area is calculated by multiplying the length of the base times the height times ½, so the formula is $A = \frac{1}{2} \times b \times h = \frac{bh}{2}$. The base is the bottom of the triangle, and the height is the distance from the base to the peak. If a problem asks one to calculate the area of a triangle, it will provide the base and height.

A circle's perimeter—also known as its circumference—is measured by multiplying the diameter (the straight line measured from one side, through the center, to the direct opposite side of the circle) by π, so the formula is $\pi \times d$. This is sometimes expressed by the formula $C = 2 \times \pi \times r$, where r is the radius of the circle. These formulas are equivalent, as the radius equals half of the diameter. The area of a circle is calculated with the formula $A = \pi \times r^2$. The test will indicate either to leave the answer with π attached or to calculate to the nearest decimal place, which means multiplying by 3.14 for π.

The perimeter of a parallelogram is measured by adding the lengths and widths together. Thus, the formula is the same as for a rectangle, $P = l + l + w + w = 2l + 2w$. However, the area formula differs from the rectangle. For a parallelogram, the area is calculated by multiplying the length by the height: $A = h \times l$

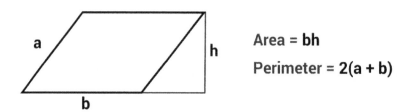

Area = bh

Perimeter = 2(a + b)

The perimeter of a trapezoid is calculated by adding the two unequal bases and two equal sides, so the formula is $P = a + b_1 + c + b_2$. Although unlikely to be a test question, the formula for the area of a trapezoid is $A = \frac{b_1 + b_2}{2} \times h$, where h equals height, and b_1 and b_2 equal the bases.

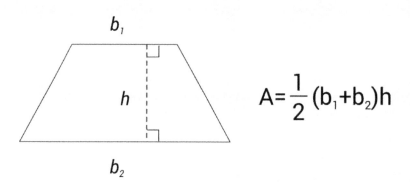

$$A = \frac{1}{2}(b_1 + b_2)h$$

Congruence and Similarity

Triangles are similar if they have the same angle measurements, and their sides are proportional to one another. Triangles are congruent if the angles of the triangles are equal in measurement and the sides of the triangles are equal in measurement.

There are five ways to show that triangles are congruent:

1. SSS (Side-Side-Side Postulate) – when all three corresponding sides are equal in length, then the two triangles are congruent.

2. SAS (Side-Angle-Side Postulate) – if a pair of corresponding sides and the angle in between those two sides are equal, then the two triangles are congruent.

3. ASA (Angle-Side-Angle Postulate) – if a pair of corresponding angles are equal and the side lengths within those angles are equal, then the two triangles are equal.

4. AAS (Angle-Angle-Side Postulate) – when a pair of corresponding angles for two triangles and a non-included side are equal, then the two triangles are congruent.

5. HL (Hypotenuse-Leg Theorem) – if two right triangles have the same hypotenuse length, and one of the other sides in each triangle are of the same length, then the two triangles are congruent.

If two triangles are discovered to be similar or congruent, this information can assist in determining unknown parts of triangles, such as missing angles and sides.

The example below involves the question of congruent triangles. The first step is to examine whether the triangles are congruent. If the triangles are congruent, then the measure of a missing angle can be found.

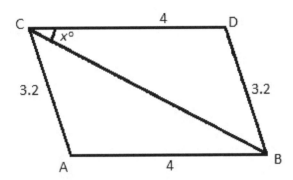

The above diagram provides values for angle measurements and side lengths in triangles *CAB* and *CDB*. Note that side *CA* is 3.2 and side *DB* is 3.2. Side *CD* is 4 and side *AB* is 4. Furthermore, line *CB* is congruent to itself by the reflexive property. Therefore, the two triangles are congruent by SSS (Side-Side-Side). Because the two triangles are congruent, all of the corresponding parts of the triangles are also congruent. Therefore, angle x is congruent to the inside of the angle for which a measurement is not provided in triangle *CAB*. Thus, 115º + 32º = 147º. A triangle's angles sum to 180º, therefore, 180º – 147º = 33º. Angle x = 33º, because the two triangles are reversed.

Surface Area and Volume

Surface area and volume are two- and three-dimensional measurements. Surface area measures the total surface space of an object, like the six sides of a cube. Questions about surface area will ask how much of something is needed to cover a three-dimensional object, like wrapping a present. Volume is the measurement of how much space an object occupies, like how much space is in the cube. Volume questions will ask how much of something is needed to completely fill the object. The most common surface area and volume questions deal with spheres, cubes, and rectangular prisms.

The formula for a cube's surface area is $SA = 6 \times s^2$, where s is the length of a side. A cube has 6 equal sides, so the formula expresses the area of all the sides. Volume is simply measured by taking the cube of the length, so the formula is $V = s^3$.

The surface area formula for a rectangular prism or a general box is SA = $2(lw + lh + wh)$, where l is the length, h is the height, and w is the width. The volume formula is $V = l \times w \times h$, which is the cube's volume formula adjusted for the unequal lengths of a box's sides.

The formula for a sphere's surface area is $SA = 4\pi r^2$, where r is the sphere's radius. The surface area formula is the area for a circle multiplied by four. To measure volume, the formula is $V = \frac{4}{3}\pi r^3$.

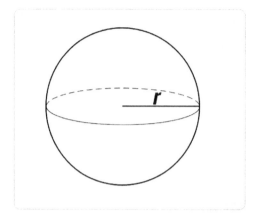

A *rectangular pyramid* is a figure with a rectangular base and four triangular sides that meet at a single vertex. If the rectangle has sides of lengths x and y, then the volume will be given by $V = \frac{1}{3}xyh$.

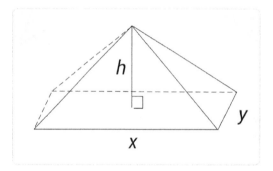

To find the surface area, the dimensions of each triangle must be known. However, these dimensions can differ depending on the problem in question. Therefore, there is no general formula for calculating total surface area.

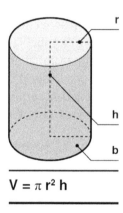

$$V = \pi\, r^2\, h$$

The formula to find the volume of a cylinder is $\pi r^2 h$. This formula contains the formula for the area of a circle (πr^2) because the base of a cylinder is a circle. To calculate the volume of a cylinder, the slices of circles needed to build the entire height of the cylinder are added together. For example, if the radius is 5 feet and the height of the cylinder is 10 feet, the cylinder's volume is calculated by using the following equation: $\pi 5^2 \times 10$. Substituting 3.14 for π, the volume is 785.4 ft³.

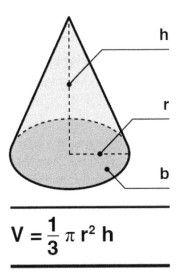

$$V = \frac{1}{3}\,\pi\, r^2\, h$$

The formula used to calculate the volume of a cone is $\frac{1}{3}\pi r^2 h$. Essentially, the area of the base of the cone is multiplied by the cone's height. In a real-life example where the radius of a cone is 2 meters and the height of a cone is 5 meters, the volume of the cone is calculated by utilizing the formula $\frac{1}{3}\pi 2^2 \times 5 = 21$. After substituting 3.14 for π, the volume is 785.4 ft³.

Solving for Missing Values in Triangles

Suppose that Lara is 5 feet tall and is standing 30 feet from the base of a light pole, and her shadow is 6 feet long. How high is the light on the pole? To figure this out, it helps to make a sketch of the situation:

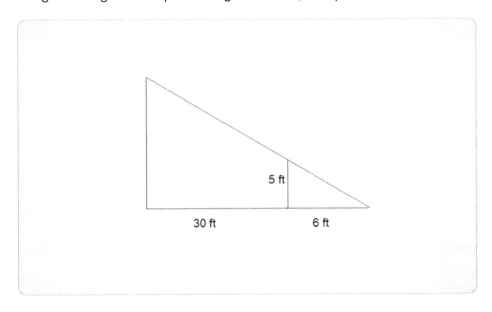

The light pole is the left side of the triangle. Lara is the 5-foot vertical line. Test takers should notice that there are two right triangles here, and that they have all the same angles as one another. Therefore, they form similar triangles. So, the ratio of proportionality between them must be found.

The bases of these triangles are known. The small triangle, formed by Lara and her shadow, has a base of 6 feet. The large triangle, formed by the light pole along with the line from the base of the pole out to the end of Lara's shadow is $30 + 6 = 36$ feet long. So, the ratio of the big triangle to the little triangle is $\frac{36}{6} = 6$. The height of the little triangle is 5 feet. Therefore, the height of the big triangle will be $6 \cdot 5 = 30$ feet, meaning that the light is 30 feet up the pole.

The Pythagorean Theorem

The *Pythagorean theorem* states that for right triangles, the sum of the squares of the two shorter sides is equal to the square of the longest side (also called the *hypotenuse*). The longest side will always be the side opposite to the 90° angle. If this side is called c, and the other two sides are a and b, then the Pythagorean theorem states that $c^2 = a^2 + b^2$. Since lengths are always positive, this also can be written as $c = \sqrt{a^2 + b^2}$. A diagram to show the parts of a triangle using the Pythagorean theorem is below.

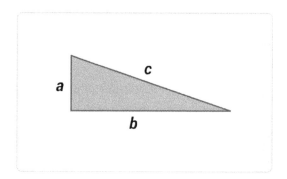

As an example of the theorem, suppose that Shirley has a rectangular field that is 5 feet wide and 12 feet long, and she wants to split it in half using a fence that goes from one corner to the opposite corner. How long will this fence need to be? To figure this out, note that this makes the field into two right triangles, whose hypotenuse will be the fence dividing it in half. Therefore, the fence length is given by $\sqrt{5^2 + 12^2} = \sqrt{169} = 13$ feet long.

One last useful relationship between the trigonometric functions introduced in the *Functions* section is the *Pythagorean identity*, which states that $\sin^2 \theta + \cos^2 \theta = 1$. Note that for trigonometric functions, the exponent is sometimes written next to the function name, so $\sin^2 \theta = (\sin \theta)^2$, and so on. The same is sometimes also done for logarithmic functions. The Pythagorean identity has two other forms which are often useful: $1 + \cot^2 \theta = \csc^2 \theta$ and $\tan^2 \theta + 1 = \sec^2 \theta$.

As mentioned, although the trigonometric functions are not one-to-one, it is possible to define inverses for them on limited domains. These are also called the *arc* functions. The inverse function for sine is called the *arcsine* and is written as either $\sin^{-1} x$ or as $\operatorname{asin} x$, and similarly for the other five trigonometric functions. The range of the arcsine and arccosecant is usually taken to be $[-\frac{\pi}{2}, \frac{\pi}{2}]$. The range of the arccosine, arcsecant, arctangent, and arccotangent are generally taken to be $[0, \pi]$. Some specific values for these inverse functions can be read off published tables.

When solving an equation using these inverses, unless the domain is specifically restricted, all possible angles which satisfy the equation must be considered. For example, when solving $\cos(x - 1) = \frac{\sqrt{2}}{2}$, arccosine is applied to both sides, which yields $x - 1 = a\cos\frac{\sqrt{2}}{2}$. From the available tables, cosine takes the value $\frac{\sqrt{2}}{2}$ for any angle $2\pi k \pm \frac{\pi}{4}$, where k is an arbitrary integer. The equation becomes $x - 1 = 2\pi k \pm \frac{\pi}{4}$, or $x = 2\pi k \pm \frac{\pi}{4} + 1$.

Performing Algebraic Operations on Functions

As mentioned, it is possible to perform algebraic operations between functions, meaning they can be added, subtracted, multiplied, or divided. In fact, all the trigonometric functions are formed this way from sine and cosine. More generally, everything stated regarding arithmetic operations on functions can be done for trigonometric and logarithmic functions. However, sometimes it will be possible to use their definition to simplify the result.

For example, given $f(x) = \sin x + 1, g(x) = \cos x$, find $\frac{f(x)}{g(x)}$. This will, of course, be $\frac{\sin x + 1}{\cos x}$; however, this can be further simplified using the identities of trigonometric functions. The expression can be rewritten as $\frac{\sin x}{\cos x} + \frac{1}{\cos x} = \tan x + \sec x$.

Identifying and Using Composite Functions

Everything previously explained about composing functions can be applied to exponential, logarithmic, and trigonometric functions as well. For example, given $f(x) = 5^x, g(x) = \cos x$, one may form the composition $(g \circ f)(x) = \cos(5^x)$. The ability to recognize such compositions will be particularly important when discussing calculus, where more examples will be considered.

Conics

The graph of an equation of the form $y = ax^2 + bx + c$ or $x = ay^2 + by + c$ is called a *parabola*.

The graph of an equation of the form $\frac{x^2}{a^2} - \frac{y^2}{b^2} = 1$ or $-\frac{x^2}{a^2} + \frac{y^2}{b^2} = 1$ is called a *hyperbola*.

The graph of an equation of the form $\frac{(x-x_0)^2}{a^2} + \frac{(y-y_0)^2}{b^2} = 1$ is called an *ellipse*. If $a = b$ then this is a circle with *radius* $r = \frac{1}{a}$.

Statistics and Probability

Center and Spread of Distributions

Descriptive statistics are utilized to gain an understanding of properties of a data set. This entails examining the center, spread, and shape of the sample data.

Center
The *center* of the sample set can be represented by its mean, median or mode. The *mean* is the average of the data set. It is calculated by adding the data values together and dividing this sum by the sample size (the number of data points). The *median* is the value of the data point in the middle when the sample is arranged in numerical order. If the sample has an even number of data points, the mean of the

two middle values is the median. The *mode* is the value which appears most often in a data set. It is possible to have multiple modes (if different values repeat equally as often) or no mode (if no value repeats).

Spread

Methods for determining the *spread* of the sample include calculating the range and standard deviation for the data. The *range* is calculated by subtracting the lowest value from the highest value in the set. The *standard deviation* of the sample can be calculated using the formula:

$$\sigma = \sqrt{\frac{\sum(x - \bar{x})^2}{n - 1}}$$

$\bar{x}$ = sample mean
n = sample size

Shape

The *shape* of the sample when displayed as a histogram or frequency distribution plot helps to determine if the sample is normally distributed (bell-shaped curve), symmetrical, or displays skewness (lack of symmetry), or kurtosis. *Kurtosis* is a measure of whether the data are heavy-tailed (high number of outliers) or light-tailed (low number of outliers).

Data Collection Methods

Statistical inference, based in probability theory, makes calculated assumptions about an entire population based on data from a sample set from that population.

Population Parameters

A population is the entire set of people or things of interest. For example, if researchers wanted to determine the number of hours of sleep per night for college females in the U.S, the population would consist of *every* college female in the country. A *sample* is a subset of the population that may be used for the study. A sample might consist of 100 students per school from 20 different colleges in the country. From the results of the survey, a sample statistic can be calculated. A *sample statistic* is a numerical characteristic of the sample data including mean and variance. A sample statistic can be used to estimate a corresponding *population parameter*, which is a numerical characteristic of the entire population.

Confidence Intervals

A population parameter estimated using a sample statistic may be very accurate or relatively inaccurate based on errors in sampling. A confidence interval indicates a range of values likely to include the true population parameter. A given confidence interval such as 95% means that the true population parameter will occur within the interval for 95% of samples.

Measurement Error

The accuracy of a population parameter based on a sample statistic may also be affected by measurement error. *Measurement error* can be divided into random error and systematic error. An example of random error for the previous scenario would be a student reporting 8 hours of sleep when she actually sleeps 7 hours per night. Systematic errors are those attributed to the measurement system. If the sleep survey gave response options of 2,4,6,8, or 10 hours. This would lead to systematic measurement error because certain values could not be accurately reported.

Evaluating Reports and Determining the Appropriateness of Data Collection Methods

The presentation of statistics can be manipulated to produce a desired outcome. For example, in the statement "four out of five dentists recommend our toothpaste", critical readers should wonder: *who are the five dentists?* While the wording is similar, this statement is very different from "four out of every five dentists recommend our toothpaste." The context of the numerical values allows one to decipher the meaning, intent, and significance of the survey or study.

When analyzing a report, the researchers who conducted the study and their intent must be considered. Was it performed by a neutral party or by a person or group with a vested interest? The sampling method and the data collection method should also be evaluated. Was it a true random sample of the population or was one subgroup over- or underrepresented? Lastly, the measurement system used to obtain the data should be assessed. Was the system accurate and precise or was it a flawed system?

Understanding and Modeling Relationships in Bivariate Data

The simplest type of correlation between two variables is a *linear correlation*. If the independent variable is x and the dependent variable is y, then a linear correlation means $y = mx + b$. If m is positive, then y will increase as x increases. While if m is negative, then y decreases while x increases. The variable b represents the value of y when x is 0.

Calculating Probabilities, Including Related Sample Spaces

Probability, represented by variable p, always has a value from 0 to 1. The total probability for all the possible outcomes (sample space) should equal 1.

The probability of a single outcome x_i can be expressed $p(x_i) = \frac{1}{n}$, where n is the total number of possible outcomes. A good example of this is a fair six-sided die, in which the possible outcomes are 1, 2, 3, 4, 5, and 6, and the individual probability of each of these six outcomes is $\frac{1}{6}$.

The probability of an outcome occurring from a range A of possible outcomes is written as $P(A)$. To compute this, the probabilities for each outcome in A are added together. To use the example of a fair six-sided die, a problem may ask one to find the probability of getting a 2 or lower when it is rolled. The possible rolls are 1, 2, 3, 4, 5, and 6. So, to get a 2 or lower, one must roll a 1 or a 2. Each probability is $\frac{1}{6}$, and adding them together to get $p(1) + p(2) = \frac{1}{6} + \frac{1}{6} = \frac{1}{3}$.

Here are a few types of probability distributions that are standard and have standard names:

- *The binomial distribution*: This distribution describes the probability of getting k successes in n trials, where each trial can either succeed or fail. If the probability of a single trial being a success is denoted by p, then, the probability of getting k successes in n trials is:

$$\frac{n!}{k!\,(n-k)!}p^k(1-p)^{n-k}$$

- *A Poisson distribution*: This describes the probability of getting k events in a fixed interval of time. If the average number of events during this time interval is denoted by λ, then the probability of getting k events during this time interval is given by $\frac{\lambda^k e^{-\lambda}}{k!}$.

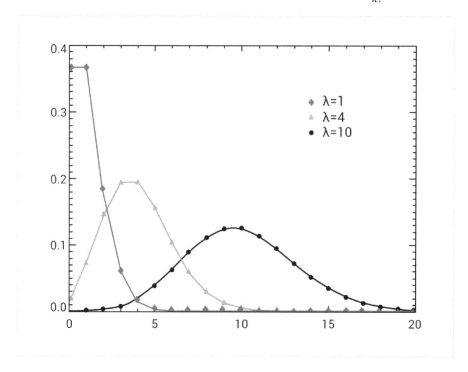

Conditional Probabilities

In some cases, it may be known that the outcome lies within the subset of possibilities B, and a problem will ask for probability that the outcome will end up being inside another subset of possibilities A. This kind of problem is called a *conditional probability*.

As an application of this, one can imagine a fair die is rolled. It is known that the roll's value lies between 1 and 4, inclusive, but the number of sides that the die has is not known (not all dice are six-sided). A problem may ask for the probability the roll was higher than 2. In this case, the total number of sides of the die is unimportant, and, since this is a fair die, the probability distribution is uniform across all possibilities. Therefore, it is possible to apply the formula $\frac{|A \cap B|}{|B|}$. $A \cap B$ means "A intersect B," and is the set of all outcomes that lie in both A and B. In this particular problem, B is {1, 2, 3, 4} and $A \cap B$ is {3, 4}. Therefore, $\frac{|A \cap B|}{|B|} = \frac{2}{4} = \frac{1}{2}$.

In many cases, changing the order of the conditional probabilities will greatly affect the outcome. For example, if a person has received a military medal, it is certain the person must have served in the military. However, given that a person served in the military, the probability of them receiving a military medal may not be very high.

In some special cases, however, the order in which the conditional probabilities are taken will not change the final probability. In this case, A and B are said to be *independent*. One situation in which one would expect that the outcomes should be independent is in rolling a pair of dice. If someone rolls two dice (a white die and a black die), then one would expect that the number that is obtained from the white die should not depend upon the number that is obtained from the black die, or vice versa. The same principle applies to a situation in which one rolls a single die repeatedly. A similar situation applies to flipping a coin repeatedly: whether the next flip is heads or tails will not depend upon what results have been obtained in previous flips.

Practice Questions

1. Which of the following is correct simplification of the expression:

$$\frac{4a^{-1}b^3}{a^4b^{-2}} * \frac{3a}{b}$$

    a. $12a^3b^5$

    b. $12\frac{b^4}{a^4}$

    c. $\frac{12}{a^4}$

    d. $7\frac{b^4}{a}$

2. What is the product of two irrational numbers?

    a. Irrational

    b. Rational

    c. Irrational or rational

    d. Complex

3. The graph shows the position of a car over a 10-second time interval. Which of the following is the correct interpretation of the graph for the interval 1 to 3 seconds?

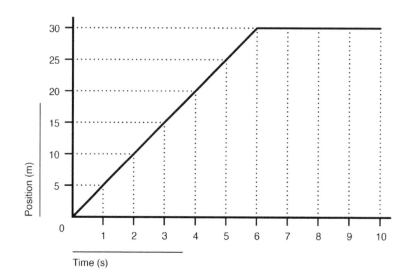

    a. The car remains in the same position.

    b. The car is traveling at a speed of 5m/s.

    c. The car is traveling up a hill.

    d. The car is traveling at 5mph.

4. How is the number -4 classified?
　　a. Real, rational, integer, whole, natural
　　b. Real, rational, integer, natural
　　c. Real, rational, integer
　　d. Real, irrational

5. After a 20% discount, Frank purchased a new refrigerator for $850. How much did he save from the original price?
　　a. $170
　　b. $212.50
　　c. $105.75
　　d. $200

6. What is the value of b in the equation: $5b - 4 = 2b + 17$?
　　a. 13
　　b. 24
　　c. 7
　　d. 21

7. What is the solution to the following problem in decimal form?
$$\frac{3}{5} \times \frac{7}{10} \div \frac{1}{2}$$
　　a. 0.042
　　b. 84%
　　c. 0.84
　　d. 0.42

8. Dwayne has received the following scores on his math tests: 78, 92, 83, and 97. What score must Dwayne get on his next math test to have an overall average of at least 90?
　　a. 89
　　b. 98
　　c. 95
　　d. 100

9. The following graph compares the various test scores of the top three students in each of these teacher's classes. Based on the graph, which teacher's students' test scores had the smallest range?

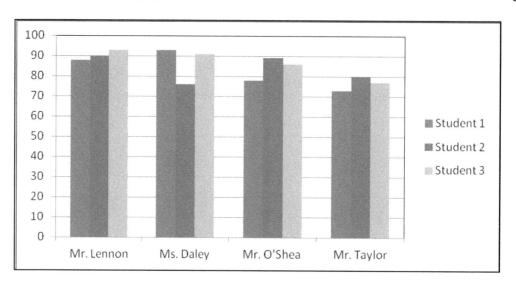

a. Mr. Lennon
b. Mr. O'Shea
c. Mr. Taylor
d. Ms. Daley

10. Which of the following augmented matrices represents the system of equations below?
$$2x - 3y + z = -5$$
$$4x - y - 2z = -7$$
$$-x + 2z = -1$$

a. $\begin{bmatrix} 2 & -3 & 1 & -5 \\ 4 & -1 & -2 & -7 \\ -1 & 0 & 2 & -1 \end{bmatrix}$

b. $\begin{bmatrix} 2 & 4 & -1 \\ -3 & -1 & 0 \\ 1 & -2 & 2 \\ -5 & -7 & -1 \end{bmatrix}$

c. $\begin{bmatrix} 2 & 4 & -1 & -5 \\ -3 & -1 & 0 & -7 \\ 2 & -2 & 2 & -1 \end{bmatrix}$

d. $\begin{bmatrix} 2 & -3 & 1 \\ 4 & -1 & -2 \\ -1 & 0 & 2 \end{bmatrix}$

11. What are the zeros of the function: $f(x) = x^3 + 4x^2 + 4x$?
   a. -2
   b. 0, -2
   c. 2
   d. 0, 2

108

12. If $g(x) = x^3 - 3x^2 - 2x + 6$ and $f(x) = 2$, then what is $g(f(x))$?
   a. -26
   b. 6
   c. $2x^3 - 6x^2 - 4x + 12$
   d. -2

13. What is the solution to the following system of equations?
$$x^2 - 2x + y = 8$$
$$x - y = -2$$
   a. $(-2, 3)$
   b. There is no solution.
   c. $(-2, 0) \ (1, 3)$
   d. $(-2, 0) \ (3, 5)$

14. Which of the following is the result after simplifying the expression: $(7n + 3n^3 + 3) + (8n + 5n^3 + 2n^4)$?
   a. $9n^4 + 15n - 2$
   b. $2n^4 + 5n^3 + 15n - 2$
   c. $9n^4 + 8n^3 + 15n$
   d. $2n^4 + 8n^3 + 15n + 3$

15. What is the product of the following expression?
$$(4x - 8)(5x^2 + x + 6)$$
   a. $20x^3 - 36x^2 + 16x - 48$
   b. $6x^3 - 41x^2 + 12x + 15$
   c. $204 + 11x^2 - 37x - 12$
   d. $2x^3 - 11x^2 - 32x + 20$

16. How could the following equation be factored to find the zeros?
$$y = x^3 - 3x^2 - 4x$$
   a. $0 = x^2(x - 4), x = 0, 4$
   b. $0 = 3x(x + 1)(x + 4), x = 0, -1, -4$
   c. $0 = x(x + 1)(x + 6), x = 0, -1, -6$
   d. $0 = x(x + 1)(x - 4), x = 0, -1, 4$

17. What is the simplified quotient of $\dfrac{5x^3}{3x^2y} \div \dfrac{25}{3y^9}$?
   a. $\dfrac{125x}{9y^{10}}$
   b. $\dfrac{x}{5y^8}$
   c. $\dfrac{5}{xy^8}$
   d. $\dfrac{xy^8}{5}$

18. Which of the following is the solution for the given equation?
$$\frac{x^2 + x - 30}{x - 5} = 11$$

   a. $x = -6$

   b. There is no solution.

   c. $x = 16$

   d. $x = 5$

19. Mom's car drove 72 miles in 90 minutes. How fast did she drive in feet per second?

   a. 0.8 feet per second

   b. 48.9 feet per second

   c. 0.009 feet per second

   d. 70. 4 feet per second

20. Solve $V = lwh$ for h.

   a. $lwV = h$

   b. $h = \dfrac{V}{lw}$

   c. $h = \dfrac{Vl}{w}$

   d. $h = \dfrac{Vw}{l}$

21. What is the domain for the function $y = \sqrt{x}$?

   a. All real numbers

   b. $x \geq 0$

   c. $x > 0$

   d. $y \geq 0$

22. If Sarah reads at an average rate of 21 pages in four nights, how long will it take her to read 140 pages?

   a. 6 nights

   b. 26 nights

   c. 8 nights

   d. 27 nights

23. The phone bill is calculated each month using the equation $c = 50g + 75$. The cost of the phone bill per month is represented by c, and g represents the gigabytes of data used that month. Identify and interpret the slope of this equation.

   a. 75 dollars per day

   b. 75 gigabytes per day

   c. 50 dollars per day

   d. 50 dollars per gigabyte

24. What is the function that forms an equivalent graph to $y = \cos(x)$?

   a. $y = \tan(x)$

   b. $y = \csc(x)$

   c. $y = \sin\left(x + \dfrac{\pi}{2}\right)$

   d. $y = \sin\left(x - \dfrac{\pi}{2}\right)$

25. If $\sqrt{1+x} = 4$, what is x?

    a. 10

    b. 15

    c. 20

    d. 25

26. What is the inverse of the function $f(x) = 3x - 5$?

    a. $f^{-1}(x) = \frac{x}{3} + 5$

    b. $f^{-1}(x) = \frac{5x}{3}$

    c. $f^{-1}(x) = 3x + 5$

    d. $f^{-1}(x) = \frac{x+5}{3}$

27. What are the zeros of $f(x) = x^2 + 4$?

    a. $x = -4$

    b. $x = \pm 2i$

    c. $x = \pm 2$

    d. $x = \pm 4i$

28. Twenty is 40% of what number?

    a. 50

    b. 8

    c. 200

    d. 5000

29. What is the simplified form of the expression $1.2 * 10^{12} \div 3.0 * 10^{8}$?

    a. $0.4 * 10^{4}$

    b. $4.0 * 10^{4}$

    c. $4.0 * 10^{3}$

    d. $3.6 * 10^{20}$

30. You measure the width of your door to be 36 inches. The true width of the door is 35.75 inches. What is the relative error in your measurement?

    a. 0.7%

    b. 0.007%

    c. 0.99%

    d. 0.1%

31. What are the y-intercept(s) for $y = x^2 + 3x - 4$?

    a. $y = 1$

    b. $y = -4$

    c. $y = 3$

    d. $y = 4$

32. Is the following function even, odd, neither, or both?
$$y = \frac{1}{2}x^4 + 2x^2 - 6$$
    a. Even
    b. Odd
    c. Neither
    d. Both

33. Which equation is not a function?
    a. $y = |x|$
    b. $y = \sqrt{x}$
    c. $x = 3$
    d. $y = 4$

34. How could the following function be rewritten to identify the zeros?
$$y = 3x^3 + 3x^2 - 18x$$
    a. $y = 3x(x+3)(x-2)$
    b. $y = x(x-2)(x+3)$
    c. $y = 3x(x-3)(x+2)$
    d. $y = (x+3)(x-2)$

35. A six-sided die is rolled. What is the probability that the roll is 1 or 2?
    a. $\frac{1}{6}$
    b. $\frac{1}{4}$
    c. $\frac{1}{3}$
    d. $\frac{1}{2}$

36. A line passes through the origin and through the point (-3, 4). What is the slope of the line?
    a. $-\frac{4}{3}$
    b. $-\frac{3}{4}$
    c. $\frac{4}{3}$
    d. $\frac{3}{4}$

37. What type of function is modeled by the values in the following table?

x	f(x)
1	2
2	4
3	8
4	16
5	32

a. Linear
b. Exponential
c. Quadratic
d. Cubic

38. An investment of $2,000 is made into an account with an annual interest rate of 5%, compounded continuously. What is the total value of the investment after eight years?
    a. $4,707
    b. $3,000
    c. $2,983.65
    d. $10,919.63

39. A ball is drawn at random from a ball pit containing 8 red balls, 7 yellow balls, 6 green balls, and 5 purple balls. What's the probability that the ball drawn is yellow?
    a. $1/26$
    b. $19/26$
    c. $7/26$
    d. 1

40. Two cards are drawn from a shuffled deck of 52 cards. What's the probability that both cards are Kings if the first card isn't replaced after it's drawn?
    a. $1/169$
    b. $1/221$
    c. $1/13$
    d. $4/13$

41. What's the probability of rolling a 6 at least once in two rolls of a die?
    a. $1/3$
    b. $1/36$
    c. $1/6$
    d. $11/36$

42. Given the set $A = \{1, 2, 3, 4, 5, 6, 7, 8, 9, 10\}$ and $B = \{1, 2, 3, 4, 5\}$, find $A - (A \cap B)$.
    n. [6, 7, 8, 9, 10]
    b. $\{1, 2, 3, 4, 5\}$
    c. $\{1, 2, 3, 4, 5, 6, 7, 8, 9, 10\}$
    d. Ø

43. An equilateral triangle has a perimeter of 18 feet. If a square whose sides have the same length as one side of the triangle is built, what will be the area of the square?
a. 6 square feet
b. 36 square feet
c. 256 square feet
d. 1000 square feet

44. In a group of 20 men, the median weight is 180 pounds and the range is 30 pounds. If each man gains 10 pounds, which of the following would be true?
a. The median weight will increase, and the range will remain the same.
b. The median weight and range will both remain the same.
c. The median weight will stay the same, and the range will increase.
d. The median weight and range will both increase.

45. For the following similar triangles, what are the values of x and y (rounded to one decimal place)?

 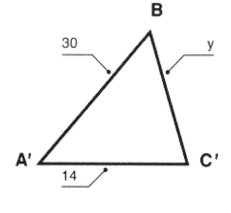

a. $x = 16.5, y = 25.1$
b. $x = 19.5, y = 24.1$
c. $x = 17.1, y = 26.3$
d. $x = 26.3, y = 17.1$

46. On Monday, Robert mopped the floor in 4 hours. On Tuesday, he did it in 3 hours. If on Monday, his average rate of mopping was p sq. ft. per hour, what was his average rate on Tuesday?
a. $\frac{4}{3}p$ sq. ft. per hour
b. $\frac{3}{4}p$ sq. ft. per hour
c. $\frac{5}{4}p$ sq. ft. per hour
d. $p + 1$ sq. ft. per hour

47. Which of the following inequalities is equivalent to $3 - \frac{1}{2}x \geq 2$?

    a. $x \geq 2$
    b. $x \leq 2$
    c. $x \geq 1$
    d. $x \leq 1$

48. For which of the following are $x = 4$ and $x = -4$ solutions?

    a. $x^2 + 16 = 0$
    b. $x^2 + 4x - 4 = 0$
    c. $x^2 - 2x - 2 = 0$
    d. $x^2 - 16 = 0$

49. What are the center and radius of a circle with equation $4x^2 + 4y^2 - 16x - 24y + 51 = 0$?

    a. Center (3, 2) and radius ½
    b. Center (2, 3) and radius ½
    c. Center (3, 2) and radius ¼
    d. Center (2, 3) and radius ¼

50. If the ordered pair $(-3, -4)$ is reflected over the x-axis, what's the new ordered pair?

    a. $(-3, -4)$
    b. $(3, -4)$
    c. $(3, 4)$
    d. $(-3, 4)$

51. If the volume of a sphere is 288π cubic meters, what are the radius and surface area of the same sphere?

    a. Radius is 6 meters and surface area is 144π square meters
    b. Radius is 36 meters and surface area is 144π square meters
    c. Radius is 6 meters and surface area is 12π square meters
    d. Radius is 36 meters and surface area is 12π square meters

52. The triangle shown below is a right triangle. What's the value of x?

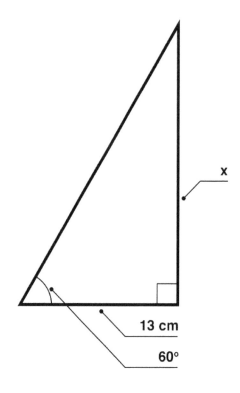

13 cm

60°

    a. $x = 1.73$
    b. $x = 0.57$
    c. $x = 13$
    d. $x = 22.49$

53. Ten students take a test. Five students get a 50. Four students get a 70. If the average score is 55, what was the last student's score?
    a. 20
    b. 40
    c. 50
    d. 60

54. A sample data set contains the following values: 1, 3, 5, 7. What's the standard deviation of the set?
    a. 2.58
    b. 4
    c. 6.23
    d. 1.1

55. A company invests $50,000 in a building where they can produce saws. If the cost of producing one saw is $40, then which function expresses the amount of money the company pays? The variable y is the money paid and x is the number of saws produced.

    a. $y = 50{,}000x + 40$
    b. $y + 40 = x - 50{,}000$
    c. $y = 40x - 50{,}000$
    d. $y = 40x + 50{,}000$

56. A pair of dice is thrown and the sum of the two scores is calculated. What's the expected value of the roll?

    a. 5
    b. 6
    c. 7
    d. 8

57. A line passes through the point (1, 2) and crosses the y-axis at $y = 1$. Which of the following is an equation for this line?

    a. $y = 2x$
    b. $y = x + 1$
    c. $x + y = 1$
    d. $y = \frac{x}{2} - 2$

58. $x^4 - 16$ can be simplified to which of the following?

    a. $(x^2 - 4)(x^2 + 4)$
    b. $(x^2 + 4)(x^2 + 4)$
    c. $(x^2 - 4)(x^2 - 4)$
    d. $(x^2 - 2)(x^2 + 4)$

59. $(4x^2 y^4)^{\frac{3}{2}}$ can be simplified to which of the following?

    a. $8x^3 y^6$
    b. $4x^{\frac{5}{2}} y$
    c. $4xy$
    d. $32x^{\frac{7}{2}} y^{\frac{11}{2}}$

60. A ball is thrown from the top of a high hill, so that the height of the ball as a function of time is $h(t) = -16t^2 + 4t + 6$, in feet. What is the maximum height of the ball in feet?

    a. 6
    b. 6.25
    c. 6.5
    d. 6.75

Answer Explanations

1. B: To simplify the given equation, the first step is to make all exponents positive by moving them to the opposite place in the fraction. This expression becomes $\frac{4b^3b^2}{a^1a^4} * \frac{3a}{b}$. Then the rules for exponents can be used to simplify. Multiplying the same bases means the exponents can be added. Dividing the same bases means the exponents are subtracted.

2. C: The product of two irrational numbers can be rational or irrational. Sometimes, the irrational parts of the two numbers cancel each other out, leaving a rational number. For example, $\sqrt{2} * \sqrt{2} = 2$ because the roots cancel each other out.

3. B: The car is traveling at a speed of five meters per second. On the interval from one to three seconds, the position changes by fifteen meters. By making this change in position over time into a rate, the speed becomes ten meters in two seconds or five meters in one second.

4. C: The number negative four is classified as a real number because it exists and is not imaginary. It is rational because it does not have a decimal that never ends. It is an integer because it does not have a fractional component. The next classification would be whole numbers, for which negative four does not qualify because it is negative.

5. B: Since $850 is the price *after* a 20% discount, $850 represents 80% of the original price. To determine the original price, set up a proportion with the ratio of the sale price (850) to original price (unknown) equal to the ratio of sale percentage:

$$\frac{850}{x} = \frac{80}{100}$$

(where x represents the unknown original price)

To solve a proportion, cross-multiply the numerators and denominators and set the products equal to each other: (850)(100) = (80)(x). Multiplying each side results in the equation 85,000 = 80x.

To solve for x, divide both sides by 80: $\frac{85,000}{80} = \frac{80x}{80}$, resulting in x = 1062.5. Remember that x represents the original price. Subtracting the sale price from the original price ($1062.50 – $850) indicates that Frank saved $212.50.

6. C: To solve for the value of b, both sides of the equation need to be equalized.

Start by cancelling out the lower value of -4 by adding 4 to both sides:

$$5b - 4 = 2b + 17$$

$$5b - 4 + 4 = 2b + 17 + 4$$

$$5b = 2b + 21$$

The variable b is the same on each side, so subtract the lower 2b from each side:

$$5b = 2b + 21$$

$$5b - 2b = 2b + 21 - 2b$$

$$3b = 21$$

Then divide both sides by 3 to get the value of b:

$$3b = 21$$

$$\frac{3b}{3} = \frac{21}{3}$$

$$b = 7$$

7. C: The first step in solving this problem is expressing the result in fraction form. Separate this problem first by solving the division operation of the last two fractions. When dividing one fraction by another, invert or flip the second fraction and then multiply the numerator and denominator.

$$\frac{7}{10} \times \frac{2}{1} = \frac{14}{10}$$

Next, multiply the first fraction with this value:

$$\frac{3}{5} \times \frac{14}{10} = \frac{42}{50}$$

Decimals are expressions of 1 or 100%, so multiply both the numerator and denominator by 2 to get the fraction as an expression of 100.

$$\frac{42}{50} \times \frac{2}{2} = \frac{84}{100}$$

In decimal form, this would be expressed as 0.84.

8. D: To find the average of a set of values, add the values together and then divide by the total number of values. In this case, include the unknown value of what Dwayne needs to score on his next test, in order to solve it.

$$\frac{78 + 92 + 83 + 97 + x}{5} = 90$$

Add the unknown value to the new average total, which is 5. Then multiply each side by 5 to simplify the equation, resulting in:

$$78 + 92 + 83 + 97 + x = 450$$

$$350 + x = 450$$

$$x = 100$$

Dwayne would need to get a perfect score of 100 in order to get an average of at least 90.

Test this answer by substituting back into the original formula.

$$\frac{78 + 92 + 83 + 97 + 100}{5} = 90$$

9. A: To calculate the range in a set of data, subtract the lowest value from the highest value. In this graph, the range of Mr. Lennon's students is 5, which can be seen physically in the graph as having the smallest difference between the highest value and the lowest value compared with the other teachers.

10. A: The augmented matrix that represents the system of equations has dimensions 4 x 3 because there are three equations with three unknowns. The coefficients of the variables make up the first three columns, and the last column is made up of the numbers to the right of the equals sign. This system can be solved by reducing the matrix to row-echelon form, where the last column gives the solution for the unknown variables.

11. B: There are two zeros for the function: $x = 0, -2$. The zeros can be found several ways, but this particular equation can be factored into $f(x) = x(x^2 + 4x + 4) = x(x + 2)(x + 2)$. By setting each factor equal to zero and solving for x, there are two solutions. On a graph these zeros can be seen where the line crosses the x-axis.

12. D: This problem involves a composition function, where one function is plugged into the other function. In this case, the $f(x)$ function is plugged into the $g(x)$ function for each x-value. The composition equation becomes $g(f(x)) = 2^3 - 3(2^2) - 2(2) + 6$. Simplifying the equation gives the answer $g(f(x)) = 8 - 3(4) - 2(2) + 6 = 8 - 12 - 4 + 6 = -2$.

13. D: This system of equations involves one quadratic function and one linear function, as seen from the degree of each equation. One way to solve this is through substitution. Solving for y in the second equation yields $y = x + 2$. Plugging this equation in for the y of the quadratic equation yields $x^2 - 2x + x + 2 = 8$. Simplifying the equation, it becomes $x^2 - x + 2 = 8$. Setting this equal to zero and factoring, it becomes $x^2 - x - 6 = 0 = (x - 3)(x + 2)$. Solving these two factors for x gives the zeros $x = 3, -2$. To find the y-value for the point, each number can be plugged in to either original equation. Solving each one for y yields the points $(3, 5)$ and $(-2, 0)$.

14. D: The expression is simplified by collecting like terms. Terms with the same variable and exponent are like terms, and their coefficients can be added.

15. A: Finding the product means distributing one polynomial onto the other. Each term in the first must be multiplied by each term in the second. Then, like terms can be collected. Multiplying the factors yields the expression $20x^3 + 4x^2 + 24x - 40x^2 - 8x - 48$. Collecting like terms means adding the x^2 terms and adding the x terms. The final answer after simplifying the expression is $20x^3 - 36x^2 + 16x - 48$.

16. D: Finding the zeros for a function by factoring is done by setting the equation equal to zero, then completely factoring. Since there was a common x for each term in the provided equation, that is factored out first. Then the quadratic that is left can be factored into two binomials $(x + 1)(x - 4)$. Setting each factor equation to zero and solving for x yields three zeros.

17. D: Dividing rational expressions follows the same rule as dividing fractions. The division is changed to multiplication, and the reciprocal is found in the second fraction. This turns the expression into $\frac{5x^3}{3x^2} * \frac{3y^9}{25}$. Multiplying across and simplifying gives the final expression: $\frac{xy^8}{5}$.

18. B: The equation can be solved by factoring the numerator into $(x + 6)(x - 5)$. Since that same factor exists on top and bottom, that factor $(x - 5)$ cancels. This leaves the equation $x + 6 = 11$. Solving the equation gives the answer $x = 5$. When this value is plugged into the equation, it yields a zero in the denominator of the fraction. Since this is undefined, there is no solution.

19. D: This problem can be solved by using unit conversion. The initial units are miles per minute. The final units need to be feet per second. Converting miles to feet uses the equivalence statement 1 mile = 5,280 feet. Converting minutes to seconds uses the equivalence statement 1 minute = 60 seconds. Setting up the ratios to convert the units is shown in the following equation $\frac{72\ miles}{90\ minutes} * \frac{1\ minute}{60\ seconds} * \frac{5280\ feet}{1\ mile} = 70.4$ feet per second. The initial units cancel out, and the new units are left.

20. B: The formula can be manipulated by dividing both the length, *l*, and the width, *w*, on both sides. The length and width will cancel on the right, leaving height by itself.

21. B: The domain is all possible input values, or x-values. For this equation, the domain is every number greater than or equal to zero. There are no negative numbers in the domain because taking the square root of a negative number results in an imaginary number.

22. D: This problem can be solved by setting up a proportion involving the given information and the unknown value. The proportion is $\frac{21\ pages}{4\ nights} = \frac{140\ pages}{x\ nights}$. Solving the proportion by cross-multiplying, the equation becomes $21x = 4 * 140$, where $x = 26.67$. Since it is not an exact number of nights, the answer is rounded up to 27 nights. Twenty-six nights would not give Sarah enough time.

23. D: The slope from this equation is 50, and it is interpreted as the cost per gigabyte used. Since the g-value represents number of gigabytes and the equation is set equal to the cost in dollars, the slope relates these two values. For every gigabyte used on the phone, the bill goes up 50 dollars.

24. C: Graphing the function $y = \cos(x)$ shows that the curve starts at $(0, 1)$, has an amplitude of 2, and a period of 2π. This same curve can be constructed using the sine graph, by shifting the graph to the left $\frac{\pi}{2}$ units. This equation is in the form $y = \sin\left(x + \frac{\pi}{2}\right)$.

25. B: Start by squaring both sides to get $1 + x = 16$. Then subtract 1 from both sides to get $x = 15$.

26. A: This inverse of a function is found by switching the x and y in the equation and solving for y. In the given equation, solving for y is done by adding 5 to both sides, then dividing both sides by 3. This answer can be checked on the graph by verifying the lines are reflected over $y = x$.

27. B: The zeros of this function can be found by using the quadratic formula, $x = \frac{-b \pm \sqrt{b^2 - 4ac}}{2a}$. Identifying a, b, and c can also be done from the equation because it is in standard form. The formula becomes $x = \frac{0 \pm \sqrt{0^2 - 4(1)(4)}}{2(1)} = \frac{\sqrt{-16}}{2}$. Since there is a negative underneath the radical, the answer is a complex number.

28. A: Setting up a proportion is the easiest way to represent this situation. The proportion becomes $\frac{20}{x} = \frac{40}{100}$, where cross-multiplication can be used to solve for x. The answer can also be found by observing the two fractions as equivalent, knowing that twenty is half of forty, and fifty is half of one-hundred.

29. C: Division with scientific notation can be solved by grouping the first terms together and grouping the tens together. The first terms can be divided, and the tens terms can be simplified using the rules for exponents. The initial expression becomes $0.4 * 10^4$. This is not in scientific notation because the first number is not between 1 and 10. Shifting the decimal and subtracting one from the exponent yields $4.0 * 10^3$.

30. A: The relative error can be found by finding the absolute error and making it a percent of the true value. The absolute error is $36 - 35.75 = 0.25$. This error is then divided by 36—the true value—to find 0.7%.

31. B: The y-intercept of an equation is found where the x-value is zero. Plugging zero into the equation for x allows the first two terms to cancel out, leaving -4.

32. A: The equation is *even* because $f(-x) = f(x)$. Plugging in a negative value will result in the same answer as when plugging in the positive of that same value. The function $f(-2) = \frac{1}{2}(-2)^4 + 2(-2)^2 - 6 = 8 + 8 - 6 = 10$ yields the same value as $f(2) = \frac{1}{2}(2)^4 + 2(2)^2 - 6 = 8 + 8 - 6 = 10$.

33. C: The equation $x = 3$ is not a function because it does not pass the vertical line test. This test is made from the definition of a function, where each x-value must be mapped to one, and only one, y-value. This equation is a vertical line, so the x-value of 3 is mapped with an infinite number of y-values.

34. A: The function can be factored to identify the zeros. First, the term $3x$ is factored out to the front because each term contains $3x$. Then, the quadratic is factored into $(x - 3)(x + 2)$.

35. C: A die has an equal chance for each outcome. Since it has six sides, each outcome has a probability of $\frac{1}{6}$. The chance of a 1 or a 2 is therefore $\frac{1}{6} + \frac{1}{6} = \frac{1}{3}$.

36. A: The slope is given by $m = \frac{y_2 - y_1}{x_2 - x_1} = \frac{0-4}{0-(-3)} = -\frac{4}{3}$.

37. B: The table shows values that are increasing exponentially. The differences between the inputs are the same, while the differences in the outputs are changing by a factor of 2. The values in the table can be modeled by the equation $f(x) = 2^x$.

38. C: The formula for continually compounded interest is $A = Pe^{rt}$. Plugging in the given values to find the total amount in the account yields the equation $A = 2000e^{0.05*8} = 2983.65$.

39. C: The sample space is made up of $8 + 7 + 6 + 5 = 26$ balls. The probability of pulling each individual ball is $^1/_{26}$. Since there are 7 yellow balls, the probability of pulling a yellow ball is $^7/_{26}$.

40. B: For the first card drawn, the probability of pulling a King is $^4/_{52}$. Since this card isn't replaced, if a King is drawn first, the probability of a King being drawn second is $^3/_{51}$. The probability of a King being drawn in both the first and second draw is the product of the two probabilities: $^4/_{52} \times {}^3/_{51} = {}^{12}/_{2652}$ which, divided by 12, equals $^1/_{221}$.

41. D: The addition rule is necessary to determine the probability because a 6 can be rolled on either roll of the die. The rule used is $P(A \text{ or } B) = P(A) + P(B) - P(A \text{ and } B)$. The probability of a 6 being individually rolled is $^1/_6$ and the probability of a 6 being rolled twice is $^1/_6 \cdot {}^1/_6 = {}^1/_{36}$. Therefore, the probability that a 6 is rolled at least once is $^1/_6 + {}^1/_6 - {}^1/_{36} = {}^{11}/_{36}$.

42. A: $(A \cap B)$ is equal to the intersection of the two sets A and B, which is $\{1, 2, 3, 4, 5\}$. $A - (A \cap B)$ is equal to the elements of A that are *not* included in the set $(A \cap B)$. Therefore, $A - (A \cap B) = \{6, 7, 8, 9, 10\}$.

43. B: An equilateral triangle has three sides of equal length, so if the total perimeter is 18 feet, each side must be 6 feet long. A square with sides of 6 feet will have an area of $6^2 = 36$ square feet.

44. A: If each man gains 10 pounds, every original data point will increase by 10 pounds. Therefore, the man with the original median will still have the median value, but that value will increase by 10. The smallest value and largest value will also increase by 10 and, therefore, the difference between the two won't change. The range does not change in value and, thus, remains the same.

45. C: Because the triangles are similar, the lengths of the corresponding sides are proportional. Therefore, $\frac{30+x}{30} = \frac{22}{14} = \frac{y+5}{y}$. This results in the equation $14(30 + x) = 22 \cdot 30$ which, when solved, gives $x = 17.1$. The proportion also results in the equation $14(y + 5) = 22y$, which, when solved, gives $y = 26.3$.

46. A: Robert accomplished his task on Tuesday in ¾ the time compared to Monday. He must have worked 4/3 as fast.

47. B: To simplify this inequality, subtract 3 from both sides to get $-\frac{1}{2}x \geq -1$. Then, multiply both sides by -2 (remembering this flips the direction of the inequality) to get $x \leq 2$.

48. D: There are two ways to approach this problem. Each value can be substituted into each equation. Choice A can be eliminated, since $4^2 + 16 = 32$. Choice B can be eliminated, since $4^2 + 4 \cdot 4 - 4 = 28$. Choice C can be eliminated, since $4^2 - 2 \cdot 4 - 2 = 6$. But, plugging in either value into $x^2 - 16$ gives $(\pm 4)^2 - 16 = 16 - 16 = 0$.

49. B: The technique of completing the square must be used to change $4x^2 + 4y^2 - 16x - 24y + 51 = 0$ into the standard equation of a circle. First, the constant must be moved to the right-hand side of the equals sign, and each term must be divided by the coefficient of the x^2 term (which is 4). The x and y terms must be grouped together to obtain $x^2 - 4x + y^2 - 6y = -\frac{51}{4}$. Next, the process of completing the square must be completed for each variable. This gives $(x^2 - 4x + 4) + (y^2 - 6y + 9) - -\frac{51}{4} +$

$4 + 9$. The equation can be written as $(x - 2)^2 + (y - 3)^2 = \frac{1}{4}$. Therefore, the center of the circle is (2, 3) and the radius is $\sqrt{1/4} = 1/2$.

50. B: When an ordered pair is reflected over an axis, the sign of one of the coordinates must change. When it's reflected over the x-axis, the sign of the x-coordinate must change. The y-value remains the same. Therefore, the new ordered pair is $(3, -4)$.

51. A: Because the volume of the given sphere is 288π cubic meters, this means $\frac{4}{3}\pi r^3 = 288\pi$. This equation is solved for r to obtain a radius of 6 meters. The surface area of a sphere is $4\pi r^2$ so, if $r = 6$ in this formula, the surface area is 144π square meters.

52. D: SOHCAHTOA is used to find the missing side length. Because the angle and adjacent side are known, $\tan 60 = \frac{x}{13}$. Making sure to evaluate tangent with an argument in degrees, this equation gives $x = 13 \tan 60 = 13 \cdot 1.73 = 22.49$.

53. A: Let the unknown score be x. The average will be $\frac{5 \cdot 50 + 4 \cdot 70 + x}{10} = \frac{530 + x}{10} = 55$. Multiply both sides by 10 to get $530 + x = 550$, or $x = 20$.

54. A: First, the sample mean must be calculated. $\bar{x} = \frac{1}{4}(1 + 3 + 5 + 7) = 4$. The standard deviation of the data set is $\sigma = \sqrt{\frac{\Sigma(x-\bar{x})^2}{n-1}}$, and $n = 4$ represents the number of data points. Therefore:

$$\sigma = \sqrt{\frac{1}{3}[(1-4)^2 + (3-4)^2 + (5-4)^2 + (7-4)^2]} = \sqrt{\frac{1}{3}(9 + 1 + 1 + 9)} = 2.58$$

55. D: For manufacturing costs, there is a linear relationship between the cost to the company and the number produced, with a y-intercept given by the base cost of acquiring the means of production, and a slope given by the cost to produce one unit. In this case, that base cost is $50,000, while the cost per unit is $40. So, $y = 40x + 50,000$.

56. D: The expected value is equal to the total sum of each product of the individual score and its probability. There are 36 possible rolls. The probability of rolling a 2 is $1/36$. The probability of rolling a 3 is $2/36$. The probability of rolling a 4 is $3/36$. The probability of rolling a 5 is $4/36$. The probability of rolling a 6 is $5/36$. The probability of rolling a 7 is $6/36$. The probability of rolling an 8 is $5/36$. The probability of rolling a 9 is $4/36$. The probability of rolling a 10 is $3/36$. The probability of rolling an 11 is $2/36$. Finally, the probability of rolling a 12 is $1/36$. Therefore, the expected value is the sum of each product of a roll and its probability, which equals 7.

57. B: From the slope-intercept form, $y = mx + b$, it is known that b is the y-intercept, which is 1. Compute the slope as $\frac{2-1}{1-0} = 1$, so the equation should be $y = x + 1$.

58. A: This has the form $t^2 - y^2$, with $t = x^2$ and $y = 4$. It's also known that $t^2 - y^2 = (t + y)(t - y)$, and substituting the values for t and y into the right-hand side gives $(x^2 - 4)(x^2 + 4)$.

59. A: Simplify this to $(4x^2y^4)^{\frac{3}{2}} = 4^{\frac{3}{2}}(x^2)^{\frac{3}{2}}(y^4)^{\frac{3}{2}}$. Now, $4^{\frac{3}{2}} = (\sqrt{4})^3 = 2^3 = 8$. For the other, recall that the exponents must be multiplied, so this yields $8x^{2\cdot\frac{3}{2}}y^{4\cdot\frac{3}{2}} = 8x^3y^6$.

60. B: The independent variable's coordinate at the vertex of a parabola (which is the highest point, when the coefficient of the squared independent variable is negative) is given by $x = -\frac{b}{2a}$. Substitute and solve for x to get $x = -\frac{4}{2(-16)} = \frac{1}{8}$. Using this value of x, the maximum height of the ball (y), can be calculated. Substituting x into the equation yields $h(t) = -16\frac{1}{8}^2 + 4\frac{1}{8} + 6 = 6.25$.

ACT Reading Test

Key Ideas and Details

Central Ideas and Themes

Topic, Main Idea, Supporting Details, and Themes
The *topic* of a text is the overall subject, and the *main idea* more specifically builds on that subject. Consider a paragraph that begins with the following: "The United States government is made of up three branches: executive, judicial, and legislative." If this sentence is divided into its essential components, there is the topic (United States Government) and the main idea (the three branches of government).

A main idea must be supported with details, which usually appear in the form of quotations, paraphrasing, or analysis. Authors should connect details and analysis to the main point. Readers should always be cautious when accepting the validity of an argument and look for logical fallacies, such as *slippery slope, straw man,* and *begging the question*. While arguments may seem sound, further analysis often reveals they are flawed. It's okay for a reader to disagree with an author.

It is important to remember that when most authors write, they want to make a point or send a message. This point or the message of a text is known as the *theme*. Authors may state themes explicitly, like in *Aesop's Fables*. More often, especially in modern literature, readers must infer the theme based on textual details. Usually after carefully reading and analyzing an entire text, the theme emerges. Typically, the longer the piece, the more numerous its themes, though often one theme dominates the rest, as evidenced by the author's purposeful revisiting of it throughout the passage.

Cultural Differences in Themes
Regardless of culture, place, or time, certain themes are universal to the human condition. Because all humans experience certain feelings and engage in similar experiences—birth, death, marriage, friendship, finding meaning, etc.—certain themes span cultures. However, different cultures have different norms and general beliefs concerning these themes. For example, the theme of maturing and crossing from childhood to adulthood is a global theme; however, the literature from one culture might imply that this happens in someone's twenties, while another culture's literature might imply that it happens in the early teenage years.

It's important for the reader to be aware of these differences. Readers must avoid being *ethnocentric*, which means believing the aspects of one's own culture to be superior to those of other cultures.

Summarizing Information Accurately

Analyzing Topics and Summary Sentences
Good writers get to the point quickly. This is accomplished by developing a strong and effective topic sentence that details the author's purpose and answers questions such as: *What does the author intend to explain or impress?* or *What does the author want the reader to believe?* The *topic sentence* is normally found at the beginning of a supporting paragraph and usually gives purpose to a single paragraph. When reading, critical readers should find the topic sentence in each paragraph. If all information points back to one sentence, it's the topic sentence.

Summary sentences offer a recap of previously discussed information before transitioning to the next point or proceeding to the closing thoughts. Summary sentences can be found at the end of supporting paragraphs and in the conclusion of a text.

Drawing Logical Inferences and Conclusions

Identifying Logical Conclusions
Determining conclusions requires being an active reader, as a reader must make a prediction and analyze facts to identify a conclusion. A reader should identify key words in a passage to determine the logical conclusion from the information presented. Consider the passage below:

> Lindsay, covered in flour, moved around the kitchen frantically. Her mom yelled from another room, "Lindsay, we're going to be late!

Readers can conclude that Lindsay's next steps are to finish baking, clean herself up, and head off somewhere with her baked goods. It's important to note that the conclusion cannot be verified factually. Many conclusions are not spelled out specifically in the text; thus, they have to be inferred and deduced by the reader.

Evaluating a Passage
Readers draw *conclusions* about what an author has presented. This helps them better understand what the writer has intended to communicate and whether they agree with what the author has offered (or not). There are a few ways to determine a logical conclusion, but careful reading is the most important. It's helpful to read a passage a few times, noting details that seem important to the piece. Sometimes, readers arrive at a conclusion that is different than what the writer intended or they may come up with more than one conclusion.

Textual evidence within the details helps readers draw a conclusion about a passage. *Textual evidence* refers to information—facts and examples—that support the main point. Textual evidence will likely come from outside sources and can be in the form of quoted or paraphrased material. In order to draw a conclusion from evidence, it's important to examine the credibility and validity of that evidence as well as how (and if) it relates to the main idea.

If an author presents a differing opinion or a *counterargument,* in order to refute it, the reader should consider how and why this information is being presented. It is meant to strengthen the original argument and shouldn't be confused with the author's intended conclusion, but it should also be considered in the reader's final evaluation.

Sometimes, authors explicitly state the conclusion that they want readers to understand. Alternatively, a conclusion may not be directly stated. In that case, readers must rely on the implications to form a logical conclusion:

> On the way to the bus stop, Michael realized his homework wasn't in his backpack. He ran back to the house to get it and made it back to the bus just in time.

In this example, although it's never explicitly stated, it can be inferred that Michael is a student on his way to school in the morning. When forming a conclusion from implied information, it's important to read the text carefully to find several pieces of evidence in the text to support the conclusion.

Summarizing is an effective way to draw a conclusion from a passage. A summary is a shortened version of the original text, written by the reader in his or her own words. Focusing on the main points of the original text and including only the relevant details can help readers reach a conclusion. It's important to retain the original meaning of the passage.

Like summarizing, *paraphrasing* can also help a reader fully understand different parts of a text. Paraphrasing calls for the reader to take a small part of the passage and list or describe its main points. However, paraphrasing is more than rewording the original passage; it should be written in the reader's own words, while still retaining the meaning of the original source. This will indicate an understanding of the original source, yet still help the reader expand on his or her interpretation.

Craft and Structure

Word and Phrase Meanings

Most experts agree that learning new words is worth the time it takes. It helps readers understand what they are reading, and it expands their vocabularies. An extensive vocabulary improves one's ability to think. When words are added to someone's vocabulary, he or she is better able to make sense of the world.

One of the fastest ways to decode a word is through context. Context, or surrounding words, gives clues as to what unknown words mean. Take the following example: *When the students in the classroom teased Johnny, he was so discombobulated that he couldn't finish a simple math problem.* Even though a reader might be unfamiliar with the word *discombobulated*, he or she can use context clues in the sentence to make sense of the word. In this case, it can be deduced that *discombobulated* means confused or distracted.

Although context clues provide a rudimentary understanding of a word, using a dictionary can provide the reader with a more comprehensive meaning of the word. Printed dictionaries list words in alphabetical order, and all versions—including those online—include a word's multiple meanings. Typically, the first definition is the most widely used or known. The second, third, and subsequent entries move toward the more unusual or archaic. Dictionaries also indicate the part(s) of speech of each word, such as noun, verb, adjective, etc.

Dictionaries are not fixed in time. The English language today looks nothing like it did in Shakespeare's time, and Shakespeare's English is vastly different from Chaucer's. The English language is constantly evolving, as evidenced by the deletion of old words and the addition of new ones. *Ginormous* and *bling-bling*, for example, can both be found in *Merriam-Webster's* latest edition, yet they were not found in prior editions.

Analyzing an Author's Rhetorical Choices

Authors utilize a wide range of techniques to tell a story or communicate information. Readers should be familiar with the most common of these techniques. Techniques of writing are also known as *rhetorical devices*.

In nonfiction writing, authors employ argumentative techniques to present their opinions to readers in the most convincing way. First of all, persuasive writing usually includes at least one type of *appeal*: an appeal to logic (logos), emotion (pathos), or credibility and trustworthiness (ethos). When writers appeal to logic, they are asking readers to agree with them based on research, evidence, and an established line of reasoning. An author's argument might also appeal to readers' emotions, perhaps by including personal stories and anecdotes (a short narrative of a specific event). A final type of appeal—appeal to authority—asks the reader to agree with the author's argument on the basis of their expertise or credentials. Three different approaches to arguing the same opinion are exemplified below:

Logic (Logos)

> Our school should abolish its current ban on cell phone use on campus. This rule was adopted last year as an attempt to reduce class disruptions and help students focus more on their lessons. However, since the rule was enacted, there has been no change in the number of disciplinary problems in class. Therefore, the rule is ineffective and should be done away with.

The above is an example of an appeal to logic. The author uses evidence to disprove the logic of the school's rule (the rule was supposed to reduce discipline problems; the number of problems has not been reduced; therefore, the rule is not working) and to call for its repeal.

Emotion (Pathos)

An author's argument might also appeal to readers' emotions, perhaps by including personal stories and anecdotes.

The next example presents an appeal to emotion. By sharing the personal anecdote of one student and speaking about emotional topics like family relationships, the author invokes the reader's empathy in asking them to reconsider the school rule.

> Our school should abolish its current ban on cell phone use on campus. If they aren't able to use their phones during the school day, many students feel isolated from their loved ones. For example, last semester, one student's grandmother had a heart attack in the morning. However, because he couldn't use his cell phone, the student didn't know about his grandmother's accident until the end of the day—when she had already passed away and it was too late to say goodbye. By preventing students from contacting their friends and family, our school is placing undue stress and anxiety on students.

Credibility (Ethos)

Finally, an appeal to authority includes a statement from a relevant expert. In this case, the author uses a doctor in the field of education to support the argument. All three examples begin from the same opinion—the school's phone ban needs to change—but rely on different argumentative styles to persuade the reader.

> Our school should abolish its current ban on cell phone use on campus. According to Dr. Bartholomew Everett, a leading educational expert, "Research studies show that cell phone usage has no real impact on student attentiveness. Rather, phones provide a valuable technological resource for learning. Schools need to learn how to integrate this new technology into their curriculum." Rather than banning phones altogether, our school should follow the advice of experts and allow students to use phones as part of their learning.

Rhetorical Questions

Another commonly used argumentative technique is asking *rhetorical questions*, which are questions that do not actually require an answer but that push the reader to consider the topic further.

> I wholly disagree with the proposal to ban restaurants from serving foods with high sugar and sodium contents. Do we really want to live in a world where the government can control what we eat? I prefer to make my own food choices.

Here, the author's rhetorical question prompts readers to put themselves in a hypothetical situation and imagine how they would feel about it.

Figurative Language

Similes and *metaphors* are part of figurative language that are used as rhetorical devices. Both are comparisons between two things, but their formats differ slightly. A simile says that two things are *similar* and makes a comparison using "like" or "as"—*A* is like *B*, or *A* is as [some characteristic] as *B*—whereas a metaphor states that two things are exactly the same—*A* is *B*. In both cases, similes and metaphors invite the reader to think more deeply about the characteristics of the two subjects and consider where they overlap. Sometimes the poet develops a complex metaphor throughout the entire poem; this is known as an extended metaphor. An example of metaphor can be found in the sentence: "His pillow was a fluffy cloud". An example of simile can be found in the first line of Robert Burns' famous poem:

> My love is like a red, red rose

This is comparison using "like," and the two things being compared are love and a rose. Some characteristics of a rose are that it is fragrant, beautiful, blossoming, colorful, vibrant—by comparing his love to a red, red rose, Burns asks the reader to apply these qualities of a rose to his love. In this way, he implies that his love is also fresh, blossoming, and brilliant.

In addition to rhetorical devices that play on the *meanings* of words, there are also rhetorical devices that use the *sounds* of words. These devices are most often found in poetry, but may also be found in other types of literature and in nonfiction writing like texts for speeches.

Alliteration and *assonance* are both varieties of sound repetition. Other types of sound repetition include: anaphora—repetition that occurs at the beginning of the sentences; epiphora—repetition occurring at the end of phrases; antimetabole—repetition of words in a succession; and antiphrasis—a form of denial of an assertion in a text.

Alliteration refers to the repetition of the first sound of each word. Recall Robert Burns' opening line:

> My love is like a red, red rose

This line includes two instances of alliteration: "love" and "like" (repeated *L* sound), as well as "red" and "rose" (repeated *R* sound). Next, assonance refers to the repetition of vowel sounds, and can occur anywhere within a word (not just the opening sound). Here is the opening of a poem by John Keats:

> When I have fears that I may cease to be

> Before my pen has glean'd my teeming brain

Assonance can be found in the words "fears," "cease," "be," "glean'd," and "teeming," all of which stress the long *E* sound. Both alliteration and assonance create a harmony that unifies the writer's language.

Another sound device is *onomatopoeia*—words whose spelling mimics the sound they describe. Words like "crash," "bang," and "sizzle" are all examples of onomatopoeia. Use of onomatopoetic language adds auditory imagery to the text.

Readers are probably most familiar with the technique of using a *pun*. A pun is a play on words, taking advantage of two words that have the same or similar pronunciation. Puns can be found throughout Shakespeare's plays, for instance:

> Now is the winter of our discontent
>
> Made glorious summer by this son of York

These lines from *Richard III* contain a play on words. Richard III refers to his brother—the newly crowned King Edward IV—as the "son of York," referencing their family heritage from the house of York. However, while drawing a comparison between the political climate and the weather (times of political trouble were the "winter," but now the new king brings "glorious summer"), Richard's use of the word "son" also implies another word with the same pronunciation, "sun"—so Edward IV is also like the sun, bringing light, warmth, and hope to England. Puns are a clever way for writers to suggest two meanings at once.

Analyzing Text Structure

Analyzing and Evaluating Text Structure
Depending on what the author is attempting to accomplish, certain formats or text structures work better than others. For example, a sequence structure might work for narration but not when identifying similarities and differences between dissimilar concepts. Similarly, a comparison-contrast structure is not useful for narration. It's the author's job to put the right information in the correct format.

Readers should be familiar with the five main literary structures:

1. *Sequence* structure (sometimes referred to as the order structure) is when the order of events proceeds in a predictable manner. In many cases, this means the text goes through the plot elements: exposition, rising action, climax, falling action, and resolution. Readers are introduced to characters, setting, and conflict in the exposition. In the rising action, there's an increase in tension and suspense. The climax is the height of tension and the point of no return. Tension decreases during the falling action. In the resolution, any conflicts presented in the exposition are solved, and the story concludes. An informative text that is structured sequentially will often go in order from one step to the next.

2. In the *problem-solution* structure, authors identify a potential problem and suggest a solution. This form of writing is usually divided into two paragraphs and can be found in informational texts. For example, cell phone, cable and satellite providers use this structure in manuals to help customers troubleshoot or identify problems with services or products.

3. When authors want to discuss similarities and differences between separate concepts, they arrange thoughts in a *comparison-contrast* paragraph structure. Venn diagrams are an effective

graphic organizer for comparison-contrast structures, because they feature two overlapping circles that can be used to organize and group similarities and differences. A comparison-contrast essay organizes one paragraph based on similarities and another based on differences. A comparison-contrast essay can also be arranged with the similarities and differences of individual traits addressed within individual paragraphs. Words such as *however*, *but*, and *nevertheless* help signal a contrast in ideas.

4. The *descriptive* writing structure is designed to appeal to one's senses. Much like an artist who constructs a painting, good descriptive writing builds an image in the reader's mind by appealing to the five senses: sight, hearing, taste, touch, and smell. However, overly descriptive writing can become tedious; sparse descriptions can make settings and characters seem flat. Good authors strike a balance by applying descriptions only to passages, characters, and settings that are integral to the plot.

5. Passages that use the *cause and effect* structure are simply asking *why* by demonstrating some type of connection between ideas. Words such as *if*, *since*, *because*, *then*, or *consequently* indicate relationship. By switching the order of a complex sentence, the writer can rearrange the emphasis on different clauses. Saying *If Sheryl is late, we'll miss the dance* is different from saying, *We'll miss the dance if Sheryl is late*. One emphasizes Sheryl's tardiness while the other emphasizes missing the dance. Paragraphs can also be arranged in a cause and effect format. Since the format—before and after—is sequential, it is useful when authors wish to discuss the impact of choices. Researchers often apply this paragraph structure to the scientific method.

Authorial Purpose and Perspective

No matter the genre or format, all authors are writing to persuade, inform, entertain, or express feelings. Often, these purposes are blended, with one dominating the rest. It's useful to learn to recognize the author's intent.

Persuasive writing is used to persuade or convince readers of something. It often contains two elements: the argument and the counterargument. The argument takes a stance on an issue, while the counterargument pokes holes in the opposition's stance. Authors rely on logic, emotion, and writer credibility to persuade readers to agree with them. If readers are opposed to the stance before reading, they are unlikely to adopt that stance. However, those who are undecided or committed to the same stance are more likely to agree with the author.

Informative writing tries to teach or inform. Workplace manuals, instructor lessons, statistical reports and cookbooks are examples of informative texts. Informative writing is usually based on facts and is often without emotion and persuasion. Informative texts generally contain statistics, charts, and graphs. Although most informative texts lack a persuasive agenda, readers must examine the text carefully to determine whether one exists within a given passage.

Stories or narratives are designed to entertain. When people go to the movies, they often want to escape for a few hours, not necessarily to think critically. Entertaining writing is designed to delight and engage the reader. However, sometimes this type of writing can be woven into more serious materials, such as persuasive or informative writing, to hook the reader before transitioning into a more scholarly discussion.

Emotional writing works to evoke the reader's feelings, such as anger, euphoria, or sadness. The connection between reader and author is an attempt to cause the reader to share the author's intended emotion or tone. Sometimes, in order to make a text more poignant, the author simply wants readers to feel the emotions that the author has felt. Other times, the author attempts to persuade or manipulate the reader into adopting their stance. While it's okay to sympathize with the author, readers should be aware of the individual's underlying intent.

Analyzing Characters' Points of View

Point of View

Point of view is another important writing device to consider. In fiction writing, point of view refers to who tells the story or from whose perspective readers are observing as they read. In nonfiction writing, the *point of view* refers to whether the author refers to himself or herself, his or her readers, or chooses not to refer to either. Whether fiction or nonfiction, the author carefully considers the impact the perspective will have on the purpose and main point of the writing.

- *First-person point of view*: The story is told from the writer's perspective. In fiction, this would mean that the main character is also the narrator. First-person point of view is easily recognized by the use of personal pronouns such as *I, me, we, us, our, my*, and *myself*.

- *Third-person point of view*: In a more formal essay, this would be an appropriate perspective because the focus should be on the subject matter, not the writer or the reader. Third-person point of view is recognized by the use of the pronouns *he, she, they*, and *it*. In fiction writing, third person point of view has a few variations.

  o *Third-person limited* point of view refers to a story told by a narrator who has access to the thoughts and feelings of just one character.

  o In *third-person omniscient* point of view, the narrator has access to the thoughts and feelings of all the characters.

  o In *third-person objective* point of view, the narrator is like a fly on the wall and can see and hear what the characters do and say, but does not have access to their thoughts and feelings.

- *Second-person point of view*: This point of view isn't commonly used in fiction or nonfiction writing because it directly addresses the reader using the pronouns *you, your*, and *yourself*. Second-person perspective is more appropriate in direct communication, such as business letters or emails.

Point of View	Pronouns used
First person	I, me, we, us, our, my, myself
Second person	You, your, yourself
Third person	He, she, it, they

Interpreting Authorial Decisions Rhetorically

There are a few ways for readers to engage actively with the text, such as making inferences and predictions. An *inference* refers to a point that is implied (as opposed to directly-stated) by the evidence presented:

> Bradley packed up all of the items from his desk in a box and said goodbye to his coworkers for the last time.

From this sentence, although it is not directly stated, readers can infer that Bradley is leaving his job. It's necessary to use inference in order to draw conclusions about the meaning of a passage. When making an inference about a passage, it's important to rely only on the information that is provided in the text itself. This helps readers ensure that their conclusions are valid.

Readers will also find themselves making predictions when reading a passage or paragraph. *Predictions* are guesses about what's going to happen next. This is a natural tendency, especially when reading a good story or watching a suspenseful movie. It's fun to try to figure out how it will end. Authors intentionally use suspenseful language and situations to keep readers interested:

> A cat darted across the street just as the car came careening around the curve.

One unfortunate prediction might be that the car will hit the cat. Of course, predictions aren't always accurate, so it's important to read carefully to the end of the text to determine the accuracy of one's predictions.

Readers should pay attention to the *sequence*, or the order in which details are laid out in the text, as this can be important to understanding its meaning as a whole. Writers will often use transitional words to help the reader understand the order of events and to stay on track. Words like *next, then, after*, and *finally* show that the order of events is important to the author. In some cases, the author omits these transitional words, and the sequence is implied. Authors may even purposely present the information out of order to make an impact or have an effect on the reader. An example might be when a narrative writer uses *flashback* to reveal information.

Drawing conclusions is also important when actively reading a passage. *Hedge phrases* such as *will, might, probably*, and *appear to be* are used by writers who want to cover their bases and make sure to show there are exceptions to their statements. *Absolute phrasing*, such as *always* and *never*, should be carefully considered, as the use of these words and their intended meanings are often incorrect.

Differentiating Between Various Perspectives and Sources of Information

Identifying the Appropriate Source for Locating Information
With a wealth of information at people's fingertips in this digital age, it's important to know not only the type of information one is looking for, but also in what medium he or she most likely to find it. Information needs to be specific and reliable. For example, if someone is repairing a car, an encyclopedia would be mostly useless. While an encyclopedia might include information about cars, an owner's manual will contain the specific information needed for repairs. Information must also be reliable or credible so that it can be trusted. A well-known newspaper may have reliable information, but a peer-reviewed journal article will have likely gone through a more rigorous check for validity. Determining bias can be helpful in determining credibility. If the information source (person, organization, or company) has something to gain from the reader forming a certain view on a topic, it's

likely the information is skewed. For example, if trying to find the unemployment rate, the Bureau of Labor Statistics is a more credible source than a politician's speech.

Primary sources are best defined as records or items that serve as evidence of periods of history. To be considered primary, the source documents or objects must have been created during the time period in which they reference. Examples include diaries, newspaper articles, speeches, government documents, photographs, and historical artifacts. In today's digital age, primary sources, which were once in print, are often are embedded in secondary sources. Secondary sources – such as websites, history books, databases, or reviews – contain analysis or commentary on primary sources. Secondary sources borrow information from primary sources through the process of quoting, summarizing, or paraphrasing.

Today's students often complete research online through electronic sources. Electronic sources offer advantages over print, and can be accessed on virtually any computer, where libraries or other research centers are limited to fixed locations and specific catalogs. Electronic sources also are efficient and yield massive amounts of data in seconds. The user can tailor a search based on key words, publication years, and article length. Lastly, many databases provide the user with instant citations, saving the user the trouble of manually assembling sources for a bibliography.

Although electronic sources yield powerful results, researchers must use caution. While there are many reputable and reliable sources on the internet, just as many are unreliable or biased sources. It's up to the researcher to examine and verify the reliability of sources. *Wikipedia*, for example, may or may not be accurate, depending on the contributor. Many databases, such as *EBSCO* or *SIRS*, offer peer-reviewed articles, meaning the publications have been reviewed for the quality and accuracy of their content.

Integration of Knowledge and Ideas

Understanding Authors' Claims

The goal of most persuasive and informative texts is to make a claim and support it with evidence. A claim is a statement made as though it is fact. Many claims are opinions; for example, "stealing is wrong." While this is generally true, it is arguable, meaning it is capable of being challenged. An initial reaction to "stealing is wrong" might be to agree; however, there may be circumstances in which it is warranted. If it is necessary for the survival of an individual or their loved ones (i.e., if they are starving and cannot afford to eat), then this assertion becomes morally ambiguous. While it may still be illegal, whether it is "wrong" is unclear.

When an assertion is made within a text, it is typically reinforced with supporting details as is exemplified in the following passage:

> The extinction of the dinosaurs has been a hot debate amongst scientists since the discovery of fossils in the eighteenth century. Numerous theories were developed in explanation, including extreme climate change, an epidemic of disease, or changes in the atmosphere. It wasn't until the late 1970s that a young geochemist, named Walter Alvarez, noticed significant changes in the soil layers of limestone he was studying in Italy. The layers contained fossilized remains of millions of small organisms within the layer that corresponded with the same period in which the dinosaurs lived. He noticed that the soil layer directly above this layer was suddenly devoid of any trace of these organisms. The soil layer directly above *this* layer was filled with an entirely new species

of organisms. It seemed the first species had disappeared at the exact same time as the dinosaurs!

With the help of his father, Walter Alvarez analyzed the soil layer between the extinct species and the new species and realized this layer was filled with an abnormal amount of *iridium* – a substance that is abundant in meteorites but almost never found on Earth. Unlike other elements in the fossil record, which take millions of years to deposit, the iridium had been laid down very abruptly. The layer also contained high levels of soot, enough to account for all of the earth's forests burning to the ground at the same time. This lead scientists to create the best-supported theory that the tiny organisms, as well as the dinosaurs and countless other species, had been destroyed by a giant asteroid that had slammed into Earth, raining tons of iridium down on the planet from a giant cosmic cloud.

Supporting Claims

Before embarking on answering these questions, readers should summarize each. This will help in locating the supporting evidence. These summaries can be written down or completed mentally; full sentences are not necessary.

Paragraph 1: Layer of limestone shows that a species of organisms disappeared at same time as the dinosaurs

Paragraph 2: Layer had high amounts of iridium and soot – scientists believe dinosaurs destroyed by asteroid.

Simply by summarizing the text, it has been plainly outlined where there will be answers to relevant questions. Although there are often claims already embedded within an educational text, a claim will most likely be given, but the evidence to support it will need to be located. Take this example question:

Q: What evidence within the text best supports the theory that the dinosaurs became extinct because of an asteroid?

The claim here is that the dinosaurs went extinct because of an asteroid. Because the text is already outlined in the summaries, it is easy to see that the evidence supporting this theory is in the second paragraph:

With the help of his father, they analyzed the soil layer between the extinct species and the new species and realized this layer was filled with an abnormal amount of *iridium* – a substance that is abundant is meteorites but almost never found on Earth. Unlike other elements in the fossil record, which take millions of years to deposit, the iridium had been laid down very abruptly. The layer also contained high levels of soot, enough to account for all of the earth's forests burning to the ground at the same time. This lead scientists to create the best-supported theory that the tiny organisms, as well as the dinosaurs and countless other species, had been destroyed by a giant asteroid that had slammed into Earth, raining tons of iridium down on the planet from a giant cosmic cloud.

Now that the evidence within the text that best supports the theory has been located, the answer choices can be evaluated:

    a. Changes in climate and atmosphere caused an asteroid to crash into Earth
    b. Walter and Luis Alvarez studied limestone with fossilized organisms
    c. A soil layer lacking organisms that existed at the same time as the dinosaurs showed low levels of iridium
    d. A soil layer lacking organisms that existed at the same time as the dinosaurs showed high levels of iridium

Answer choice (a) is clearly false as there is nothing within the text that claims that climate changes caused an asteroid to crash into Earth. This kind of answer choice displays an incorrect use of detail. Although the passage may have contained the words "change," "climate," and "atmosphere," these terms were manipulated to form an erroneous answer.

Answer choice (b) is incorrect because while the scientists did study limestone with fossilized organisms, and in doing so they discovered evidence that led to the formation of the theory, this is not the actual evidence itself. This is an example of an out-of-scope answer choice: a true statement that may or may not have been in the passage, but that isn't the whole answer or isn't the point.

Answer choice (c) is incorrect because it is the opposite of the correct answer. Assuming the second paragraph was summarized correctly, it is already known that the soil layer contained *high* levels of iridium, not low levels. Even if the paragraph was not summarized that way, the final sentence states that "tons of iridium rained down on the planet." So, answer choice (c) is false.

Answer choice (d) is correct because it matches the evidence found in the second paragraph.

Differentiating Between Facts and Opinions

Fact and Opinion, Biases, and Stereotypes

It is important to distinguish between facts and opinions when reading a piece of writing. When an author presents facts, such as statistics or data, readers should be able to check those facts to verify that they are accurate. When authors share their own thoughts and feelings about a subject, they are expressing their opinions.

Authors often use words like *think, feel, believe,* or *in my opinion* when expressing an opinion, but these words won't always appear in an opinion piece, especially if it is formally written. An author's opinion may be backed up by facts, which gives it more credibility, but that opinion should not be taken as fact. A critical reader should be suspect of an author's opinion, especially if it is only supported by other opinions.

Fact	Opinion
There are nine innings in a game of baseball.	Baseball games run too long.
James Garfield was assassinated on July 2, 1881.	James Garfield was a good president.
McDonald's® has stores in 118 countries.	McDonald's® has the best hamburgers.

Critical readers examine the facts used to support an author's argument. They check the facts against other sources to be sure those facts are correct. They also check the validity of the sources used to be sure those sources are credible, academic, and/or peer-reviewed. When an author uses another person's opinion to support his or her argument, even if it is an expert's opinion, it is still only an opinion and should not be taken as fact. A strong argument uses valid, measurable facts to support ideas. Even then, the reader may disagree with the argument.

An authoritative argument may use the facts to sway the reader. In the example of global warming, many experts differ in their opinions of which alternative fuels can be used to aid in offsetting it. Because of this, a writer may choose to only use the information and experts' opinions that supports his or her viewpoint. For example, if the argument is that wind energy is the best solution, the author will use facts that support this idea. That same author may leave out relevant facts on solar energy. The way the author uses facts can influence the reader, so it's important to consider the facts being used, how those facts are being presented, and what information might be left out.

Authors can also demonstrate *bias* if they ignore an opposing viewpoint or present their side in an unbalanced way. A strong argument considers the opposition and finds a way to refute it. Critical readers should look for an unfair or one-sided presentation of the argument and be skeptical, as a bias may be present. Even if this bias is unintentional, if it exists in the writing, the reader should be wary of the validity of the argument.

Readers should also look for the use of stereotypes that refer to specific groups. *Stereotypes* are often negative connotations about a person or place and should always be avoided. When a critical reader finds stereotypes in a piece of writing, he or she should immediately be critical of the argument and consider the validity of anything the author presents. Stereotypes reveal a flaw in the writer's thinking and may suggest a lack of knowledge or understanding about the subject.

Using Evidence to Make Connections Between Different Texts

When analyzing two or more texts, there are several different aspects that need to be considered, particularly the styles (or the artful way in which the authors use diction to deliver a theme), points of view, and types of argument. In order to do so, one should compare and contrast the following elements between the texts:

- Style: narrative, persuasive, descriptive, informative, etc.
- Tone: sarcastic, angry, somber, humorous, etc.
- Sentence structure: simple (1 clause) compound (2 clauses), complex-compound (3 clauses)
- Punctuation choice: question marks, exclamation points, periods, dashes, etc.
- Point of view: first person, second person, third person
- Paragraph structure: long, short, both, differences between the two
- Organizational structure: compare/contrast, problem/solution, chronological, etc.

The following two poems and the essay concern the theme of death and are presented to demonstrate how to evaluate the above elements:

"Queen Mab," Percy Bysshe Shelley

How wonderful is Death,

Death, and his brother Sleep!

One, pale as yonder waning moon

With lips of lurid blue;

The other, rosy as the morn

When throned on ocean's wave

It blushes o'er the world;

Yet both so passing wonderful!

"After Great Pain, A Formal Feeling Comes," Emily Dickinson

After great pain, a formal feeling comes –

The Nerves sit ceremonious, like Tombs –

The stiff Heart questions 'was it He, that bore,'

And 'Yesterday, or Centuries before'?

The Feet, mechanical, go round –

A Wooden way

Of Ground, or Air, or Ought –

Regardless grown,

A Quartz contentment, like a stone –

This is the Hour of Lead –

Remembered, if outlived,

As Freezing persons, recollect the Snow –

First – Chill – then Stupor – then the letting go –

The Process of Dying

Death occurs in several stages. The first stage is the pre-active stage, which occurs a few days to weeks before death, in which the desire to eat and drink decreases, and the person may feel restless, irritable, and anxious. The second stage is the active stage, where the skin begins to cool, breathing becomes difficult as the lungs become congested (known as the "death rattle"), and the person loses control of their bodily fluids.

Once death occurs, there are also two stages. The first is clinical death, when the heart stops pumping blood and breathing ceases. This stage lasts approximately 4-6 minutes, and during this time, it is possible for a victim to be resuscitated via CPR or a defibrillator. After 6 minutes however, the oxygen stores within the brain begin to deplete, and the victim enters biological death. This is the point of no return, as the cells of the brain and vital organs begin to die, a process that is irreversible.

Now, using the outline above, the similarities and differences between the three passages are considered:

1. *Style*: The two poems are both descriptive as they focus on descriptions and sensations to convey their messages and do not follow any sort of timeline. The third selection is an expository style, presenting purely factual evidence on death, completely devoid of emotion.

2. *Tone*: Readers should notice the differences in the word choices between the two poems. Percy Shelley's word choices—"wonderful," "rosy," "blushes," "ocean"—surrounding death indicates that he views death in a welcoming manner as his words carry positive charges. The word choices by Dickinson, however, carry negative connotations—"pain," "wooden," "stone," "lead," "chill," "tombs"—which indicates an aversion to death. In contrast, the expository passage has no emotionally-charged words of any kind, and seems to view death simply as a process that happens, neither welcoming nor fearing it. The tone in this passage, therefore, is neutral.

3. *Sentence Structure*: Shelley's poem is composed mostly of compound sentences, which flow easily into one another. If read aloud, it sounds almost fluid, like the waves of the ocean he describes in his poem. His sentence structure mirrors the ease in which he views death. Dickinson's poem, on the other hand, is mostly simple sentences that are short and curt. They do not flow easily into one another, possibly representing her hesitancy and discomfort in her views of death. The expository passage contains many complex-compound sentences, which are used to accommodate lots of information. The structure of these sentences contributes to the overall informative nature of the selection.

4. *Punctuation Choice*: Shelley uses commas, semicolons, and exclamation points in his poem, which, combined with his word choices and sentence structure, contributes to the overall positive tone of the poem. Dickinson uses lots of dashes, which make the poem feel almost cutting and jagged, which contributes to the overall negative tone of her poem. The expository text uses only commas and periods, which adds to the overall neutral tone of the selection.

5. *Point of View*: The point of view in all three selections is third person. In the two poems, there are no obvious pronouns; however, they both are presented in the third-person point of view, as Shelley speaks of Death in the third person, and Dickinson refers to "freezing persons." Generally, if there are no first- or second-person pronouns in a selection, the view is third person. The informational selection also uses third-person point of view, as it avoids any first- or second-person pronouns.

6. *Paragraph/Stanza Structure*: Shelley's poem is one stanza long, making it inherently simple in nature. The simplicity of the single stanza is representative (again) of the comfort in which the author finds the topic of death. Dickinson's poem is much lengthier, and comparatively, could signify

the difficulty of letting go of the death of a loved one. The paragraph structure of the essay is much longer than the two, and is used to fit in a lot more information than the poems, as the poems are trying to convey emotion, and the essay is presenting facts.

7. *Organizational Structure*: Shelley's poem uses a compare and contrast method to illustrate the similarities between death and sleep: that death is merely a paler, bluer brother to the warm and rosy sleep. Dickinson's structure, however, is descriptive, focusing primarily on feelings and sensations. The expository passage, on the other hand, is chronologically-organized, as it follows a timeline of events that occur in stages.

When analyzing the different structures, it may be helpful to make a table and use single words to compare and contrast the texts:

Elements	Queen Mab	After Great Pain	Process of Dying
Style	Descriptive	Descriptive	Expository
Tone	Warm	Cold	Neutral
Sentence Structure	Fluid	Jagged	Long
Punctuation Choice	!	–	.
Point of View	Third	Third	Third
Paragraph Structure	Short	Longer	Longest
Organizational Structure	Compare-Contrast	Descriptive	Chronological

Using this table, the differences become very clear. Although the two poems are both about death, their word tone, sentence structure, punctuation choices, and organization depict differences in how the authors perceive death, while the elements in the expository text clearly indicate an objective view of death. It should be noted that these are only a handful of the endless possible interpretations the reader could make.

Analyzing How Authors Construct Arguments

Constructing Arguments Through Evidence
Using only one form of supporting evidence is not nearly as effective as using a variety to support a claim. Presenting only a list of statistics can be boring to the reader, but providing a true story that's both interesting and humanizing helps. In addition, one example isn't always enough to prove the writer's larger point, so combining it with other examples in the writing is extremely effective. Thus, when reading a passage, readers should not just look for a single form of supporting evidence.

For example, although most people can't argue with the statement, "Seat belts save lives", its impact on the reader is much greater when supported by additional content. The writer can support this idea by:

- Providing statistics on the rate of highway fatalities alongside statistics of estimated seat belt usage.

- Explaining the science behind car accidents and what happens to a passenger who doesn't use a seat belt.

- Offering anecdotal evidence or true stories from reliable sources on how seat belts prevent fatal injuries in car crashes.

Another key aspect of supporting evidence is a *reliable source*. Does the writer include the source of the information? If so, is the source well-known and trustworthy? Is there a potential for bias? For example, a seat belt study done by a seat belt manufacturer may have its own agenda to promote.

Logical Sequence
Even if the writer includes plenty of information to support his or her point, the writing is only effective when the information is in a logical order. *Logical sequencing* is really just common sense, but it's an important writing technique. First, the writer should introduce the main idea, whether for a paragraph, a section, or the entire text. Then he or she should present evidence to support the main idea by using transitional language. This shows the reader how the information relates to the main idea and to the sentences around it. The writer should then take time to interpret the information, making sure necessary connections are obvious to the reader. Finally, the writer can summarize the information in the closing section.

NOTE: Although most writing follows this pattern, it isn't a set rule. Sometimes writers change the order for effect. For example, the writer can begin with a surprising piece of supporting information to grab the reader's attention, and then transition to the main idea. Thus, if a passage doesn't follow the logical order, readers should not immediately assume it's wrong. However, most writing that has a nontraditional beginning usually settles into a logical sequence.

Practice Test

1. There are two major kinds of cameras on the market right now for amateur photographers. Camera enthusiasts can either purchase a digital single-lens reflex (DSLR) camera or a compact system camera (CSC). The main difference between a DSLR and a CSC is that the DSLR has a full-sized sensor, which means it fits in a much larger body. The CSC uses a mirrorless system, which makes for a lighter, smaller camera. While both take quality pictures, the DSLR generally has better picture quality due to the larger sensor. CSCs still take very good quality pictures and are more convenient to carry than a DSLR. This makes the CSC an ideal choice for the amateur photographer looking to step up from a point-and-shoot camera.

The main difference between the DSLR and CSC is:
  a. The picture quality is better in the DSLR.
  b. The CSC is less expensive than the DSLR.
  c. The DSLR is a better choice for amateur photographers.
  d. The DSLR's larger sensor makes it a bigger camera than the CSC.

2. When selecting a career path, it's important to explore the various options available. Many students entering college may shy away from a major because they don't know much about it. For example, many students won't opt for a career as an actuary, because they aren't exactly sure what it entails. But in doing so, they are missing out on a career that is very lucrative and in high demand. Actuaries work in the insurance field and assess risks and premiums. The average salary of an actuary is $100,000 per year. Another career option students may avoid, due to lack of knowledge of the field, is a hospitalist. This is a physician that specializes in the care of patients in a hospital, as opposed to those seen in private practices. The average salary of a hospitalist is upwards of $200,000. It pays to do some digging and find out more about these lesser-known career fields.

An actuary is:
  a. A doctor who works in a hospital.
  b. The same as a hospitalist.
  c. An insurance agent who works in a hospital.
  d. A person who assesses insurance risks and premiums.

3. Hard water occurs when rainwater mixes with minerals from rock and soil. Hard water has a high mineral count, including calcium and magnesium. The mineral deposits from hard water can stain hard surfaces in bathrooms and kitchens as well as clog pipes. Hard water can stain dishes, ruin clothes, and reduce the life of any appliances it touches, such as hot water heaters, washing machines, and humidifiers. One solution is to install a water softener to reduce the mineral content of water, but this can be costly. Running vinegar through pipes and appliances and using vinegar to clean hard surfaces can also help with mineral deposits.

From this passage, it can be concluded that:
  a. Hard water can cause a lot of problems for homeowners.
  b. Calcium is good for pipes and hard surfaces.
  c. Water softeners are easy to install.
  d. Vinegar is the only solution to hard water problems.

4. Coaches of kids' sports teams are increasingly concerned about the behavior of parents at games. Parents are screaming and cursing at coaches, officials, players, and other parents. Physical fights have even broken out at games. Parents need to be reminded that coaches are volunteers who give up their time and energy to help kids develop in their chosen sport. The goal of kids' sports teams is to learn and develop skills, but it's also to have fun. When parents are out of control at games and practices, it takes the fun out of the sport.

From this passage, it can be concluded that:
    a. Coaches are modeling good behavior for kids.
    b. Organized sports are not good for kids.
    c. Parents' behavior at their kids' games needs to change.
    d. Parents and coaches need to work together.

5. While scientists aren't entirely certain why tornadoes form, they have some clues into the process. Tornadoes are dangerous funnel clouds that occur during large thunderstorms. When warm, humid air near the ground meets cold, dry air from above, a column of the warm air can be drawn up into the clouds. Winds at different altitudes blowing at different speeds make the column of air rotate. As the spinning column of air picks up speed, a funnel cloud is formed. This funnel cloud moves rapidly and haphazardly. Rain and hail inside the cloud cause it to touch down, creating a tornado. Tornadoes move in a rapid and unpredictable pattern, making them extremely destructive and dangerous. Scientists continue to study tornadoes to improve radar detection and warning times.

The main purpose of this passage is to:
    a. Show why tornadoes are dangerous
    b. Explain how a tornado forms
    c. Compare thunderstorms to tornadoes
    d. Explain what to do in the event of a tornado

6. Samuel teaches at a high school in one of the biggest cities in the United States. His students come from diverse family backgrounds. Samuel observes that the best students in his class are from homes where parental supervision is minimal. The parents of the bottom five students are the most involved, by a large margin. There are 24 students in his class. Samuel is going to write an academic paper based on his students' family backgrounds and academic performance. The paper will argue that parental involvement is not an important factor in academic success.

Which of the following statements best describes Samuel's sample size?
    a. The sample is biased because he has first-hand experience and personal knowledge of its participants.
    b. The sample contains too few members to make meaningful claims applicable to a large group.
    c. The sample contains too many members to understand the context and specifics of any given student's situation.
    d. The sample is unbiased and appropriately-sized to draw conclusions on the role of parental supervision in education.

7. Annabelle Rice started having trouble sleeping. Her biological clock was suddenly amiss and she began to lead a nocturnal schedule. She thought her insomnia was due to spending nights writing a horror story, but then she realized that even the idea of going outside into the bright world scared her to bits. She concluded she was now suffering from heliophobia.

Which of the following most accurately describes the meaning of the underlined word in the sentence above?
   a. Fear of dreams
   b. Fear of sunlight
   c. Fear of strangers
   d. Anxiety spectrum disorder

8. Many people are unsure of exactly how the digestive system works. Digestion begins in the mouth where teeth grind up food and saliva breaks it down, which makes it easier for the body to absorb. Next, the food moves to the esophagus, and it is pushed into the stomach. The stomach is where food is stored and broken down further by acids and digestive enzymes, preparing it for passage into the intestines. The small intestine is where the nutrients are taken from food and passed into the blood stream. Other essential organs, like the liver, gall bladder, and pancreas, aid the stomach in breaking down food and absorbing nutrients. Finally, food waste is passed into the large intestine, where it is eliminated by the body.

What is the purpose of this passage?
   a. To explain how the liver works.
   b. To show why it is important to eat healthy foods.
   c. To explain how the digestive system works.
   d. To show how nutrients are absorbed by the small intestine.

9. Which of these descriptions gives the most detailed and objective support for the claim that drinking and driving is unsafe?
   a. A dramatized television commercial reenacting a fatal drinking and driving accident, including heart-wrenching testimonials from loved ones
   b. The Department of Transportation's press release noting the additional drinking and driving special patrol units that will be on the road during the holiday season
   c. Congressional written testimony on the number of drinking and driving incidents across the country and their relationship to underage drinking statistics, according to experts
   d. A highway bulletin warning drivers of the penalties associated with drinking and driving

10. A famous children's author recently published a historical fiction novel under a pseudonym; however, it did not sell as many copies as her children's books. In her earlier years, she had majored in history and earned a graduate degree in Antebellum American History, which is the timeframe of her new novel. Critics praised this newest work far more than the children's series that made her famous. In fact, her new novel was nominated for the prestigious Albert J. Beveridge Award, but still isn't selling like her children's books, which fly off the shelves because of her name alone.

Which one of the following statements might be accurately inferred based on the above passage?
    a. The famous children's author produced an inferior book under her pseudonym.
    b. The famous children's author is the foremost expert on Antebellum America.
    c. The famous children's author did not receive the bump in publicity for her historical novel that it would have received if it were written under her given name.
    d. People generally prefer to read children's series than historical fiction.

Questions 11-14 are based on the following passage:

Smoking is Terrible

Smoking tobacco products is terribly destructive. A single cigarette contains over 4,000 chemicals, including 43 known carcinogens and 400 deadly toxins. Some of the most dangerous ingredients include tar, carbon monoxide, formaldehyde, ammonia, arsenic, and DDT. Smoking can cause numerous types of cancer including throat, mouth, nasal cavity, esophagus, stomach, pancreas, kidney, bladder, and cervical.

Cigarettes contain a drug called nicotine, one of the most addictive substances known to man. Addiction is defined as a compulsion to seek the substance despite negative consequences. According to the National Institute of Drug Abuse, nearly 35 million smokers expressed a desire to quit smoking in 2015; however, more than 85 percent of those addicts will not achieve their goal. Almost all smokers regret picking up that first cigarette. You would be wise to learn from their mistake if you have not yet started smoking.

According to the U.S. Department of Health and Human Services, 16 million people in the United States presently suffer from a smoking-related condition and nearly nine million suffer from a serious smoking-related illness. According to the Centers for Disease Control and Prevention (CDC), tobacco products cause nearly six million deaths per year. This number is projected to rise to over eight million deaths by 2030. Smokers, on average, die ten years earlier than their nonsmoking peers.

In the United States, local, state, and federal governments typically tax tobacco products, which leads to high prices. Nicotine addicts sometimes pay more for a pack of cigarettes than for a few gallons of gas. Additionally, smokers tend to stink. The smell of smoke is all-consuming and creates a pervasive nastiness. Smokers also risk staining their teeth and fingers with yellow residue from the tar.

Smoking is deadly, expensive, and socially unappealing. Clearly, smoking is not worth the risks.

11. Which of the following best describes the passage?
    a. Narrative
    b. Persuasive
    c. Expository
    d. Technical

12. Which of the following statements most accurately summarizes the passage?
    a. Tobacco is less healthy than many alternatives.
    b. Tobacco is deadly, expensive, and socially unappealing, and smokers would be much better off kicking the addiction.
    c. In the United States, local, state, and federal governments typically tax tobacco products, which leads to high prices.
    d. Tobacco products shorten smokers' lives by ten years and kill more than six million people per year.

13. The author would be most likely to agree with which of the following statements?
    a. Smokers should only quit cold turkey and avoid all nicotine cessation devices.
    b. Other substances are more addictive than tobacco.
    c. Smokers should quit for whatever reason that gets them to stop smoking.
    d. People who want to continue smoking should advocate for a reduction in tobacco product taxes.

14. Which of the following represents an opinion statement on the part of the author?
    a. According to the Centers for Disease Control and Prevention (CDC), tobacco products cause nearly six million deaths per year.
    b. Nicotine addicts sometimes pay more for a pack of cigarettes than a few gallons of gas.
    c. They also risk staining their teeth and fingers with yellow residue from the tar.
    d. Additionally, smokers tend to stink. The smell of smoke is all-consuming and creates a pervasive nastiness.

15. In 2015, 28 countries, including Estonia, Portugal, Slovenia, and Latvia, scored significantly higher than the United States on standardized high school math tests. In the 1960s, the United States consistently ranked first in the world. Today, the United States spends more than $800 billion dollars on education, which exceeds the next highest country by more than $600 billion dollars. The United States also leads the world in spending per school-aged child by an enormous margin.

If these statements above are factual, which of the following statements must be correct?
    a. Outspending other countries on education has benefits beyond standardized math tests.
    b. The United States' education system is corrupt and broken.
    c. The standardized math tests are not representative of American academic prowess.
    d. Spending more money does not guarantee success on standardized math tests.

16. Osteoporosis is a medical condition that occurs when the body loses bone or makes too little bone. This can lead to brittle, fragile bones that easily break. Bones are already porous, and when osteoporosis sets in, the spaces in bones become much larger, causing them to weaken. Both men and women can contract osteoporosis, though it is most common in women over age 50. Loss of bone can be silent and progressive, so it is important to be proactive in preventing the disease.

What is the main purpose of this passage?
    a. To discuss some of the ways people contract osteoporosis.
    b. To describe different treatment options for those with osteoporosis.
    c. To explain how to prevent osteoporosis.
    d. To define osteoporosis.

17. Which of the following is a primary source?
    a. A critic's summary and review of a new book on the life of Abraham Lincoln
    b. A peer-reviewed scientific journal's table of contents
    c. A report containing the data, summary, and conclusions of a recent gene splicing study
    d. A news article quoting recent groundbreaking research into curing cancer

Question 18 is based on the following passage:

Cynthia keeps to a strict vegetarian diet, which is part of her religion. She absolutely cannot have any meat or fish dishes. This is more than a preference; her body has never developed the enzymes to process meat or fish, so she becomes violently ill if she accidentally eats any of the offending foods.

Cynthia is attending a full day event at her college next week. When at an event that serves meals, she always likes to bring a platter of vegetarian food for herself and to share with other attendees who have similar dietary restrictions. She requested a menu in advance to determine when her platter might be most useful to vegetarians. Here is the menu:

Breakfast: Hazelnut coffee or English breakfast tea, French toast, eggs, and bacon strips

Lunch: Assorted sandwiches (vegetarian options available), French fries, and baked beans

Cocktail hour: Alcoholic beverages, fruit, and cheese

Dinner: Roasted pork loin, seared trout, and bacon-bit topped macaroni and cheese

18. If Cynthia wants to pick the meal where there would be the least options for her and fellow vegetarians, during what meal should she bring the platter?
    a. Breakfast
    b. Lunch
    c. Cocktail hour
    d. Dinner

Questions 19-21 are based on the following passage:

George Washington emerged out of the American Revolution as an unlikely champion of liberty. On June 14, 1775, the Second Continental Congress created the Continental

Army, and John Adams, serving in the Congress, nominated Washington to be its first commander. Washington fought under the British during the French and Indian War, and his experience and prestige proved instrumental to the American war effort. Washington provided invaluable leadership, training, and strategy during the Revolutionary War. He emerged from the war as the embodiment of liberty and freedom from tyranny.

After vanquishing the heavily favored British forces, Washington could have pronounced himself as the autocratic leader of the former colonies without any opposition, but he famously refused and returned to his Mount Vernon plantation. His restraint proved his commitment to the fledgling state's republicanism. Washington was later unanimously elected as the first American president. But it is Washington's farewell address that cemented his legacy as a visionary worthy of study.

In 1796, President Washington issued his farewell address by public letter. Washington enlisted his good friend, Alexander Hamilton, in drafting his most famous address. The letter expressed Washington's faith in the Constitution and rule of law. He encouraged his fellow Americans to put aside partisan differences and establish a national union. Washington warned Americans against meddling in foreign affairs and entering military alliances. Additionally, he stated his opposition to national political parties, which he considered partisan and counterproductive.

Americans would be wise to remember Washington's farewell, especially during presidential elections when politics hits a fever pitch. They might want to question the political institutions that were not planned by the Founding Fathers, such as the nomination process and political parties themselves.

19. Which of the following statements is logically based on the information contained in the passage above?
    a. George Washington's background as a wealthy landholder directly led to his faith in equality, liberty, and democracy.
    b. George Washington would have opposed America's involvement in the Second World War.
    c. George Washington would not have been able to write as great a farewell address without the assistance of Alexander Hamilton.
    d. George Washington would probably not approve of modern political parties.

20. Which of the following statements is the best description of the author's purpose in writing this passage about George Washington?
    a. To inform American voters about a Founding Father's sage advice on a contemporary issue and explain its applicability to modern times
    b. To introduce George Washington to readers as a historical figure worthy of study
    c. To note that George Washington was more than a famous military hero
    d. To convince readers that George Washington is a hero of republicanism and liberty

21. In which of the following materials would the author be the most likely to include this passage?
    a. A history textbook
    b. An obituary
    c. A fictional story
    d. A newspaper editorial

Scientist: Last year was the warmest ever recorded in the last 134 years. During that time, the ten warmest years have all occurred since 2000. This correlates directly with the recent increases in carbon dioxide as large countries like China, India, and Brazil continue developing and industrializing. No longer do just a handful of countries burn massive amounts of carbon-based fossil fuels; it is quickly becoming the case throughout the whole world as technology and industry spread.

Politician: Yes, but there is no causal link between increases in carbon emissions and increasing temperatures. The link is tenuous and nothing close to certain. We need to wait for all of the data before drawing hasty conclusions. For all we know, the temperature increase could be entirely natural. I believe the temperatures also rose dramatically during the dinosaurs' time, and I do not think they were burning any fossil fuels back then.

22. What is one point on which the scientist and politician agree?
    a. Burning fossil fuels causes global temperatures to rise.
    b. Global temperatures are increasing.
    c. Countries must revisit their energy policies before it's too late.
    d. Earth's climate naturally goes through warming and cooling periods.

23. Raul is going to Egypt next month. He has been looking forward to this vacation all year. Since childhood, Raul has been fascinated with pyramids, especially the Great Pyramid of Giza, which is the oldest of the Seven Wonders of the Ancient World. According to religious custom, Egyptian royalty is buried in the tombs located within the pyramid's great labyrinths. Since it has been many years since Raul read about the pyramid's history, he wants to read a book describing how and why the Egyptians built the Great Pyramid thousands of years ago.

Which of the following guides would be the best for Raul?
    a. *A Beginner's Guide to Giza*, a short book describing the city's best historical sites, published by the Egyptian Tourism Bureau (2015)
    b. *The Life of Zahi Hawass*, the autobiography of one of Egypt's most famous archaeologists who was one of the first explorers at Giza (2014)
    c. *A History of Hieroglyphics*, an in-depth look at how archaeologists first broke the ancient code, published by the University of Giza's famed history department (2013)
    d. *Who Built the Great Pyramids?,* a short summary of the latest research and theories on the ancient Egyptians' religious beliefs and archaeological skills, written by a team of leading experts in the field (2015)

Questions 24-28 are based on the following passage:

Christopher Columbus is often credited for discovering America. This is incorrect. First, it is impossible to "discover" somewhere where people already live; however, Christopher Columbus did explore places in the New World that were previously untouched by Europe, so the term "explorer" would be more accurate. Another correction must be made, as well: Christopher Columbus was not the first European explorer to reach the present-day Americas! Rather, it was Leif Erikson who first came to the New World and contacted the natives, nearly five hundred years before Christopher Columbus.

Leif Erikson, the son of Erik the Red (a famous Viking outlaw and explorer in his own right), was born in either 970 or 980, depending on which historian you seek. His own family, though, did not raise Leif, which was a Viking tradition. Instead, one of Erik's prisoners taught Leif reading and writing, languages, sailing, and weaponry. At age 12, Leif was considered a man and returned to his family. He killed a man during a dispute shortly after his return, and the council banished the Erikson clan to Greenland.

In 999, Leif left Greenland and traveled to Norway where he would serve as a guard to King Olaf Tryggvason. It was there that he became a convert to Christianity. Leif later tried to return home with the intention of taking supplies and spreading Christianity to Greenland, however his ship was blown off course and he arrived in a strange new land: present day Newfoundland, Canada.

When he finally returned to his adopted homeland Greenland, Leif consulted with a merchant who had also seen the shores of this previously unknown land we now know as Canada. The son of the legendary Viking explorer then gathered a crew of 35 men and set sail. Leif became the first European to touch foot in the New World as he explored present-day Baffin Island and Labrador, Canada. His crew called the land "Vinland," since it was plentiful with grapes.

During their time in present-day Newfoundland, Leif's expedition made contact with the natives whom they referred to as Skraelings (which translates to "wretched ones" in Norse). There are several secondhand accounts of their meetings. Some contemporaries described trade between the peoples. Other accounts describe clashes where the Skraelings defeated the Viking explorers with long spears, while still others claim the Vikings dominated the natives. Regardless of the circumstances, it seems that the Vikings made contact of some kind. This happened around 1000, nearly five hundred years before Columbus famously sailed the ocean blue.

Eventually, in 1003, Leif set sail for home and arrived at Greenland with a ship full of timber. In 1020, seventeen years later, the legendary Viking died. Many believe that Leif Erikson should receive more credit for his contributions in exploring the New World.

24. Which of the following best describes how the author generally presents the information?
    a. Chronological order
    b. Comparison-contrast
    c. Cause effect
    d. Conclusion-premises

25. Which of the following is an opinion, rather than historical fact, expressed by the author?
   a. Leif Erikson was definitely the son of Erik the Red; however, historians debate the year of his birth.
   b. Leif Erikson's crew called the land "Vinland," since it was plentiful with grapes.
   c. Leif Erikson deserves more credit for his contributions in exploring the New World.
   d. Leif Erikson explored the Americas nearly five hundred years before Christopher Columbus.

26. Which of the following most accurately describes the author's main conclusion?
   a. Leif Erikson is a legendary Viking explorer.
   b. Leif Erikson deserves more credit for exploring America hundreds of years before Columbus.
   c. Spreading Christianity motivated Leif Erikson's expeditions more than any other factor.
   d. Leif Erikson contacted the natives nearly five hundred years before Columbus.

27. Which of the following best describes the author's intent in the passage?
   a. To entertain
   b. To inform
   c. To alert
   d. To suggest

28. Which of the following can be logically inferred from the passage?
   a. The Vikings disliked exploring the New World.
   b. Leif Erikson's banishment from Iceland led to his exploration of present-day Canada.
   c. Leif Erikson never shared his stories of exploration with the King of Norway.
   d. Historians have difficulty definitively pinpointing events in the Vikings' history.

This article discusses the famous poet and playwright William Shakespeare. Read it and answer questions 29-32:

People who argue that William Shakespeare is not responsible for the plays attributed to his name are known as Anti-Stratfordians (from the name of Shakespeare's birthplace, Stratford-upon-Avon). The most common Anti-Stratfordian claim is that William Shakespeare simply was not educated enough or from a high enough social class to have written plays overflowing with references to such a wide range of subjects like history, the classics, religion, and international culture. William Shakespeare was the son of a glove-maker, he only had a basic grade school education, and he never set foot outside of England—so how could he have produced plays of such sophistication and imagination? How could he have written in such detail about historical figures and events, or about different cultures and locations around Europe? According to Anti-Stratfordians, the depth of knowledge contained in Shakespeare's plays suggests a well-traveled writer from a wealthy background with a university education, not a countryside writer like Shakespeare. But in fact, there is not much substance to such speculation, and most Anti-Stratfordian arguments can be refuted with a little background about Shakespeare's time and upbringing.

First of all, those who doubt Shakespeare's authorship often point to his common birth and brief education as stumbling blocks to his writerly genius. Although it is true that Shakespeare did not come from a noble class, his father was a very *successful* glove-maker and his mother was from a very wealthy land owning family—so while Shakespeare may have had a country upbringing, he was certainly from a well-off family and would have been educated accordingly. Also, even though he did not attend university, grade school education in Shakespeare's time was actually quite rigorous and exposed students to classic drama through writers like Seneca and Ovid. It is not unreasonable to believe that Shakespeare received a very solid foundation in poetry and literature from his early schooling.

Next, Anti-Stratfordians tend to question how Shakespeare could write so extensively about countries and cultures he had never visited before (for instance, several of his most famous works like *Romeo and Juliet* and *The Merchant of Venice* were set in Italy, on the opposite side of Europe!). But again, this criticism does not hold up under scrutiny. For one thing, Shakespeare was living in London, a bustling metropolis of international trade, the most populous city in England, and a political and cultural hub of Europe. In the daily crowds of people, Shakespeare would certainly have been able to meet travelers from other countries and hear firsthand accounts of life in their home country. And, in addition to the influx of information from world travelers, this was also the age of the printing press, a jump in technology that made it possible to print and circulate books much more easily than in the past. This also allowed for a freer flow of information across different countries, allowing people to read about life and ideas from throughout Europe. One needn't travel the continent in order to learn and write about its culture.

29. Which sentence contains the author's thesis?
   a. People who argue that William Shakespeare is not responsible for the plays attributed to his name are known as Anti-Stratfordians.
   b. But in fact, there is not much substance to such speculation, and most Anti-Stratfordian arguments can be refuted with a little background about Shakespeare's time and upbringing.
   c. It is not unreasonable to believe that Shakespeare received a very solid foundation in poetry and literature from his early schooling.
   d. Next, Anti-Stratfordians tend to question how Shakespeare could write so extensively about countries and cultures he had never visited before.

30. In the first paragraph, "How could he have written in such detail about historical figures and events, or about different cultures and locations around Europe?" is an example of which of the following?
   a. Hyperbole
   b. Onomatopoeia
   c. Rhetorical question
   d. Appeal to authority

31. How does the author respond to the claim that Shakespeare was not well-educated because he did not attend university?
   a. By insisting upon Shakespeare's natural genius
   b. By explaining grade school curriculum in Shakespeare's time
   c. By comparing Shakespeare with other uneducated writers of his time
   d. By pointing out that Shakespeare's wealthy parents probably paid for private tutors

32. The word "bustling" in the third paragraph most nearly means
    a. Busy
    b. Foreign
    c. Expensive
    d. Undeveloped

The next article is for questions 33-35:

The Myth of Head Heat Loss

It has recently been brought to my attention that most people believe that 75% of your body heat is lost through your head. I had certainly heard this before, and am not going to attempt to say I didn't believe it when I first heard it. It is natural to be gullible to anything said with enough authority. But the "fact" that the majority of your body heat is lost through your head is a lie.

Let me explain. Heat loss is proportional to surface area exposed. An elephant loses a great deal more heat than an anteater, because it has a much greater surface area than an anteater. Each cell has mitochondria that produce energy in the form of heat, and it takes a lot more energy to run an elephant than an anteater.

So, each part of your body loses its proportional amount of heat in accordance with its surface area. The human torso probably loses the most heat, though the legs lose a significant amount as well. Some people have asked, "Why does it feel so much warmer when you cover your head than when you don't?" Well, that's because your head, because it is not clothed, is losing a lot of heat while the clothing on the rest of your body provides insulation. If you went outside with a hat and pants but no shirt, not only would you look silly, but your heat loss would be significantly greater because so much more of you would be exposed. So, if given the choice to cover your chest or your head in the cold, choose the chest. It could save your life.

33. Why does the author compare elephants and anteaters?
    a. To express an opinion
    b. To give an example that helps clarify the main point
    c. To show the differences between them
    d. To persuade why one is better than the other

34. Which of the following best describes the tone of the passage?
    a. Harsh
    b. Angry
    c. Casual
    d. Indifferent

35. The author appeals to which branch of rhetoric to prove his or her case?
    a. Factual evidence
    b. Emotion
    c. Ethics and morals
    d. Author qualification

The next article is for questions 36-40:

The Old Man and His Grandson

There was once a very old man, whose eyes had become dim, his ears dull of hearing, his knees trembled, and when he sat at table he could hardly hold the spoon, and spilt the broth upon the table-cloth or let it run out of his mouth. His son and his son's wife were disgusted at this, so the old grandfather at last had to sit in the corner behind the stove, and they gave him his food in an earthenware bowl, and not even enough of it. And he used to look towards the table with his eyes full of tears. Once, too, his trembling hands could not hold the bowl, and it fell to the ground and broke. The young wife scolded him, but he said nothing and only sighed. Then they brought him a wooden bowl for a few half-pence, out of which he had to eat.

They were once sitting thus when the little grandson of four years old began to gather together some bits of wood upon the ground. 'What are you doing there?' asked the father. 'I am making a little trough,' answered the child, 'for father and mother to eat out of when I am big.'

The man and his wife looked at each other for a while, and presently began to cry. Then they took the old grandfather to the table, and henceforth always let him eat with them, and likewise said nothing if he did spill a little of anything.
(*Grimms' Fairy Tales*, p. 111)

36. Which of the following most accurately represents the theme of the passage?
    a. Respect your elders
    b. Children will follow their parents' example
    c. You reap what you sow
    d. Loyalty will save your life

37. How is the content in this selection organized?
    a. Chronologically
    b. Problem and solution
    c. Compare and contrast
    d. Order of importance

38. Which character trait most accurately reflects the son and his wife in this story?
    a. Compassion
    b. Understanding
    c. Cruelty
    d. Impatience

39. Where does the story take place?
    a. In the countryside
    b. In America
    c. In a house
    d. In a forest

40. Why do the son and his wife decide to let the old man sit at the table?
    a. Because they felt sorry for him
    b. Because their son told them to
    c. Because the old man would not stop crying
    d. Because they saw their own actions in their son

Answer Explanations

1. D: The passage directly states that the larger sensor is the main difference between the two cameras. Choices A and B may be true, but these answers do not identify the major difference between the two cameras. Choice C states the opposite of what the paragraph suggests is the best option for amateur photographers, so it is incorrect.

2. D: An actuary assesses risks and sets insurance premiums. While an actuary does work in insurance, the passage does not suggest that actuaries have any affiliation with hospitalists or working in a hospital, so all other choices are incorrect.

3. A: The passage focuses mainly on the problems of hard water. Choice B is incorrect because calcium is not good for pipes and hard surfaces. The passage does not say anything about whether water softeners are easy to install, so Choice C is incorrect. Choice D is also incorrect because the passage does offer other solutions besides vinegar.

4. C: The main point of this paragraph is that parents need to change their poor behavior at their kids' sporting events. Choice A is incorrect because the coaches' behavior is not mentioned in the paragraph. Choice B suggests that sports are bad for kids, when the paragraph is about parents' behavior, so it is incorrect. While Choice D may be true, it offers a specific solution to the problem, which the paragraph does not discuss.

5. B: The main point of this passage is to show how a tornado forms. Choice A is incorrect because while the passage does mention that tornadoes are dangerous, it is not the main focus of the passage. While thunderstorms are mentioned, they are not compared to tornadoes, so Choice C is incorrect. Choice D is incorrect because the passage does not discuss what to do in the event of a tornado.

6. B: Samuel wants to write an academic paper based on his 24 students. His best students come from homes where parental supervision is minimal, while the worst come from parents with extensive involvement. His conclusion is counterintuitive and probably the result of a small sample size. Choices A and D having to do with bias, is not the issue, nor is Choice C. Samuel's experience with these students is not applicable to students in general; rather, it is a tiny sample size relative to the millions of school children in the United States. The correct answer is B since the sample contains too few members to make meaningful claims applicable to a large group.

7. B: The passage indicates that Annabelle has a fear of going outside into the daylight. Thus, *heliophobia* must refer to a fear of bright lights or sunlight. Choice B is the only answer that describes this.

8. C: The purpose of this passage is to explain how the digestive system works. Choice A focuses only on the liver, which is a small part of the process and not the focus of the paragraph. Choice B is off-track because the passage does not mention healthy foods. Choice D only focuses on one part of the digestive system.

9. C: The answer we seek has both the most detailed and objective information. Choice A describing a television commercial with a dramatized reenactment is not particularly detailed. Choice B, a notice to the public informing them of additional drinking and driving units on patrol, is not detailed and objective information. Choice D, a highway bulletin, does not present the type of information required. Choice C is the correct answer. The number of incidents and their relationship to a possible cause are both detailed and objective information.

10. C: We are looking for an inference—a conclusion that is reached on the basis of evidence and reasoning—from the passage that will likely explain why the famous children's author did not achieve her usual success with the new genre (despite the book's acclaim). Choice A is wrong because the statement is false according to the passage. Choice B is wrong because, although the passage says the author has a graduate degree on the subject, it would be an unrealistic leap to infer that she is the foremost expert on Antebellum America. Choice D is wrong because there is nothing in the passage to lead us to infer that people generally prefer a children's series to historical fiction. In contrast, Choice C can be logically inferred since the passage speaks of the great success of the children's series and the declaration that the fame of the author's name causes the children's books to "fly off the shelves." Thus, she did not receive any bump from her name since she published the historical novel under a pseudonym, and Choice C is correct.

11. B: Narrative, Choice A, means a written account of connected events. Think of narrative writing as a story. Choice C, expository writing, generally seeks to explain or describe some phenomena, whereas Choice D, technical writing, includes directions, instructions, and/or explanations. This passage is definitely persuasive writing, which hopes to change someone's beliefs based on an appeal to reason or emotion. The author is aiming to convince the reader that smoking is terrible. They use health, price, and beauty in their argument against smoking, so Choice B, persuasive, is the correct answer.

12. B: The author is clearly opposed to tobacco. He cites disease and deaths associated with smoking. He points to the monetary expense and aesthetic costs. Choice A is wrong because alternatives to smoking are not even addressed in the passage. Choice C is wrong because it does not summarize the passage; rather, it is just a premise. Choice D is wrong because, while these statistics do support the argument, they do not represent a summary of the piece. Choice C is the correct answer because it states the three critiques offered against tobacco and expresses the author's conclusion.

13. C: We are looking for something the author would agree with, so it will almost certainly be anti-smoking or an argument in favor of quitting smoking. Choice A is wrong because the author does not speak against means of cessation. Choice B is wrong because the author does not reference other substances, but does speak of how addictive nicotine—a drug in tobacco—is. Choice D is wrong because the author certainly would not encourage reducing taxes to encourage a reduction of smoking costs, thereby helping smokers to continue the habit. Choice C is correct because the author is definitely attempting to persuade smokers to quit smoking.

14. D: Here, we are looking for an opinion of the author's rather than a fact or statistic. Choice A is wrong because quoting statistics from the Centers of Disease Control and Prevention is stating facts, not opinions. Choice B is wrong because it expresses the fact that cigarettes sometimes cost more than a few gallons of gas. It would be an opinion if the author said that cigarettes were not affordable. Choice C is incorrect because yellow stains are a known possible adverse effect of smoking. Choice D is correct as an opinion because smell is subjective. Some people might like the smell of smoke, they might not have working olfactory senses, and/or some people might not find the smell of smoke akin to "pervasive nastiness," so this is the expression of an opinion. Thus, Choice D is the correct answer.

15. D: Outspending other countries on education could have other benefits, but there is no reference to this in the passage, so Choice A is incorrect. Choice B is incorrect because the author does not mention corruption. Choice C is incorrect because there is nothing in the passage stating that the tests are not genuinely representative. Choice *D* is accurate because spending more money has not brought success. The United States already spends the most money, and the country is not excelling on these tests. Choice *D* is the correct answer.

16. D: The main point of this passage is to define osteoporosis. Choice *A* is incorrect because the passage does not list ways that people contract osteoporosis. Choice *B* is incorrect because the passage does not mention any treatment options. While the passage does briefly mention prevention, it does not explain how, so Choice *C* is incorrect.

17. C: A primary source is an artifact, document, recording, or other source of information that is created at the time under study. Think of a primary source as the original representation of the information. In contrast, secondary sources make conclusions or draw inferences based on primary sources, as well as other secondary sources. Choice *A*, therefore, a critic's summary and review of a new book is a secondary source; additionally, the book itself may be a secondary source. Choice *B*, a table of contents, is a secondary source since it refers to other information. Choice *D*, a news article quoting research, is also a secondary source. Therefore, a report of the groundbreaking research itself, Choice *C*, is correct.

18. D: Cynthia needs to select the meal with the least vegetarian options. Although the breakfast menu, Choice *A*, includes bacon, there is also coffee, tea, French toast, and eggs available. Choice *B*, lunch, includes an option for vegetarian sandwiches along with the French fries and baked beans. The cocktail hour, Choice *C*, does not contain meat or fish. In contrast, the dinner is a vegetarian's nightmare: nothing suitable is offered. Thus, dinner, Choice *D*, is the best answer.

19. D: Although Washington is from a wealthy background, the passage does not say that his wealth led to his republican ideals, so Choice *A* is not supported. Choice *B* also does not follow from the passage. Washington's warning against meddling in foreign affairs does not mean that he would oppose wars of every kind, so Choice *B* is wrong. Choice *C* is also unjustified since the author does not indicate that Alexander Hamilton's assistance was absolutely necessary. Choice *D* is correct because the farewell address clearly opposes political parties and partisanship. The author then notes that presidential elections often hit a fever pitch of partisanship. Thus, it is follows that George Washington would not approve of modern political parties and their involvement in presidential elections.

20. A: The author finishes the passage by applying Washington's farewell address to modern politics, so the purpose probably includes this application. Choice *B* is wrong because George Washington is already a well-established historical figure; furthermore, the passage does not seek to introduce him. Choice *C* is wrong because the author is not fighting a common perception that Washington was merely a military hero. Choice *D* is wrong because the author is not convincing readers. Persuasion does not correspond to the passage. Choice *A* states the primary purpose.

21. D: Choice *A* is wrong because the last paragraph is not appropriate for a history textbook. Choice *B* is false because the piece is not a notice or announcement of Washington's death. Choice *C* is clearly false because it is not fiction, but a piece of historical writing. Choice *D* is correct. The passage is most likely to appear in a newspaper editorial because it cites information relevant and applicable to the present day, which is a popular format in editorials.

22. B: The scientist and politician largely disagree, but the question asks for a point where the two are in agreement. The politician would not concur that burning fossil fuels causes global temperatures to rise; thus, Choice *A* is wrong. He would not agree with Choice *C* suggesting that countries must revisit their energy policies. By inference from the given information, the scientist would likely not concur that

Earth's climate naturally goes through warming and cooling cycles; so, Choice *D* is incorrect. However, both the scientist and politician would agree that global temperatures are increasing. The reason for this is in dispute. The politician thinks it is part of the Earth's natural cycle; the scientist thinks it is from the burning of fossil fuels. However, both acknowledge an increase, so Choice *B* is the correct answer.

23. D: Raul wants a book that describes how and why ancient Egyptians built the Great Pyramid of Giza. Choice *A* is incorrect because it focuses more generally on Giza as a whole, rather than the Great Pyramid itself. Choice *B* is close but incorrect because it is an autobiography that will largely focus on the archaeologist's life. Choice *C* is wrong because it focuses on hieroglyphics; it is not directly on point. Choice *D*, the book directly covering the building of the Great Pyramids, should be most helpful.

24. D: The passage does not proceed in chronological order since it begins by pointing out Leif Erikson's explorations in America, so Choice *A* does not work. Although the author compares and contrasts Erikson with Christopher Columbus, this is not the main way in which the information is presented; therefore, Choice *B* does not work. Neither does Choice *C* because there is no mention of or reference to cause and effect in the passage. However, the passage does offer a conclusion (Leif Erikson deserves more credit) and premises (first European to set foot in the New World and first to contact the natives) to substantiate Erikson's historical importance. Thus, Choice *D* is correct.

25. C: Choice *A* is wrong because it describes facts: Leif Erikson was the son of Erik the Red and historians debate Leif's date of birth. These are not opinions. Choice *B* is wrong; that Erikson called the land "Vinland" is a verifiable fact, as is Choice *D* because he did contact the natives almost 500 years before Columbus. Choice *C* is the correct answer because it is the author's opinion that Erikson deserves more credit. That, in fact, is his conclusion in the piece, but another person could argue that Columbus or another explorer deserves more credit for opening up the New World to exploration. Rather than being an indisputable fact, it is a subjective value claim.

26. B: Choice *A* is wrong because the author aims to go beyond describing Erikson as a mere legendary Viking. Choice *C* is wrong because the author does not focus on Erikson's motivations, let alone name the spreading of Christianity as his primary objective. Choice *D* is wrong because it is a premise that Erikson contacted the natives 500 years before Columbus, which is simply a part of supporting the author's conclusion. Choice *B* is correct because, as stated in the previous answer, it accurately identifies the author's statement that Erikson deserves more credit than he has received for being the first European to explore the New World.

27. B: Choice *A* is wrong because the author is not in any way trying to entertain the reader. Choice *D* is wrong because he goes beyond a mere suggestion; "suggest" is too vague. Although the author is certainly trying to alert the readers (make them aware) of Leif Erikson's underappreciated and unheralded accomplishments, the nature of the writing does not indicate the author would be satisfied with the reader merely knowing of Erikson's exploration (Choice *C*). Rather, the author would want the reader to be informed about it, which is more substantial (Choice *B*).

28. D: Choice *A* is wrong because the author never addresses the Vikings' state of mind or emotions. Choice *B* is wrong because the author does not elaborate on Erikson's exile and whether he would have become an explorer if not for his banishment. Choice *C* is wrong because there is not enough information to support this premise. It is unclear whether Erikson informed the King of Norway of his finding. Although it is true that the King did not send a follow-up expedition, he could have simply chosen not to expend the resources after receiving Erikson's news. It is not possible to logically infer whether Erikson told him. Choice *D* is correct because there are two examples—Leif Erikson's date of birth and what happened during the encounter with the natives—of historians having trouble pinning down important dates in Viking history.

29. B: The thesis is a statement that contains the author's topic and main idea. The main purpose of this article is to use historical evidence to provide counterarguments to Anti-Stratfordians. *A* is simply a definition; Choice *C* is a supporting detail, not a main idea; and Choice *D* represents an idea of Anti-Stratfordians, not the author's opinion. The sentence in Choice *B* is the author's thesis.

30. C: This question requires readers to be familiar with different types of rhetorical devices. A rhetorical question is a question that is asked not to obtain an answer but to encourage readers to more deeply consider an issue.

31. B: This question asks readers to refer to the organizational structure of the article and demonstrate understanding of how the author provides details to support their argument. The author of this passage responds to the claim that Shakespeare was not well-educated because he did not attend university by explaining grade school curriculum in Shakespeare's time, choice B. This particular detail can be found in the second paragraph: "even though he did not attend university, grade school education in Shakespeare's time was actually quite rigorous."

32. A: This is a vocabulary question that can be answered using context clues. Other sentences in the paragraph describe London as "the most populous city in England" filled with "crowds of people," giving an image of a *busy* city full of people. *B* is incorrect because London was in Shakespeare's home country, not a foreign one. Choice *C* is not mentioned in the passage. Choice *D* is not a good answer choice because the passage describes how London was a popular and important city, probably not an underdeveloped one.

33. B: Choice *B* is correct because the author is trying to demonstrate the main idea, which is that heat loss is proportional to surface area, and so the author compares two animals with different surface areas to clarify the main point. Choice *A* is incorrect because the author uses elephants and anteaters to prove a point—that heat loss is proportional to surface area—not to express an opinion. Choice *C* is incorrect because although the author does use them to show differences, they do so in order to give examples that prove the above points, so Choice *C* is not the best answer. Choice *D* is incorrect because there is no language to indicate favoritism between the two animals.

34. C: Because of the way that the author addresses the reader, and also the colloquial language that the author uses (i.e., "let me explain," "so," "well," didn't," "you would look silly," etc.), Choice *C* is the best answer because it has a much more casual tone than the usual informative article. Choice *A* may be a tempting choice because the author says the "fact" that most of one's heat is lost through their head is a "lie," and that someone who does not wear a shirt in the cold looks silly, but it only happens twice within all the diction of the passage and it does not give an overall tone of harshness. Choice *B* is incorrect because again, while not necessarily nice, the language does not carry an angry charge. The author is clearly not indifferent to the subject because of the passionate language that he or she uses, so Choice *D* is incorrect.

35. A: The author gives logical examples and reasons in order to prove that most of one's heat is not lost through their head; therefore, Choice *A* is correct. Choice *B* is incorrect because there is not much emotionally-charged language in this selection, and even the small amount present is greatly outnumbered by the facts and evidence. Choice *C* is incorrect because there is no mention of ethics or morals in this selection. Choice *D* is incorrect because the author never qualifies himself or herself as someone who has the authority to be writing on this topic.

161

36. B: *A* is incorrect because it does not fit with the primary purpose of this passage, which is to tell a story of how a child plans to treat his parents when he sees the way they treat his grandfather. It is trying to remind readers to treat others with respect because that is how one wants to be treated, and that this does not apply only to elderly people. Choice *B* fits most appropriately with the primary purpose, since the son and wife see that they will be treated unfairly because they witness that their child plans to do it to them when they are older. To "reap what you sow" means that there are repercussions for every action. This may seem like the correct answer; however, the parents do not actually have to eat out of a trough later in life. They don't actually experience any repercussions. Even though it may be argued that the boy is being loyal to his grandfather, this does not fit with the primary purpose. The boy also never mentions that his actions are because he cares for his grandfather; rather, he simply mirrors the behaviors of his parents.

37. A: *A* is correct because it follows a series of events that happen in order, one right after the other. First the grandfather spills his food, then his son puts him in a corner, then the child makes a trough for his parents to eat out of when he's older, and finally the parents welcome the old man back to the table. Choice *B* is incorrect as even though it could be argued that the way they treat the old man is a problem, there really isn't a solution to the problem, even though they stop treating him badly. Also, problem and solution styles generally do not follow a chronological timeline. Choice *C* is incorrect because events in the passage are not compared and contrasted; this is not a primary organizational structure of the passage. Choice *D* is incorrect because there is no language to indicate that one person or event is more important than the other.

38. C: Although they do show him compassion in the end, it is not because they feel compassionate for him, but instead, it is because they recognize that their son plans to treat them the way they are treating the old man when they are older. So, they treat the old man the way they would want to be treated. Understanding is not the overall attitude they feel toward the old man, and it is only in realizing the cruelty of their behavior that they understand how they have been treating him. Choice *C* is correct because it condenses the actions of the son and his wife into a single word. Refusing to let the old man sit at the table when he clearly needs help and looks at the table with tear-filled eyes is a cruel thing to do. Choice *D* may be tempting to pick as they *are* impatient with him, but it's not the best answer. People can be impatient without being cruel.

39. C: Choice *A* is incorrect as there is no descriptive language to indicate that they are in the countryside. *B* is incorrect because the passage has no language or descriptions to indicate they are in America. Choice *C* is correct because the setting contains elements of a house: a table, a stove, and a corner. Choice *D* may be tempting as there is mention of "bits of wood upon the ground," but as there are no other elements of a forest in the story, this is not the correct answer.

40. D: The parents allow the old man to sit at the table because their son starts to make them a trough, so their motivation in letting him eat at the table is not because they feel sorry for him, but because they don't want their son to treat them that way when they are old. This makes Choice *A* incorrect. Their son did not tell them to let the old man sit at the table, so Choice *B* is incorrect. In the story, it mentions that even after the old man has eyes full of tears, the wife gave him a cheap wooden bowl to eat out of, so clearly his crying did not make them stop treating him badly, making Choice *C* incorrect. Choice *D* is correct because the parents let the old man sit at the table as a result of the boy mimicking their behavior.

ACT Science Test

The ACT science exam tests analytical skills associated with interpreting scientific principles of the natural world. The content may be from biology, the earth sciences, chemistry, or physics. The test presents scientific concepts in the form of passages of three different formats. A total of 40 multiple-choice questions related to the passage are to be completed in 35 minutes.

Test-takers are often surprised to discover that detailed knowledge of science content isn't required to achieve success on the ACT science test. In fact, the test is designed to determine how well an individual is able to analyze, compare, and generalize information. For example, the test doesn't seek to determine if one possesses an extensive knowledge of elephant biology. Instead, the exam might ask one to compare two scientists' differing opinions about elephant communication. In this case, the test taker is *not* required to possess any knowledge about elephants or the manner in which they communicate. All of the information needed to answer the questions will be presented in the passage. The test taker must read the passage, compare the differing hypotheses, analyze the graphical information, and generate conclusions.

Three Types of Passages

Data representation
Scientific data will be presented in tables, graphs, diagrams, or models. These passages account for 30% to 40% of the ACT Science Test. These passages typically contain 5 or 6 questions designed to test one's ability to interpret scientific data represented in a graphical format instead of written text. These questions do *not* necessarily examine scientific content knowledge (e.g., the equation for photosynthesis); rather, they test students' ability to interpret raw data represented in a table or graph. Therefore, it's possible to do well on this portion of the exam without a detailed understanding of the scientific topic at hand. Questions may ask for factual information, identification of data trends, or graph calculations. For example:

- Based on the attached graph, how did Study 1 differ from Study 2?
- What is the nature of the relationship between Experiment 1 and Experiment 2?
- What is *x* at the given *y*-value?

Research summaries
These passages account for 45% to 55% of the ACT Science Test. Passages present the design, implementation, and conclusion of various scientific experiments. These passages typically contain 5 or 6 questions designed to test one's ability to identify the following:

- What question is the experiment trying to answer?
- What is the researcher's predicted answer to the question?
- How did the researchers test the hypotheses?
- Based on data obtained from the experiments, was the prediction correct?
- What would happen if . . .?
- 2 X 2 Matrix questions: "Yes, because . . ." or "No, because . . ."

Conflicting viewpoints
This section will present a disagreement between two scientists about a specific scientific hypothesis or concept. These passages account for 15% to 20% of the ACT Science Test. The opinions of each

researcher are presented in two separate passages. There are two formats for these questions. The test taker must demonstrate an understanding of the content, or compare and contrast the main differences between the two opinions. For example:

- Based on the data presented by Scientist 1, which of the following is correct?
- What is the main difference between the conclusions of Expert A and Expert B?

Elements of Science Passages

Short answer questions
Short answer questions are usually one to five words long and require the reader to recall basic facts presented in the passage.

An example answer choice: "Research group #1 finished last."

Long answer questions
Long answer questions are composed of one to three sentences that require the reader to make comparisons, summaries, generalizations, or conclusions about the passage.

An example answer choice: "Scientist 2 disagreed with Scientist 1 on the effects of Bisphenol A pollution and its presumed correlation to birth defects in mice and humans. Scientist 2 proposes that current environmental Bisphenol A levels are not sufficient to cause adverse effects on human health."

Fact questions
Fact questions are the most basic type of question on the test. They ask the reader to recall a specific term, definition, number, or meaning.

An example question/answer: "Which of the following organisms was present in fresh water samples from Pond #1?"
    a. Water flea
    b. Dragonfly nymph
    c. Snail
    d. Tadpole

Graphs
There are five different graph types used in the ACT Science Test to represent the passage data. There will be at least one of each type included in the test. The five types include: illustrative graphs, bar graphs, scatter plots, line graphs, and region graphs. Most ACT Science passages will include two or more of the five graph types.

The illustrative graph provides a graphic representation or picture of some process. Questions may address specific details of the process depicted in the graph.

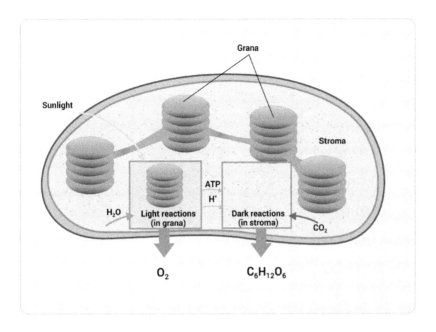

Bar graphs depict the passage data as parallel lines of varying heights. ACT bar graphs will be printed in black and white. Data may be oriented vertically or horizontally. Questions may ask, "During the fall season, in what habitat do bears spend the most time?"

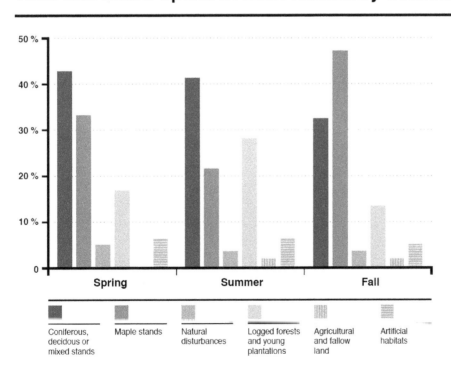

Bar graphs can also be horizontal, like the graph below.

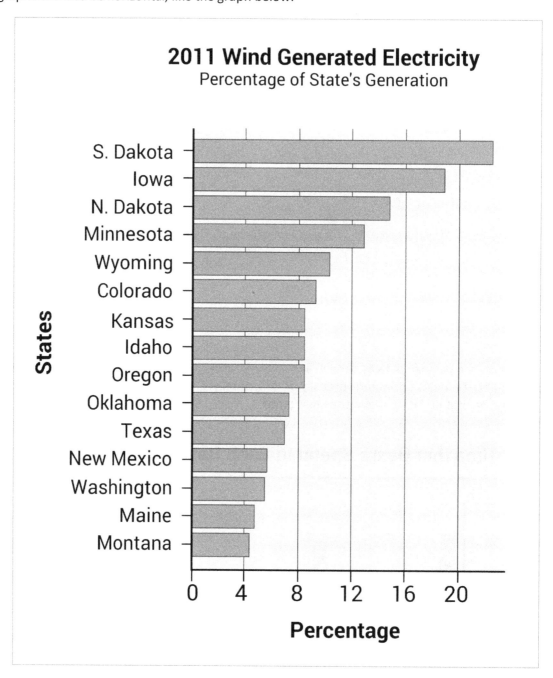

2011 Wind Generated Electricity
Percentage of State's Generation

Scatter plots provide a visual representation of the passage data along the x- and y-axes. This representation indicates the nature of the relationship between the two variables. It is important to note that correlation doesn't equal causation. The relationship may be linear, curvilinear, positive, negative, inverse, or there may be no relationship. Questions may ask "What is the relationship between x and y?"

Line graphs are scatter plots that compare and contrast the relationships between two or more data sets. The horizontal axis represents the passage data sets that are compared over time. The vertical axis is the scale for measurement of that data. The scale points are equidistant from one another. There will always be a title for the line graph. Questions related to line graphs might ask," Which of the following conclusions is supported by the provided graph of tropical storms?"

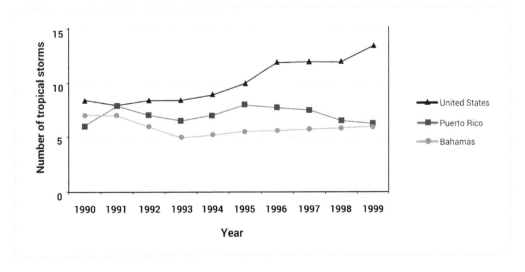

A region graph is a visual representation of the passage data set used to display the properties of a given substance under different conditions or at different points in time. Questions relating to this graph may ask, "According to the figure, what is the temperature range associated with liquid nitrogen?"

Nitrogen Phases

Tables

ACT Science Test tables present passage data sets in tabular form. The independent variable is positioned on the left side, while the dependent variable is on the right side of the table. The content of ACT Science tables is always discussed in the corresponding passage. Knowledge of all table content isn't required.

Sample Table for Analysis

Data type	Seismic sources							
	Individual faults						Area/volume sources	
	Location	Activity	Length	Dip	Depth	Style	Area	Depth
Geological/Remote Sensing								
Detailed mapping	X	X	X	X		X		
Geomorphic data	X	X	X			X	X	
Quaternary surface rupture	X	X	X			X		
Fault trenching data	X	X		X		X		
Paleoliquefaction data	X	X					X	
Borehole data	X	X		X		X		
Aerial photography	X	X	X					
Low sun-angle photography	X	X	X					
Stellite imagery	X		X				X	
Regional structure	X			X		X	X	
Balanced Cross Section	X			X	X		X	
Geophysical/Geodetic								
Regional potential field data	X		X				X	X
Local potential field data	X		X	X	X	X		
High resolution reflection data	X	X		X		X		
Standard reflexing data	X			X		X		
Deep crustal reflection data	X			X	X		X	X
Tectonic geodetic/strain data	X	X		X	X	X	X	X
Reginal stress data						X	X	
Seismological								
Reflected crustal phase data								X
Pre-instrumental earthquake data	X	X			X	X	X	
Teleseismic earthquake data							X	
Regional network seismicity data	X	X	X	X	X		X	X
Local network seismicity data	X	X	X	X	X			X
Focal mechanism data				X		X		

169

Answer Choice Elimination Techniques

The ability to quickly and effectively eliminate incorrect answer choices is one of the most important skills to develop before sitting for the exam. The following tips and strategies are designed to help in this effort.

First, test takers should look for answer choices that make absolute "all-or-nothing" statements, as they are usually incorrect answers. Key word clues to incorrect answer choices include: always, never, everyone, no one, all, must, and none. An example of a possible incorrect answer choice is provided below:

> *"The use of antibiotics should be discontinued indefinitely as they are always over-prescribed."*

An example of a possible correct answer choice:

> *"The use of antibiotics should be closely monitored by physician review boards in order to prevent the rise of drug-resistant bacteria."*

Test takers should look for unreasonable, awkward, or irrational answer choices and they should pay special attention to irrelevant information that isn't mentioned in the passage. If the answer choice relates to an idea or position that isn't clearly presented in the passage, it's likely incorrect.

Answer choices that seem too broad or generic and also those that are very narrow or specific are also important to note. For example, if a question relates to a summarization of the passage, test takers should look for answers that encompass a broad representation of the presented ideas, facts, concepts, etc. On the other hand, if a question asks about a specific word, number, data point, etc. the correct answer will likely be more narrow or specific.

Highly Technical Questions

The goal of the ACT Science Test is to measure scientific reasoning skills, not scientific content knowledge. Therefore, candidates shouldn't "cram" for this section using complex scientific concepts from textbooks or online courses. Instead, they should focus on understanding the format of the exam and the manner in which ideas are presented and questions are asked.

> *Example question about two scientists' conflicting viewpoints:*

> Scientist 1: Reproductive success in red-tailed hawks has been drastically reduced as a consequence of widespread release of endocrine-disrupting chemicals such as dichloro-diphenyl-trichloroethane (DDT).

> Scientist 2: The reproductive fitness of red-tailed hawks is only mildly reduced by the weak effects of DDT, but it is highly sensitive to another class of chemicals called polychlorinated biphenyls (PCBs).

Considering the two viewpoints of the passage, which of the following statements is true?

    a. Red-tailed hawks are an endangered species due the effects of over-hunting and the release of toxic chemicals such as DDT and PCBs.

    b. PCBs must not be the cause of red-tailed hawk reproductive problems because polychlorinated biphenyls do not affect female reproductive organs.

    c. Scientist 2 proposes that PCBs are likely the cause of red-tailed hawk reproductive problems since DDT is only mildly toxic.

    d. DDT is a persistent organic pesticide and should be avoided.

Answer A: INCORRECT. This answer is irrational. Neither scientist mentioned anything about hunting or red-tailed hawks being endangered.

Answer B: INCORRECT. This answer is also irrational. Neither scientist proposes that PCBs do not affect female reproductive organs.

Answer C: CORRECT. This answer makes the most sense. It's true that Scientist 2 believes that PCBs cause reproductive problems in red-tailed hawks because DDT is only mildly toxic.

Answer D: INCORRECT. This answer is very narrow and specific. The phrase "persistent organic pesticide" isn't mentioned at all in the passage.

Again, the reader didn't need to know anything about dichloro-diphenyl-trichloroethane, polychlorinated biphenyls, red-tailed hawks, reproductive biology, or endocrine-disrupting chemicals to answer the question correctly. Instead, the test taker must consider both viewpoints and make comparisons or generalizations between the two.

Time Management

Using time efficiently is a critical factor for success on the ACT Science Test. Test takers may find the following strategies to be helpful when preparing for the exam:

- There are 40 questions and only 35 minutes, which leaves about 50 seconds for each question. This may seem daunting; however, it's important to consider that multiple questions apply to a single passage, graph, etc. Therefore, it may be possible to answer some in less than 50 seconds, leaving extra time for more demanding questions.

- It's important to read the entire passage before answering the questions and to consider all facts, conflicting viewpoints, hypotheses, conclusions, opinions, etc.

- Be sure to review only the information presented in the passages, as the questions will relate solely to this content.

- Don't get stuck on difficult questions. The exam is designed with a mix of easy and hard questions. Make sure to get all the easy ones answered, and then go back to focus on more difficult questions.

- Try to quickly eliminate answer choices that are obviously incorrect.

General Tips for Success

Before taking the exam, successful test takers practice answering questions from all of the different formats. Being able to quickly identify what one is being asked to do saves valuable time.

Test takers should read each passage completely and make notes or underline important information, such as:

- What is the hypothesis of an experiment?
- What is the result of the experiment?
- What is the experimental question?
- What information led to the researcher's viewpoint?
- What is the main difference between the two experiments?
- What is the main difference of opinion between two researchers?

Test takers should be mindful of the time. There are 40 questions that must be completed in 35 minutes. It is recommended that test takers quickly look at the questions before reading the associated passage. This will provide a general idea of which parts of the passage to read carefully. Test takers should answer all of the questions.

Practice Questions

Passage I

Questions 1-5 pertain to the following information:

Worldwide, fungal infections of the lung account for significant mortality in individuals with compromised immune function. Three of the most common infecting agents are *Aspergillus, Histoplasma*, and *Candida*. Successful treatment of infections caused by these agents depends on an early and accurate diagnosis. Three tests used to identify specific markers for these mold species include ELISA (enzyme-linked immunosorbent assay), GM Assay (Galactomannan Assay), and PCR (polymerase chain reaction).

Two important characteristics of these tests include sensitivity and specificity. Sensitivity relates to the probability that the test will identify the presence of the infecting agent, resulting in a true positive result. Higher sensitivity equals fewer false-positive results. Specificity relates to the probability that if the test doesn't detect the infecting agent, the test is truly negative for that agent. Higher specificity equals fewer false-negatives.

Figure 1 shows the timeline for the process of infection from exposure to the pathogen to recovery or death.

Figure 1:
Natural History of the Process of Infection

Figure 2 (below) shows the sensitivity and specificity for ELISA, GM assay and PCR related to the diagnosis of infection by *Aspergillus*, *Histoplasma* and *Candida*.

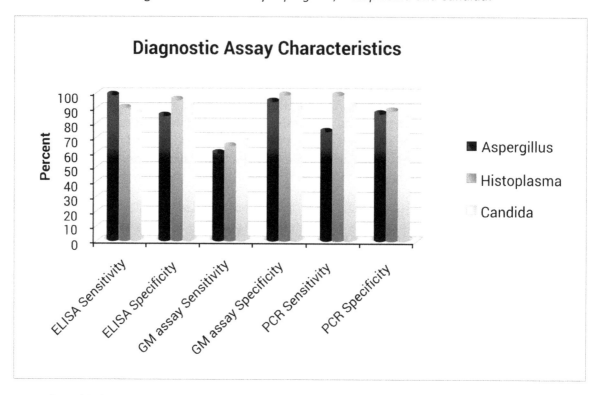

The table below identifies the process of infection in days from exposure for each of the species.

Process of Infection - Days Since Pathogen Exposure			
	Aspergillus	Histoplasma	Candida
Sub-clinical Disease	Day 90	Day 28	Day 7
Detection Possible	Day 118	Day 90	Day 45
Symptoms Appear	Day 145	Day100	Day 120

Figure 3 (below) identifies the point at which each test can detect the organism. Time is measured in days from the time an individual is exposed to the pathogen.

Point at Which Pathogen is Detected ELISA, GM assay, & PCR

Comparison of Time of Detection

1. Which of the following statements is supported by Figure 2?
    a. For *Candida*, the GM assay will provide the most reliable results.
    b. ELISA testing for *Aspergillus* is the most specific of the three tests.
    c. PCR is the most sensitive method for testing *Histoplasma*.
    d. True positive rates were greater than 75% for all three testing methods.

2. In reference to the table and Figure 3, which pathogen can be detected earlier in the disease process, and by which method?
    a. *Candida* by PCR testing
    b. *Aspergillus* by ELISA testing
    c. *Candida* by GM assay
    d. *Histoplasma* by PCR testing

3. In reference to Figure 2, which statement is correct?
    a. There is a 20% probability that ELISA testing will NOT correctly identify the presence of *Histoplasma*.
    b. When GM assay testing for *Candida* is conducted, there is a 31% probability that it will NOT be identified if the organism is present.
    c. The probability that GM assay testing for *Aspergillus* will correctly identify the presence of the organism is 99%.
    d. The false-negative probabilities for each of the three testing methods identified in Figure 2 indicate that the organism will be detected when present less than 70% of the time.

4. Physicians caring for individuals with suspected *Histoplasma* infections order diagnostic testing prior to instituting treatment. PCR testing results will not be available for 10 days. GM assay results can be obtained more quickly. The physicians opt to wait for the PCR testing. Choose the best possible rationale for that decision.

   a. The treatment will be the same regardless of the test results.

   b. The individual was not exhibiting any disease symptoms.

   c. The probability of PCR testing identifying the presence of the organism is greater than the GM assay.

   d. The subclinical disease phase for *Histoplasma* is more than 100 days.

5. Referencing the data in Figures 2 and 3, if ELISA testing costs twice as much as PCR testing, why might it still be the best choice to test for *Candida*?

   a. ELISA testing detects the presence of *Candida* sooner than PCR testing.

   b. ELISA testing has fewer false-positives than PCR testing.

   c. There is only a 69% probability that PCR testing will correctly identify the presence of *Candida*.

   d. PCR testing is less sensitive than ELISA testing for *Candida*.

Passage II

Questions 6-12 pertain to the following information:

Scientists disagree about the cause of Bovine Spongiform Encephalopathy (BSE), also known as "mad cow disease." Two scientists discuss different explanations about the cause of the disease.

Scientist 1

Mad cow disease is a condition that results in the deterioration of brain and spinal cord tissue. This deterioration manifests as sponge-like defects or holes that result in irreversible damage to the brain. The cause of this damage is widely accepted to be the result of an infectious type of protein, called a prion. Normal prions are located in the cell wall of the central nervous system and function to preserve the myelin sheath around the nerves. Prions are capable of turning normal proteins into other prions by a process that is still unclear, thereby causing the proteins to be "refolded" in abnormal and harmful configurations. Unlike viruses and bacteria, the harmful prions possibly don't contain DNA or RNA, based on the observation of infected tissues in the laboratory that remain infected after immersion in formaldehyde or exposure to ultraviolet light. The transformation from normal to abnormal protein structure and function in a given individual is thought to occur as the result of proteins that are genetically weak or abnormally prone to mutation, or through transmission from another host through food, drugs or organ transplants from infected animals. The abnormal prions also don't trigger an immune response. After prions accumulate in large enough numbers, they form damaging conglomerations that result in the sponge-like holes in tissues, which eventually cause the loss of proper brain function and death.

Figure 1 depicts formation of abnormal prions that results from the abnormal (right) folding of amino acids.

Figure 1:
Configurations of Normal and Abnormal Prions

Normal Prion | Diseased (Abnormal) Prion
Amino acids in alpha helix
Amino acids in sheet form
Amino acids in alpha helix
Amino acids in beta helix

<u>Scientist 2</u>

The degeneration of brain tissue in animals afflicted with mad cow disease is widely considered to be the result of prion proteins. This theory fails to consider other possible causes, such as viruses. Recent studies have shown that infected tissues often contain small particles that match the size and density of viruses. In order to demonstrate that these viral particles are the cause of mad cow disease, researchers used chemicals to inactivate the viruses. When the damaged, inactivated viruses were introduced into healthy tissue, no mad cow disease symptoms were observed. This result indicates that viruses are likely the cause of mad cow disease. In addition, when the infected particles from an infected animal are used to infect a different species, the resulting particles are identical to the original particles. If the infecting agent was a protein, the particles would not be identical because proteins are species-specific. Instead, the infective agent is viewed as some form of a virus that has its own DNA or RNA configuration and can reproduce identical infective particles.

6. Which statement below best characterizes the main difference in the scientists' opinions?
    a. The existence of species-specific proteins
    b. Transmission rates of mad cow disease
    c. The conversion process of normal proteins into prions
    d. The underlying cause of mad cow disease

7. Which of the following statements is INCORRECT?
    a. Scientist 2 proposes that viruses aren't the cause of mad cow disease because chemicals inactivated the viruses.
    b. Scientist 1 suggests that infectious proteins called prions are the cause of mad cow disease.
    c. Scientist 1 indicates that the damaging conglomerations formed by prions eventually result in death.
    d. Scientist 2 reports that infected tissues often contain particles that match the size profile of viruses.

8. which of the following is true according to Scientist 1?
    a. Normal proteins accumulate in large numbers to produce damaging conglomerations.
    b. Prions can change normal proteins into prions.
    c. Species-specific DNA sequences of infected tissues indicate that proteins cause mad cow disease.
    d. Prions are present only in the peripheral nervous system of mammals.

9. Which of the following statements would be consistent with the views of BOTH scientists?
    a. Resulting tissue damage is reversible.
    b. The infecting agent is composed of sheets of amino acids in an alpha helix configuration.
    c. Species-specific DNA can be isolated from infected tissue.
    d. Cross-species transmission of the illness is possible.

10. How does the "conglomeration" described in the passage affect function?
    a. Synapses are delayed
    b. Sponge-like tissue formations occur
    c. Space-occupying lesions compress the nerves
    d. The blood supply to surrounding tissues is decreased

11. What evidence best supports the views of Scientist 2?
    a. Species-specific DNA is present in the infected particles.
    b. Prions are present in the cell membrane.
    c. Prions can trigger an immune response.
    d. The infected particles were inactivated and didn't cause disease.

12. Which of the following statements is supported by this passage?
    a. Scientist 1 favors the claim that viruses are the cause of mad cow disease.
    b. Prions are a type of infectious virus.
    c. The process that results in the formation of the abnormal prion is unclear.
    d. Mad cow disease is caused by normal proteins.

Passage III

Questions 13-17 pertain to the following information:

Scientists have long been interested in the effect of sleep deprivation on overeating and obesity in humans. Recently, scientists discovered that increased levels of the endocannabinoid 2-Arachidonoylglycerol (2-AG) in the human body is related to overeating. The endocannabinoids play an important role in memory, mood, the reward system, and metabolic processes including glucose metabolism and generation of energy. The endocannabinoid receptors CB1-R and CB2-R are protein receptors located on the cell membrane in the brain, the spinal cord and, to a lesser extent, in the peripheral neurons and the organs of the immune system. The two principal endogenous endocannabinoids are AEA (Anandamide) and 2-Arachidonoylglycerol (2-AG). The endocannabinoids can affect the body's response to chronic stress, mediate the pain response, decrease GI motility, and lessen the inflammatory response in some cancers.

Figure 1 (below) identifies the chemical structure of the endogenous cannabinoids including 2-AG.

Figure 1:
Chemical Structure of Common Endogenous Cannabinoids

The Five-Best known Endocannabinoids Showing the Common 19 - C Backbone Structure and specific R-group Constituents

Anandamide	2 - Arachidonoyl- glycerol	Noladin Ether
O ‖ C–N OH	O ‖ C–O OH OH	C–O OH OH

N-arachidonoyl-dopamine	Virodhamine	EC backbone structure
O ‖ C–N OH OH	O ‖ C–O NH$_2$	R

Recent research has also examined the relationship between sleep deprivation and the levels of 2-AG present in blood, as these conditions relate to obesity. The circadian fluctuations of 2-AG are well-known. Levels normally increase in late afternoon and evening. This physiological increase is thought to contribute to late-day snacking behaviors even after adequate calories have been consumed. The relationship between sleep deprivation and 2-AG appears to relate to the effect of 2-AG on the stress response, represented by sleep deprivation in this study. In order to examine this relationship, university scientists conducted an experiment to identify the influence of injections of 2-AG and sleep deprivation on overeating in a population of non-obese male and female participants that ranged in age from 20 – 40 years old. To accomplish this, human research subjects (participants) were allowed to eat their favorite junk foods in addition to consuming sufficient calories each day. All of the participants were injected daily with a solution of either sterile normal saline or 2-AG. Daily weight gain was recorded for the three treatment groups that included: participants A - E who received sterile normal saline injections, participants F - J who received 2-AG injections, and participants K - O who received 2-AG injections and were limited to 4.5 hours of sleep each night for 7 nights. The results of the three trials are shown below.

Figure 2 identifies the daily weight gain (in grams) of participants receiving sterile normal saline injections.

Daily Weight Gain for Patients Receiving Sterile Normal Saline Injections

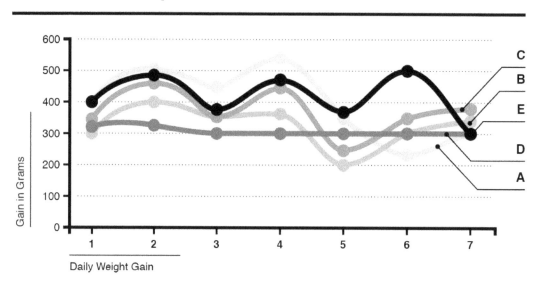

Figure 3 identifies the daily weight gain for participants receiving 2-AG injections.

Figure 3:
Daily Weight Gain for Participants Receiving Daily 2-AG Injections

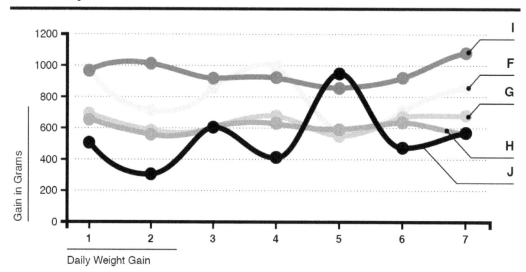

Figure 4 identifies the daily weight gain for participants receiving daily injections of 2-AG who were also limited to 4.5 hours sleep per night for 7 consecutive nights.

Figure 4:

Daily Weight Gain for Participants Receiving Daily 2-AG Injections Who Were Limited to 4.5 Hours of Sleep Per Night for 7 Consecutive Nights

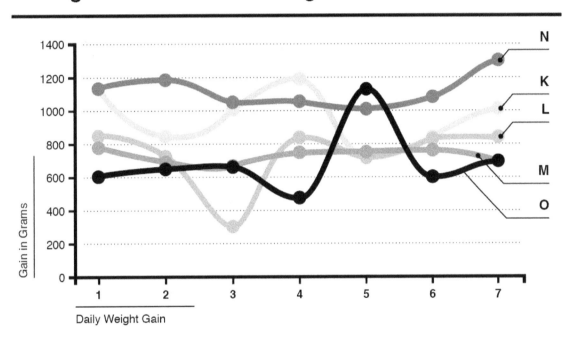

Figure 5 (below) identifies the participants' average daily weight gain by trial.

13. What was the main hypothesis for this study?
    a. 2-AG injections combined with sleep deprivation will result in weight gain.
    b. 2-AG injections will increase food intake beyond satiety.
    c. Sleep deprivation will result in weight gain.
    d. The placebo effect of the sterile normal saline will influence eating behavior.

14. Do the study results support the hypothesis? Choose the best answer.
    a. No, participants in trials 1 and 3 all gained weight.
    b. Yes, participants in trial 1 gained more weight daily than participants in trial 3.
    c. No, the average weight gain of participants in trial 2 and trial 3 was the same.
    d. Yes, all trial 3 participants gained more weight than trial 1 participants.

15. Describe the study results for participants D and H.
    a. Participant H gained more than one pound each day.
    b. Weight gain for each participant was inconsistent with the study hypothesis.
    c. There was significant fluctuation in the daily weight gain for both participants.
    d. Participant D's average daily weight was two times participant H's average daily weight gain.

16. According to the researchers, which of the following best describes the influence of sleep deprivation on eating behaviors?
    a. The total number of sleep hours is unrelated to the degree of body stress.
    b. Sleep deprivation stimulates the release of endogenous cannabinoids that may increase food intake.
    c. Deprivation of any variety triggers the hunger response.
    d. Sleep deprivation increases eating behaviors in the early morning hours.

17. According to the passage, how does 2-AG influence eating behaviors?
    a. Circadian fluctuations result in increased levels of 2-AG in the afternoon and evening.
    b. Endogenous cannabinoids like 2-AG increase gastric motility, which stimulates the hunger response.
    c. The sedation that results from the presence of 2-AG limits food intake.
    d. Endogenous cannabinoids block the opioid system, which decreases food-seeking behaviors.

Passage IV

Questions 18-22 pertain to the following passage:

A national wholesale nursery commissioned research to conduct a cost/benefit analysis of replacing existing fluorescent grow lighting systems with newer LED lighting systems. LEDs (light-emitting diodes) are composed of various semi-conductor materials that allow the flow of current in one direction. This means that LEDs emit light in a predictable range, unlike conventional lighting systems that give off heat and light in all directions. The wavelength of light of a single LED is determined by the properties of the specific semi-conductor. For instance, the indium gallium nitride system is used for blue, green, and cyan LEDs. As a result, growing systems can be individualized for the specific wavelength requirements for different plant species. In addition, LEDs don't emit significant amounts of heat compared to broadband systems, so plant hydration can be controlled more efficiently.

Figure 1 identifies the visible spectrum with the wavelength expressed in nanometers.

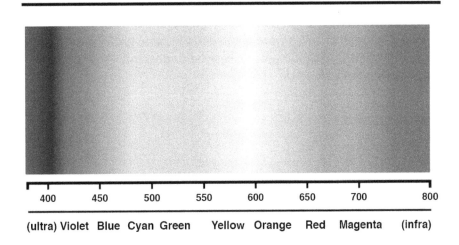

Figure 1:
The Visible Spectrum (Wavelength in Nanometers)

400   450   500   550   600   650   700   800

(ultra) Violet Blue Cyan Green   Yellow Orange   Red   Magenta   (infra)

Figure 2 (below) identifies the absorption rates of different wavelengths of light.

Researchers conducted three trials and hypothesized that LEDs would result in greater growth rates than conventional lighting or white light. They also hypothesized that using a combination of red, blue, green, and yellow wavelengths in the LED lighting system would result in a greater growth rate than using red or blue wavelengths alone. Although green and yellow wavelengths are largely reflected by the plant (Figure 2), the absorption rate is sufficient to make a modest contribution to plant growth. Fifteen Impatiens walleriana seed samples were planted in the same growing medium. Temperature, hydration, and light intensity were held constant. Plant height in millimeters was recorded as follows.

Figure 3 identifies the plant growth rate in millimeters with light wavelengths of 440 nanometers.

Figure 3:
Plant Growth Rate (mm) with Light wavelengths of 440 nm

Figure 4 (below) identifies the plant growth rate in mm with light wavelengths of 650 nanometers.

Figure 4:
Plant Growth Rate (mm) with Light wavelengths of 650 nm

Figure 5 (below) identifies the plant growth rate in millimeters with combined light wavelengths of 440, 550, and 650 nanometers.

Figure 5:

Plant Growth Rate (mm) with Combined Light wavelengths of 440, 550, and 650 nm

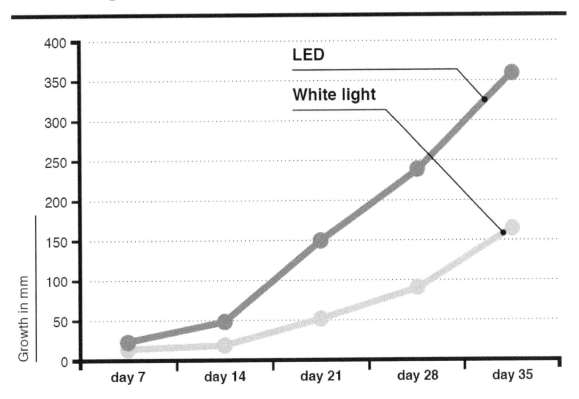

Figure 6 (below) identifies average daily plant growth rate in millimeters.

18. If the minimum plant height required for packaging a plant for sale is 150 millimeters, based on plant growth, how much sooner will the LED plants be packaged compared to the white light plants?
  a. 14 days
  b. 21 days
  c. 35 days
  d. 42 days

19. Plants reflect green and yellow light wavelengths. Do the results of the three trials support the view that plants also absorb and use green and yellow light wavelengths for growth?
  a. Yes, green and yellow light wavelengths were responsible for plant growth in trial 3.
  b. No, white light alone was responsible for measurable plant growth.
  c. Yes, the growth rates in trial 3 were greater than the rates in trials 1 and 2.
  d. No, only the red and blue wavelengths were effective in stimulating plant growth.

20. When did the greatest rate of growth occur for both groups in trial 1 and trial 2?
  a. From 7 days to 14 days
  b. From 28 days to 35 days
  c. From 21 days to 28 days
  d. From 14 days to 21 days

21. If an LED lighting system costs twice as much as a white light system, based only on the average daily growth rate as noted above, would it be a wise investment?
  a. No, because multiple different semi-conductors would be necessary.
  b. Yes, growth rates are better with LEDs.
  c. No, the LED average daily growth rate was not two times greater than the white light rate.
  d. Yes, LEDs use less electricity and water.

22. If the researchers conducted an additional trial, trial 4, to measure the effect of green and yellow wavelengths on plant growth, what would be the probable result?
    a. The growth rate would exceed trial 1.
    b. The growth rate would equal trial 3.
    c. The growth rate would be the same as trial 2.
    d. The growth rate would be less than trial 1 or trial 2.

Passage V

Questions 23-28 pertain to the following passage:

Mangoes are a tropical fruit that grow on trees native to Southern Asia called the *Mangifera*. Mangoes are now grown in most frost-free tropical and subtropical locations around the world. India and China harvest the greatest numbers of mangoes. A major problem the mango industry faces each year is the destruction of fruit after harvest. This destruction is the result of spoilage or rotting that occurs during long shipping and storage times.

To prevent the spoilage of mangoes, fruits are stored and shipped in climate-controlled containers. Ideally, mangoes should be stored at around 5 °C, which is about the same temperature as a home refrigerator. Although storage at 5 °C is highly effective at preventing spoilage, the monetary costs associated with maintaining this temperature during long shipping times are prohibitive.

Fruit companies spend large amounts of money to learn about the underlying cause of spoilage and possible methods to prevent loss of their product. Anthracnose, an infection that causes mango decay, is caused by *Colletotrichum,* a type of fungus that has been identified as a major contributor to mango spoilage. This fungus, which may remain dormant on green fruit, grows on the surface of the mango and can penetrate the skin and cause spoilage. The infection first appears during the flowering period as small black dots that progress to dark brown or black areas as ripening occurs. Humidity and excessive rainfall increase the severity of this infection. Previous studies established that colony sizes smaller than 35 millimeters after 4 weeks of travel resulted in acceptable amounts of spoilage.

Currently, several additional pre-treatment measures aimed at prevention are employed to slow decay of the fruit from the harvest to the marketplace. Industry researchers examined the individual and collective benefits of two of these processes, including post-harvest hot water treatment and air cooling at varied transport temperatures in order to identify optimum post-harvest procedures.

Table 1 identifies the observed mango decay in millimeters at 5 °C, 7.5 °C, and 10 °C with two pre-treatment processes over time measured in days since harvest of the fruit.

Table 1: Days Since Harvest

	2	4	6	8	10	12	14	16	18	20	22	24	26	28
5° C														
Water	1	4	7	9	11	12	14	19	22	23	25	27	28	30
Air	0	2	3	6	8	9	11	12	13	15	16	17	18	19
7.5°C														
Water	2	3	4	5	6	8	9	11	12	13	14	15	16	27
Air	0	2	5	6	7	9	10	15	22	23	24	27	32	39
10°C														
Water	2	3	5	7	8	11	12	14	22	35	42	44	47	62
Air	1	2	4	6	7	9	10	15	19	23	27	29	35	44

Figure 1 (below) identifies the observed mango decay of fruit stored at 5 °C measured in millimeters, with two pretreatment processes, over time measured in days since harvest of the fruit.

Figure 1:
5 °C Mango Decay Rates

Figures 2 (below) identifies the observed mango decay of fruit stored at 7.5 °C, measured in millimeters, with two pretreatment processes, over time measured in days since harvest of the fruit.

Figure 2:
7.5 °C Mango Decay Rates

Figures 3 (below) identifies the observed mango decay of fruit stored at 10 °C measured in millimeters, with two pretreatment processes, over time measured in days since harvest of the fruit.

Figures 3:
10 °C Mango Decay Rates

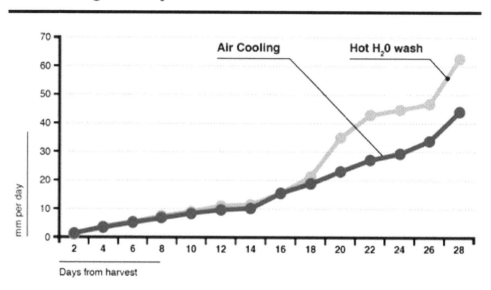

Figure 4 (below) identifies fruit decay measured in millimeters at 5 °C, 7.5 °C, and 10 °C with the combined pre-treatments over 28 days.

Figure 4:
Mango Decay Rates at 5 °C, 7.5 °C, and 10 °C with the Combined Pre-Treatments (Air Cooling & Water Bath)

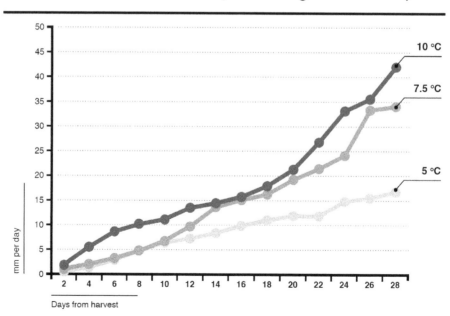

23. According to the passage above, which of the following statements is false?
    a. The optimal temperature for storing mangos is 5 °C.
    b. Anacardiaceae Magnifera is responsible for mango spoilage.
    c. Storing fruit at 5 °C is costly.
    d. Long distance shipping is a critical factor in mango spoilage.

24. If the mangoes were shipped from India to the U.S., and the trip was expected to take 20 days, which model would be best according to the data in Table 1?
    a. The 10 °C model, because fungal levels were acceptable for both pre-treatments.
    b. The 5 °C, model because it's more cost-effective.
    c. The 7.5 °C model, because this temperature is less expensive to maintain, and the fungal levels were acceptable.
    d. No single model is better than the other two models.

25. According to Figures 1 – 3 above, the largest one-day increase in fruit decay occurred under which conditions?
    a. Air cooling at 10 °C
    b. Hot water wash at 10 °C
    c. Air cooling at 7.5 °C
    d. Hot water wash at 7.5 °C

26. Which pre-treatment method reached unacceptable fungal levels first?
    a. Hot water wash at 7.5 °C
    b. Air cooling at 5 °C
    c. Hot water wash at 10 °C
    d. Air cooling at 10 °C

27. The researchers were attempting to identify the best shipping conditions for mangoes for a 28-day trip from harvest to market. Referencing Figures 1 - 4, which conditions would be the most cost-effective?
    a. Air cooling pre-treatment at 5 °C
    b. Air cooling and hot water wash pre-treatment at 5 °C
    c. Hot water wash pre-treatment at 7.5 °C
    d. Air cooling at 10 °C

28. Shipping mangoes at 5 °C is costly. According to the researchers' findings, is shipping mangoes at 5 °C more cost effective than 7.5 °C for trips lasting more than 28 days when combined air cooling and hot water wash treatments are applied?
    a. Yes, shipping at 7.5 °C combined with both pre-treatments resulted in an unacceptable fungal infection rate.
    b. Yes, fungal infection rates were below 35 mm for both pre-treatments 5 °C.
    c. No, air cooling pre-treatment was acceptable at 10 °C, and it's less expensive to ship fruit at 10 °C.
    d. No, hot water wash rates were lower than air cooling at 5 °C.

Passage VI

Questions 29-34 pertain to the following passage.

Scientists recently discovered that circadian rhythms help regulate sugar consumption by brown adipose tissue. The results of this study suggest that circadian rhythms and fat cells work together to warm the body in preparation for early morning activities involving cold weather. A circadian rhythm refers to life processes controlled by an internal "biological clock" that maintains a 24-hour rhythm. Sleep is controlled by one's circadian rhythm. To initiate sleep, the circadian rhythm stimulates the pineal gland to release the hormone melatonin, which causes sleepiness. Importantly, the circadian rhythm discerns when to begin the process of sleep based on the time of day. During the daytime, sunlight stimulates special cells within the eye, photosensitive retinal ganglion cells, which, in turn, allow the "biological clock" to keep track of how many hours of sunlight there are in a given day.

Brown adipose tissue (BAT) is a type of fat that plays an important role in thermogenesis, a process that generates heat. In humans and other mammals, there are two basic types of thermogenesis: shivering thermogenesis and non-shivering thermogenesis. Shivering thermogenesis involves physical movements, such as shaky hands or clattering teeth. Heat is produced as a result of energy being burned during physical activity. Non-shivering thermogenesis doesn't require physical activity; instead, it utilizes brown adipose tissue to generate heat. Brown fat cells appear dark because they contain large numbers of mitochondria, the organelles that burn sugar to produce energy and heat.

Researchers know that brown adipose tissue (BAT) is essential for maintaining body temperature. A new discovery in humans has shown that circadian rhythms cause BAT to consume more sugar in the early-morning hours. This spike in sugar consumption causes more heat to be produced in BAT. Scientists propose that our human ancestors could have benefited from extra body heat during cold hunts in the morning.

Perhaps more significantly, these new findings may suggest a role for BAT in the prevention of Type 2 Diabetes. Two important questions remain; to what degree does BAT affect blood glucose levels, and is it possible to increase BAT in a given individual? The demonstrated increase in sugar consumption and heat production of BAT is thought to be related to insulin-sensitivity. To examine the first question, researchers conducted three trials to examine the relationship between brown fat and blood glucose levels at different points in the day. PET scanning was used to estimate total body brown fat in 18 non-diabetic participants. Total body brown fat expressed as a proportion of total body fat (either 5%, 10%, or 20%) was the basis for group selection. The researchers hypothesized that the blood glucose levels would be inversely related to the percentage of BAT. Resulting data is included below.

Figure 1 (below) identifies the circadian cycle of blood glucose.

Figure 1:
Normal Circadian Plasma Glucose Levels

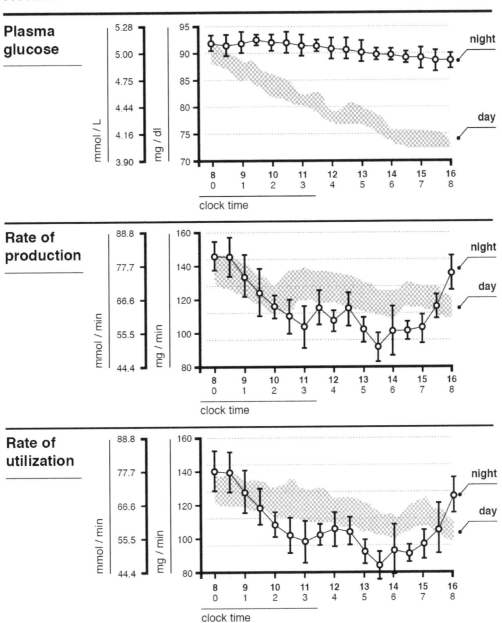

Figure 2 (below) identifies the resulting blood glucose measurements for participants with 5% total brown body fat.

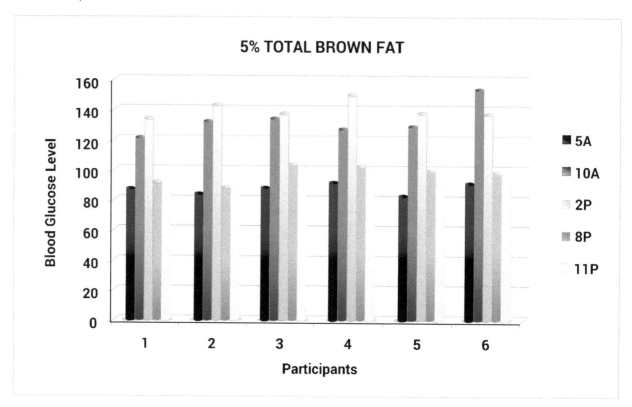

Figure 3 (below) identifies the resulting blood glucose measurements for participants with 10% total brown body fat.

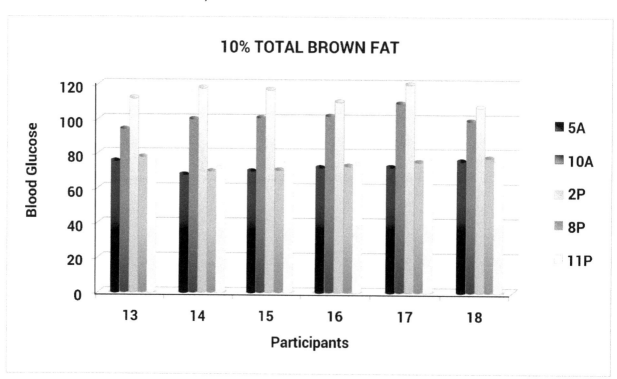

Figure 4 (below) identifies the resulting blood glucose measurements for participants with 20% total brown body fat.

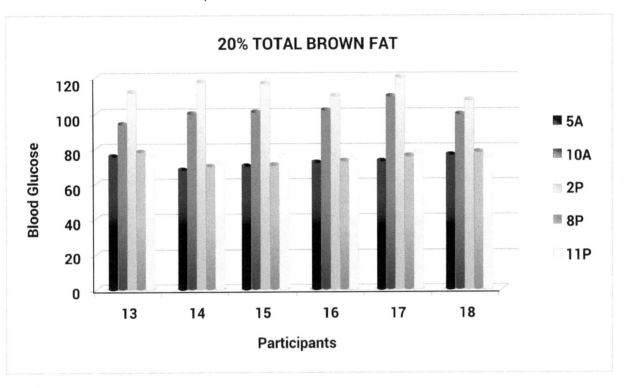

Figure 5 (below) identifies the average blood glucose measurements for the three trials.

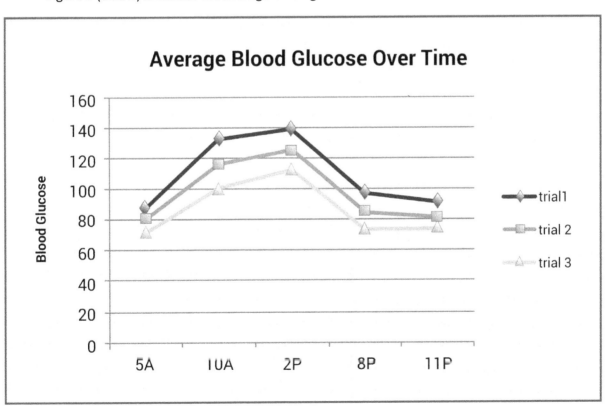

29. Which of the following describes the relationship of the research results in Figure 5?
    a. Positive correlation among the three trials
    b. Curvilinear relationship
    c. Weak negative relationship
    d. No demonstrated relationship

30. Which of the following statements concerning mitochondria is INCORRECT?
    a. Mitochondrial function is diminished in the presence of elevated blood glucose levels.
    b. Mitochondria are responsible for the color of brown fat.
    c. Mitochondria are capable of reproduction in response to energy needs.
    d. Mitochondria are responsible for binding oxygen in mature red blood cells.

31. According to Figure 5, participants' blood sugars were highest at what time of day?
    a. 5 a.m., because heat is generated early in the morning
    b. 8 p.m., because the participants ate less for dinner than lunch
    c. 11 p.m., because brown adipose tissue is not active at night
    d. 2 p.m., because the effects of the early-morning activity of the brown adipose tissue had diminished

32. Circadian rhythms control sleep by doing which of the following?
    a. Stimulating the pineal gland to release ganglia
    b. Stimulating the release of melatonin
    c. Suppressing shivering during cold mornings
    d. Instructing brown adipose tissue to release sugar

33. Which Participant in trial 1 had the highest average blood sugar for the group?
    a. 1
    b. 3
    c. 4
    d. 6

34. Is the data in Figure 5 consistent with the daytime plasma glucose trend in Figure 1?
    a. Yes, Figure 5 blood glucose readings declined from a morning to afternoon.
    b. No, blood glucose readings peaked at 2 p.m..
    c. Yes, morning glucose readings were higher in group 1.
    d. No, nighttime levels fluctuated between 100 and 110.

Passage VII

Questions 35-40 pertain to the following passage:

A biome is a major terrestrial or aquatic environment that supports diverse life forms. Freshwater biomes—including lakes, streams and rivers, and wetlands—account for 0.01% of the Earth's fresh water. Collectively, they are home to 6% of all recognized species. Standing water bodies may vary in size from small ponds to the Great Lakes. Plant life in lakes is specific to the zone of the lake that provides the optimal habitat for a specific species, based on the depth of the water as it relates to light. The photic layer is the shallower layer where light is available for photosynthesis. The aphotic layer is deeper, and the levels of sunlight are too low for photosynthesis. The benthic layer is the bottom-most layer, and its inhabitants are nourished by materials from the photic layer. Light-sensitive cyanobacteria and microscopic algae are two forms of phytoplankton that exist in lakes. As a result of nitrogen and phosphorous from agriculture and sewage run-off, algae residing near the surface can multiply abnormally so that available light is diminished to other species. Oxygen supplies may also be reduced when large numbers of algae die.

Recently, concerns have been raised about the effects of agriculture and commercial development on the quality of national freshwater bodies. In order to estimate the effect of human impact on freshwater, researchers examined plant life from the aphotic layer of three freshwater lakes of approximately the same size located in three different environments. Lake A was located in a remote forested area of western Montana. Lake B was located in central Kansas. Lake C was located in a medium-size city on the west coast of Florida. The researchers hypothesized that the microscopic algae and cyanobacteria populations from Lake A would approach appropriate levels for the size of the lake. They also hypothesized that the remaining two samples would reveal abnormal levels of the phytoplankton. In addition, the researchers measured the concentration of algae at different depths at four different times in another lake identified as having abnormal algae growth. These measurements attempted to identify the point at which light absorption in the photic layer was no longer sufficient for the growth of organisms in the aphotic layer. Resulting data is identified below.

Figure 1 (below) illustrates the zones of the freshwater lake.

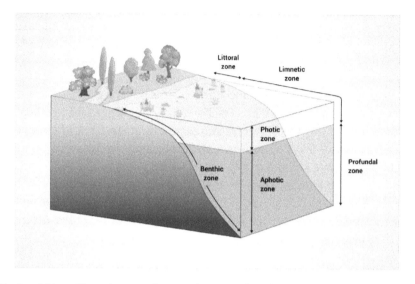

Figure 2 (below) identifies algae and cyanobacteria levels in parts per million for Lake A over six measurements.

normal: Algae 50 p.p.m. Cyanobacteria 35 p.p.m.

Figure 3 (below) identifies algae and cyanobacteria levels in parts per million for Lake B over six measurements.

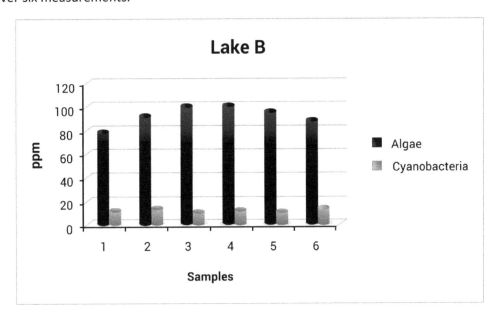

normal: Algae 50 p.p.m. Cyanobacteria 35 p.p.m.

Figure 4 (below) identifies algae and cyanobacteria levels in parts per million for Lake C over six measurements.

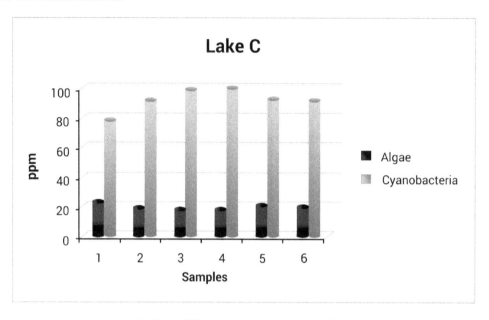

normal: Algae 50 p.p.m. Cyanobacteria 35 p.p.m.

Figure 5 (below) identifies cyanobacteria levels at different depths over time.

35. Based on Figure 2, was the researchers' hypothesis confirmed?

a. No, the phytoplankton levels were not elevated in the first trial.
b. Yes, the phytoplankton levels were raised above normal in each sample.
c. No, the Lake A numbers were normal.
d. Yes, algae levels were above normal in Lake C.

36. In Lake B, cyanobacteria were decreased and algae were increased. Which of the following is a possible explanation for this finding?
a. The overgrowth of algae decreased the light energy available for cyanobacteria growth.
b. Lake B experienced severe flooding, causing the water levels in the lake to rise above normal.
c. Agricultural chemical residue depleted the food source for cyanobacteria.
d. Cyanobacteria cannot survive in the cold winter weather in Lake B.

37. What common factor might explain the results for Lake B and Lake C?
a. Population concentration
b. Average humidity of the locations
c. Average heat index
d. Excess nitrogen and phosphorous in the ground water

38. As algae levels increase above normal, what happens to organisms in the aphotic level?
a. Growth is limited but sustained.
b. Species eventually die due to decreased oxygenation.
c. Cyanobacteria increase to unsafe levels.
d. Aerobic bacteria multiply.

39. Referencing Figures 2 and 3, which environment would favor organisms in the benthic layer of the corresponding lake?
a. Figure 4, because the cyanobacteria are protective.
b. Figure 3, because increased numbers of Algae provide more light.
c. Figure 4, because cyanobacteria are able to survive.
d. Figure 3, because the levels of both species are normal.

40. Which of the following statements is supported by the data in Figure 5?
a. Algae growth is greater in July than April.
b. Cyanobacteria can't exist at 20 meters in this lake.
c. There's insufficient light in the aphotic layer at 3 meters to support algae growth.
d. Cyanobacteria growth rates are independent of algae growth at 1 meter.

Answer Explanations

1. C: There is a 99% probability of PCR testing identifying *Histoplasma*. GM assay was more specific for identifying *Aspergillus,* 95% to 85%. True positive is defined by sensitivity. The sensitivity of GM assay testing is less than 70%.

2. D: *Histoplasma* is detectable 90 days from exposure. PCR testing is able to detect *Histoplasma* 91 days from exposure—one day after sufficient organisms exist for detection. *Candida* is detectable 45 days from exposure. PCR testing is able to detect *Candida* 72 days from exposure—27 days after a sufficient number of organisms exist for detection. *Aspergillus* is detectable 118 days from exposure. ELISA testing is able to detect *Aspergillus* 134 days from exposure—16 days after a sufficient number of organisms exist for detection. *Candida* is detectable 45 days from exposure. GM assay testing is able to detect *Candida* 56 days from exposure—11 days after a sufficient number of organisms exist for detection.

3. B: The probability that the GM assay will identify *Candida* is 69%. Therefore, there's a 31% probability that it won't be identified. ELISA sensitivity and specificity for *Histoplasma* are both greater than 80%. False-negative probabilities are represented by the specificity of a given testing method. The sensitivity and specificity for GM assay testing for *Aspergillus* is 9% and 96% respectively. All testing methods had greater than 90% specificity for the organisms.

4. C: The sensitivity of PCR testing for *Histoplasma* is 99%, and the test can identify the organism one day after it reaches a detectable colony size. The sensitivity for GM assay testing for *Histoplasma* is 65%. If physicians rely on GM assay testing, they may determine that the individual doesn't have the *Histoplasma* infection. Treatment will depend on the presence or absence of the infection as indicated by testing. Waiting for PCR testing is based on the sensitivity of the test, not the individual's current symptoms. The subclinical phase of *Histoplasma* is 28 days.

5. A: ELISA testing detects *Candida* three days after the organism is present in sufficient numbers to be recognized. PCR detects the organism more than three weeks after it is first detectable. ELISA testing sensitivity for *Candida* is 87% and PCR testing is 92%. However, the ability to identify the presence of the organism earlier in the process of infection (allowing early intervention) outweighs the differences in the probability of identifying the presence of the organism. There's a 92% probability that PCR testing will identify the presence of *Candida*. PCR testing is more sensitive than ELISA: 92% versus 87%

6. D: The main difference in the scientists' opinions is related to the cause of mad cow disease. The existence of species-specific proteins was used by Scientist 2 to support viral infection as the cause of the disease. Transmission rates of the disease and the conversion of normal proteins to prions were not debated in the passage.

7. A: Scientist 2 proposed that viruses were the cause of mad cow disease because chemicals inactivated the viruses. The remaining choices are correct.

8. B: According to Scientist 1, abnormal prions are capable of "refolding" normal proteins in harmful prions. Abnormal proteins accumulate to produce the damaging conglomerations. Scientist 2 didn't find species-specific DNA and used this fact to support viruses as the cause of mad cow disease. According to Scientist 1, prions are located in the central nervous system, not the peripheral nervous system.

9. D: Mad cow disease can be spread between animal species and from animals to humans through consumption of diseased animal products. The resulting damage to the central nervous system is irreversible and will eventually cause the death of the animal. Scientist 2 would not agree that the infecting agent contained amino acids, as they form proteins, and Scientist 2 believes that a virus causes the disease. Scientist 2 demonstrated that the infected tissue of animals that were infected by a different species didn't contain species-specific DNA, which would have been the expected outcome if the infecting agent were a protein.

10. C: The accumulated masses of abnormal prions eventually form sponge-like holes in the brain and spinal cord that result in death. The passage doesn't mention the effects of the synapses, nerves, or blood supply.

11. D: The absence of disease resulting from the inactivated viral particles best supports the views of Scientist 2. There were no species-specific DNA sequences found in the infected particles. Scientist 2 didn't support the existence of prions as the cause of mad cow disease.

12. C: The actual process of "refolding" the normal protein into the abnormal protein isn't clear from this passage. Scientist 1 claims that prions cause the disease. Prions are an abnormal protein, not a virus. Scientist 1 claims that mad cow disease is caused by abnormal proteins.

13. C: The main hypothesis for this study involved the influence of 2-AG levels combined with sleep deprivation on eating behaviors. The combination of the two conditions, not each one separately, constitutes the main hypothesis. The passage didn't discuss a placebo effect in the normal saline injection group.

14. D: The study results support the hypothesis because the participants who received 1-AG injections and were sleep deprived gained more weight than participants who received sterile normal saline injections. The remaining choices do not support the hypothesis.

15. A: Participant H gained more than 1 pound (450g) per day. There was little fluctuation in the day-to-day weight gain for each participant. Participant H in trial 2 gained more weight than participant D in trial 1.

16. B: Sleep deprivation increases the levels and duration of action of 2-AG, an endogenous cannabinoid, especially in the late afternoon. The stress effect increases with the degree of sleep deprivation. The passage doesn't discuss a relationship between sleep deprivation and the hunger response. Eating behaviors are increased in late afternoon as a result of the extended duration of 2-AG action.

17. A: Circadian fluctuations increase the levels of 2-AG during the afternoon and evening. This increase is believed to stimulate food intake beyond the point of satiety. Endogenous cannabinoids decrease gastric motility. 2-AG may have a calming effect on mood, but food intake is still increased in the presence of afternoon and evening levels of 2-AG. Endogenous cannabinoids work with the opioid system to mediate the pain response, not food-seeking behaviors.

18. A: In trial 3, the plants grown with the combined-wavelength LED's reached 150 millimeters by day 21. The plants grown with white light reached 160 millimeters by day 35.

19. C: In trial 3, with LED lighting that included green and yellow wavelengths, plant growth was greater than trial 1 or trial 2 with either blue or red wavelengths. However, from the available information, it can only be said that green and yellow wavelengths *contributed to* plant growth in trial 3, but not that green and yellow wavelengths *alone* were responsible for plant growth in trial 3. There was plant growth in all lighting conditions.

20. B: In trial 1, from day 28 to day 35, white light growth increased by 71 millimeters, and red light increased by 78 millimeters. In trial 2, from day 28 to day 35, white light growth increased by 71 millimeters, and blue light increased by 78 millimeters.

21. C: The average daily growth with LED lighting was not twice the white light average daily growth. LED systems did result in better growth rates and they do require less water and electricity. However, the question is based only recorded average daily growth, and that rate was not double the white light rate.

22. D: The passage says that green and yellow wavelengths are reflected by the plant. Therefore, it's expected that those wavelengths would result in slower growth than the blue or red wavelengths, which are absorbed.

23. B: *Anacardiaceae Magnifera* is the genus and family name for the mango. The *Colletotrichum* fungus causes the spoilage. The remaining choices are correct.

24. C: According to Table 1, at 20 days, the fungal level at 7.5 °C was the same as the fungal level at 5 °C. Because the 7.5 °C temperature is less expensive than the 5 °C temperature, the 7.5°C model is best. The 10°C model is less expensive than the 7.5 °C, but fungal levels are greater. Only the 7.5 °C and 5 °C models had acceptable fungal levels at 20 days.

25. B: The hot water wash pre-treatment fungal level increased by 15 millimeters from day 26 to day 28 at 10 °C. It was the single largest one-day increase across the trials. Air cooling at 10 °C increased by 5 millimeters from day 14 to day 16. Air cooling at 7.5 °C increased by 7 millimeters from day 26 to day 28. Hot water wash at 7.5 °C increased 11 millimeters from day 26 to day 28.

26. C: The hot water wash fungal level at 10 °C reached 35 millimeters on day 20. The maximum fungal level for air cooling at 5 °C was 19 millimeters, and at 10 °C, 35 millimeters on day 26. The maximum fungal level for hot water at 7.5 °C was 36 millimeters on day 28.

27. C: The fungal levels were acceptable with the hot water wash at 7.5 °C, and the 7.5 °C temperature is less expensive to maintain. Air cooling and hot water wash pre-treatment at 5 °C resulted in acceptable fungal levels, but the 5 °C temperature is costlier. Fungal levels were not acceptable at 28 days at 10 °C.

28. B: Shipping mangoes at 5 °C is costly, but for the 28-day trip, the fungal levels were only acceptable in the 5 °C model. Air cooling fungal rates at 5 °C were lower than the hot water wash rates, but each was acceptable. Fungal rates at 7.5 °C and 10 °C were unacceptable.

29. A: The correlation was positive, because when one variable increased, the other increased, and when one variable decreased, the other decreased. There are two forms for a curvilinear relationship. In one curvilinear relationship, when variable 1 increases, a second variable increases as well, but only to a certain point, and then variable 2 decreases as variable 1 continues to increase. In the other form, variable 1 increases while variable 2 decreases to a certain point, after which both variables increase. In a negative relationship, high values for one variable are associated with low values for the second variable.

30. D: Mitochondrial activity is suppressed by elevated blood glucose levels. Mitochondria use sugar to produce cellular energy, and the presence of large numbers of mitochondria in BAT gives BAT a brownish color. Mitochondria contain DNA and can reproduce additional mitochondria when additional energy is required. In the body, mature red blood cells are the only cells that don't contain mitochondria.

31. D: Blood sugars for all groups identified in Figure 5 were highest at 2 p.m.

32. B: Circadian rhythms control sleep by stimulating the release of melatonin from the pineal gland. Ganglia are nerve cells, not hormones, that affect sleep. BAT doesn't release sugar; it utilizes sugar for heat production. Shivering on cold mornings is a desirable form of thermogenesis, but isn't associated with sleep.

33. D: The average blood sugar for participant 6 was 115. Participant 1 was 105, participant 3 was 112, and participant 4 was 82.

34. B: The daytime blood glucose levels in Figure 1 decreased as the day progressed. The blood glucose levels in Figure 5 peaked for the day at 2 p.m. Night blood glucose levels didn't reach 100. Group I's levels are irrelevant to the question.

35. A: Based only on Figure 2, the researchers' hypothesis wasn't confirmed. Subsequent trials confirmed the hypothesis.

36. A: Increased algae levels can block sunlight, limiting growth of species inhabiting lower zones. The passage doesn't identify the effects of rainfall or cold temperatures on phytoplankton growth, so Choices B and D are incorrect. The passage identifies the effect of phosphorous and nitrogen residue on algae growth, but not as a food source for cyanobacteria.

37. D: The passage identifies freshwater contamination by phosphorous and nitrogen as the most common cause of algae overgrowth. Population density would be more common in Florida than Kansas.

38. B: As algae levels increase above normal, organisms in the aphotic level plants don't receive adequate light for normal growth and oxygen levels are decreased, resulting in the death of oxygen-dependent species.

39. C: Algae block the sunlight, which limits growth.

40. A: Algae growth was greater in July, which limited the amount of light reaching the lower zones of the lake, decreasing the levels of cyanobacteria. Cyanobacteria existed in less-than-normal concentrations at 20 meters, but there were measurable levels of the organisms. Algae growth at 3 meters wasn't measured. The passage states that cyanobacteria growth is associated with algae growth, not independent of algae growth.

ACT Writing Test

For some people, a writing test can seem very intimidating, perhaps even as scary as public speaking. However, with a little planning and practice, there's no reason to be afraid. Let's look at some strategies to help test takers do their best.

What to Expect

The test contains a topic followed by three possible viewpoints. Read everything carefully, and brainstorm an opinion on the topic. Then, write an essay that clearly evaluates all three viewpoints and states and supports the opinion using relevant facts and personal experiences along with creativity and critical thinking.

The assignment must be completed within a 30-minute time frame. Thirty minutes may not seem like a lot of time, but it is sufficient for organizing thoughts and putting the best words forward. Keep in mind that there is no right or wrong answer to the writing test. The important thing is to approach the response in an organized, clear, and direct way. In other words, be sure the writing makes sense.

So, how is that done?

Before the Big Day

Practice. Practice. Practice. While the concept of practice may seem unappealing, it is important to be aware of its value. Just as skills in any sport will likely improve with practice, creating sample writings will exercise "writing muscles" and will likely elevate skills and proficiency. Any kind of writing practice is advantageous, but essay writing is particularly relevant.

It also helps to be aware of how long it takes to comprehend and complete an essay assignment such as the ACT Test to determine if it is necessary to work faster.

Another tip is to ask others for their opinion. Feedback is a very important tool for becoming aware of strengths and weaknesses. Ultimately, the best opportunity for success is to work on being both a reader and a writer.

Keys to Good Writing

Use proper grammar, spelling, punctuation, and other formal writing techniques. This isn't an email or a text to send to friends with *lol* and *l8r,* where the only punctuation marks are in emojis, and the only capital letters are for shouting. There's nothing wrong with typing that way in a text, but this is a different kind of writing. It's closer to a speech, so start thinking more formally about how to express thoughts.

Explain thoughts in an organized way. Writers shouldn't assume that readers share the same knowledge or thoughts. It is necessary to explain the opinion that an idea is "bad" or "good," even if it seems obvious. Make sure the reasons are relevant and consistent—writing won't be credible if an argument contradicts a previous statement.

On Test Day

Brainstorm

Don't just start writing! Writing lacks direction if thoughts and ideas aren't organized first. So, before writing a single sentence of the opening paragraph, take a few minutes to brainstorm. Write down anything and everything related to the topic. Don't filter out anything, no matter how silly it might seem; it's impossible to know what ideas might grow into a full argument. It might be a good idea to use the scratch paper provided to jot down ideas and organize them, grouping similar ideas together. At this point, keep in mind that the people scoring the test will be looking for variety, creativity, and imagination—in the examples, in the ways the points are made, and especially in the perspectives.

While forming thoughts on the topic, imagine someone who disagrees. What arguments would that person make? How would he or she see the topic? Write down those ideas. Keep in mind that there are often many ways to justify the same position. So, imagine people who may agree but for completely different reasons, and write down what they might say as well. Including diverse viewpoints will show a well-rounded understanding of the topic.

Lastly, when brainstorming, don't forget that, although covering multiple viewpoints is key to good writing, truly *great* writing comes from bringing personal experience to the content. If the topic can be related to something personal (and still make a relevant, organized point), the writing will be more memorable—and probably earn a higher score.

Inventory

Keep brainstorming until the ideas stop flowing (but keep an eye on the clock—don't go over five minutes, or it may be difficult to get the actual writing done). Then, take a deep breath, and look at the ideas. Look for those that have a lot of information and strategies to support them, even if they're not the most exciting ones. At this point, it may be necessary to start cutting ideas that don't have enough material to back them up.

An *angle,* or pattern, should start to emerge—a common theme to pull the most promising ideas together. Keep this overarching direction in mind while deciding what to keep and what to drop. Once again, good writing comes from having well-developed and supported ideas, but *great* writing finds a way to connect all those ideas into a single big idea.

Organize

After deciding what written material to use, start putting it all in order. Look for ideas that flow logically. Seek out similarities or differences that draw certain thoughts together into a natural sequence. If one area looks weak or needs more support, either come up with some convincing evidence to strengthen it or take it out. Don't include anything that can't be backed up or that doesn't fit in the flow of the main idea.

Manage the Clock

Don't let the clock be the enemy. By now, it should be possible to see how many points there are and how much time is left. Do some simple math to figure out how much time there is to develop each idea. Don't forget to leave some time to review and proofread the writing (proofreading will be covered later).

Write

After all the preparation work is done, writers should have a clear idea of what they want to say. Keep in mind that there are certain things the scorers are looking for to show that the writing is well-thought-out. Also, be sure to write legibly, as the score could be lowered if the handwriting is poor.

Introduction

The opening paragraph is the introduction. It should include the following basic components:

- *A short restatement of the topic.* Don't just copy the writing prompt; rephrase it to suit the ideas. Make it look like the topic was created to make the points.

- *A personal opinion, or a statement of the overall big theme.* This will help set up the reader to understand how the smaller ideas fit into the big picture.

- *Smaller ideas.* They will serve as road maps for the audience. Telling readers how to navigate the ideas is like letting them see a "movie trailer" for the writing. They'll know what the writing is about, and they'll be interested to see how the ideas are developed.

Body

This is the meat of the writing and what all the brainstorming time has been spent preparing for. But by now, the ideas aren't bouncing around; they're neatly lined up, in order, ready to be released on the page. So, start writing!

Don't rush. With all these ideas, it's easy to start rushing to get them all down at once. This can lead to long, complicated, hard-to-follow sentences with lots of ideas crammed in. That's not good writing. Remember, hard work went into organizing the thoughts, and all the ideas are there. So, slow down. Make each point, one at a time, in the clearest, most direct way possible. Look for ways to connect ideas. Transition sentences that lead from one concept to another are a great way to provide flow and can prevent the writing from sounding like a collection of unrelated statements.

Conclusion

All the points have been made, developed, and connected to one another. Now it's time to write a conclusion. Conclusions sometimes seem silly and repetitive, but they really do serve an important purpose. State the opinion again and the main reasons behind it. Revisit the big idea here, and possibly restate the small ideas in a very basic way. Don't go through the details again—that's already been done. Also, don't present any *new* information or ideas in the conclusion. Simply summarize what's been said, and wrap it up into a neat package for the reader.

Proofread

Everyone makes mistakes in the heat of writing on an exam: a misspelled word, a sentence that doesn't make sense, or a paragraph that seems disjointed and confusing. Be sure to leave a few minutes (at the end) to go back and reread the writing. Read slowly, trying to hear the words. It may feel silly, but moving the lips will help internalize the flow and make it easier to catch writing problems. Most mistakes are quick fixes, and any writer will be glad to have gone back and corrected them.

Also, be sure to delete any notes left while working through the assignment or any text from the brainstorming session. The formatting (indented paragraphs, for example) should be consistent. Leave readers with a document that looks appealing and "clean"—without mistakes—before they read a single word.

Final Thoughts

When time runs out, it will probably feel like there was room for improvement. That's normal. In fact, scorers understand the difficulties of creating organized, coherent writing in a timed situation under pressure. No one expects the writing to be perfect. With that in mind, here are some ideas for test takers to consider while working through the writing test:

- *Don't panic.* This is doable. Stop if it feels like brain overload is setting in and drawing a blank is imminent. Take a deep breath, and remember the process. Don't force it. It's even okay to stop for a 30-second "mental vacation" to clear the mind.

- *Make the clock work.* Brainstorming and dividing the task into smaller chunks allows for viewing the remaining time in the least stressful way. If writing an entire essay in 30 minutes is overwhelming, just focus on finishing the next paragraph.

- *Don't try to impress anyone.* Don't use fancy words just because they're familiar—writers shouldn't use any word that they're not 100 percent sure about. Also, don't add more writing just to make the essay longer. What's important is clear, organized writing. If the ideas have been brainstormed, developed, and written in a logical order, it will be possible to put a lot of meaning into very few words.

In the end, by following these procedures, writing an easy-to-follow and well-thought-out response on the test should be no trouble. Remember: This can be done!

Good luck, and good writing!

FREE Test Taking Tips DVD Offer

To help us better serve you, we have developed a Test Taking Tips DVD that we would like to give you for FREE. **This DVD covers world-class test taking tips that you can use to be even more successful when you are taking your test.**

All that we ask is that you email us your feedback about your study guide. Please let us know what you thought about it – whether that is good, bad or indifferent.

To get your **FREE Test Taking Tips DVD**, email freedvd@studyguideteam.com with "FREE DVD" in the subject line and the following information in the body of the email:

     a. The title of your study guide.

     b. Your product rating on a scale of 1-5, with 5 being the highest rating.

     c. Your feedback about the study guide. What did you think of it?

     d. Your full name and shipping address to send your free DVD.

If you have any questions or concerns, please don't hesitate to contact us at freedvd@studyguideteam.com.

Thanks again!

CPSIA information can be obtained
at www.ICGtesting.com
Printed in the USA
LVHW02s1721151117
556417LV00002B/5/P

9 781628 45